A Guide to

SUNKEN SHIPS

in American Waters

Barkentine wrecked on reef is swamped and dashed by pounding surf.

A GUIDE TO
SUNKEN SHIPS
IN AMERICAN WATERS

by

ADRIAN L. LONSDALE
LCdr. U.S. Coast Guard

and

H. R. KAPLAN
U.S. Coast Guard

Compass Publications Inc.
Arlington, Virginia

COMPASS PUBLICATIONS, INC.
617 LYNN BLDG., 1111 N. 19TH ST.
ARLINGTON, VIRGINIA 22209

DEDICATION

to man's friend and
implacable foe —
the sea

Preface

FOR THE thousands of persons interested in sunken ships in American continental waters, this book should prove a valuable source. Within the covers of a single, conveniently arranged volume, the authors have provided information on approximately 1,100 shipwrecks along our coasts, the Great Lakes and larger rivers. Also included are copies of sections of appropriate U.S. Coast and Geodetic Survey charts for plotting wrecks referred to in the text. So far as I know, never before has anyone provided so comprehensive a treatment of this engrossing subject. As an additional feature, the authors have included interesting textual material on the background and history of the areas covered.

An appraisal of this book in manuscript form gives an early indication of its ultimate value as a much-needed reference work. Sunken wrecks have a romantic appeal, in addition to economic interest, as evidenced by the substantial volume of requests received regularly by the Bureau on the subject. Much of this interest obviously stems from the continuing advancement in the techniques of SCUBA diving and the natural lure of possible discovery of sunken treasure. This book will be a valuable addition to literature on the subject and should find many interested readers.

H. Arnold Karo, Rear Admiral

Director, U. S. Coast and Geodetic Survey

TABLE OF CONTENTS

Dedication .... **v**

Preface .... **vii**

Introduction .... **xii**

Chapter 1 — Northeastern Coast 1

Maine, New Hampshire, Massachusetts,

Rhode Island, Connecticut, and New York.

The Saga of Cape Cod, **3**; The *Portland* Mystery, **5**; Tragedy off the Long Island Coast, **5**; The *Larchmont* Disaster, **6**; Tabulation of Sunken Ships on Coast of Maine and New Hampshire, **10**; Tabulation of Sunken Ships on Coast of Massachusetts, **11**; Tabulation of Sunken Ships on Coast of Rhode Island, **17**; Tabulation of Sunken Ships on Coast of Connecticut and New York, **18**; U.S. Coast and Geodetic Survey Charts Covering Northeastern Coast, **21**.

Chapter 2 — Middle Atlantic Coast 23

New Jersey, Delaware, Maryland,

Virginia, and North Carolina.

The Treasure of the *Republic,* **26**; Shipwreck for Profit, **32**; Hatteras, Cape of Storms, **33**; Tabulation of Sunken Ships on Coast of New Jersey, **36**; Tabulation of Sunken Ships on Coast of Delaware, **43**; Tabulation of Sunken Ships on Coast of Maryland, **44**; Tabulation of Sunken Ships on Coast of Virginia, **45**; Tabulation of Wrecks on Coast of North Carolina, **49**; U.S. Coast and Geodetic Survey Charts Covering Middle Atlantic Coast, **55**.

Chapter 3 — Southeastern Coast 57

South Carolina, Georgia, and Florida.

Wreck of the *Valentine*, **62**, The Key West Story, **64**; Tabulation of Sunken Ships on Coast of South Carolina, **70**; Tabulation of Sunken Ships on Coast of Georgia and Florida, **71**; U.S. Coast and Geodetic Survey Charts Covering Southeastern Coast, **75**.

Chapter 4 — Gulf of Mexico 77

Florida, Alabama, Mississippi,
Louisiana, and Texas.

The Legend of Jean Lafitte, **82**; Valor at Galveston, **88**; Tabulation of Sunken Ships on Coast of Florida, **91**; Tabulation of Sunken Ships on Coast of Alabama, **92**; Tabulation of Sunken Ships on Coast of Mississippi and Louisiana, **93**; Tabulation of Sunken Ships on Coast of Texas, **94**; U.S. Coast and Geodetic Survey Charts Covering Gulf of Mexico, **96**.

Chapter 5 — Great Lakes 99

Lake Ontario, Lake Erie, Detroit River,
Lake Huron, Lake Superior, Lake Michigan.

The Unlikeliest Thanksgiving, **106**; Tabulation of Sunken Ships in Lake Ontario and Lake Erie, **113**; Tabulation of Sunken Ships in Detroit River and Lake Huron, **115**; Tabulation of Sunken Ships in Lake Superior, **116**; Tabulation of Sunken Ships in Lake Michigan, **118**; U.S. Army Corps of Engineers Charts Covering Great Lakes, **120**.

Chapter 6 — Great Rivers 123

Illinois River, Kanawha River, Mississippi
River, Cumberland River, Tennessee River,
Allegheny River, Missouri River, Monongahela
River, and Ohio River.

Cheating the Ohio, **125**; Soldier Rest; Thy Warfare O'er, **128**; Tabulation of Sunken Ships in Illinois River, and Middle and Upper Mississippi River, **132**; Tabulation of Sunken Ships in Lower Mississippi River, **133**; Tabulation of Sunken Ships in Kanawha River, Cumberland River, Tennessee River and Missouri River, **134**; Tabulation of Sunken Ships in Allegheny River, Monongahela River and Ohio River, **135**.

Chapter 7 — Pacific Coast 139

California, Oregon,
and Washington.

The Mystery of the Chinese Silver, **148**; The Shoestring Rescue, **149**; Tabulation of Sunken Ships on Coast of California, **155**; Tabulation of Sunken Ships on Coast of Oregon, **159**; Tabulation of Sunken Ships on Coast of Washington, **162**; U.S. Coast and Geodetic Survey Charts covering Pacific Coast, **164**.

Chapter 8 — Northern Pacific 167

Alaska

Alaskan Treasure Trove, **171**; Tragedy of the Aleutians, **172**; Tabulation of Sunken Ships off Coast of Alaska, **177**; U.S. Coast and Geodetic Survey Charts covering Northern Pacific **180**.

Appendices

Appendix A — Questions and Answers on Your Rights 183

Appendix B — Where to Obtain Charts 185

Introduction

SOMEWHERE OFF the Florida Keys at the bottom of the South Atlantic lie the remains of an English merchant ship. She was sent there long ago by one of the many sea robbers who roamed what was then known as the "Spanish Main." For centuries, the tides of the Atlantic have washed over her rotting timbers. Her fittings and cannon are crusted over with generations of marine growth. Yet locked in one of her ancient chests, her treasure remains intact: thousands of silver pieces minted during the reign of Elizabeth. So far as we know, they are still there, waiting to be claimed by some bold adventurer willing to take the risk.

This is of course, a highly romanticized example of sunken treasure. In today's world, "pieces of eight" and silver bullion aren't likely to be found outside the pages of adventure books. Nevertheless it is still true that the coasts of the United States, the Great Lakes, and the shores of some of the larger rivers are dotted with sunken vessels of all descriptions. Their cargo may not be as exotic as that of the old English merchant ship, and their sinkings may have occurred under less dramatic circumstances. Yet the fact remains that the sea is still a vast storehouse of the remains of ships and their cargoes.

Nor is the interest in sunken ships purely romantic. We believe that the information in this book has a very practical value for those with a more professional interest such as salvage companies, the merchant marine industries, college and school libraries, historians, and, in fact, anyone interested in this fascinating aspect of marine history.

With this thought in mind we have sought to provide a handy, convenient reference book. For convenience, we have listed shipwrecks geographically, in tabular form, giving a quick resumé of all pertinent facts. They include the name, type, and tonnage of the vessel; the most reliable information of the vessel's position available; and, whenever possible, the cargo carried and the depth of the water in which it lies. Also, we have included in the appendices some of the main elements of salvage laws, and a listing of the sources from which charts may be obtained. For the most part, we have restricted ourselves to major ships, but have occasionally made exceptions in cases of unusual interest. Some of these are presented in narrative form.

Our data have been gathered from a wide variety of sources, most of it coming from government reports. Although we believe these sources to be reliable, we cannot vouch for their total accuracy in all cases.

Here are the terms and abbreviations appearing in the text:

Bk.	—Bark	Sch.	—Schooner
Str.	—Steamer	Shp.	—Sailing Ship
Ftr.	—Freighter	M/V	—Motor Vessel
USS	—United States Ship	Twr.	—Trawler
Coll.	—Collier	Bge.	—Barge
SS	—Steamship	Yct.	—Yacht
Tkr.	—Tanker	Dge.	—Dredge
	Frg.	—Frigate	

Where known, the position of each wreck included in the Great Rivers chapter are noted in the tables by the number of miles distant from the mouth of the river, in conformity with the river charts which denote mileage from the river mouth. (You will note that the Mississippi River is divided into two segments: the Middle and Upper Mississippi, and the Lower Mississippi. The line of demarcation is at Cairo, Ill., where the Ohio and Mississippi Rivers meet. Mileages listed in the table for the Middle and Upper Mississippi River are given from that point.)

In the great majority of cases, sunken vessels along the coasts and in Great Lakes are located by latitude and longitude. However, for some wrecks, locations cannot be determined by latitude and longitude. In such cases an approximate location is given. In this book all latitudes are north and all longitudes are west.

Let's say that you wish to plot the location of the passenger liner *Republic*. The *Republic* was reported to have carried $3,000,000 in American ten dollar gold coins known as Eagles. According to old Coast Guard records, it sank at Latitude 40-25.5 North and Longitude 69-40.0 West. To plot the wreck, draw a horizontal line from 40-25.5 on the right hand scale of C. & G. S. Chart No. 1108 and a vertical line from 69-40.0 on the bottom scale. Where the two lines intersect is the reported position where the vessel sank.

You will notice on the chart that all the wreck marks are not identified in the tables. This is because little information is available or because the sunken vessel may have been a small trawler, tug or other vessel not important enough to have been considered for inclusion. In other cases such as the *Republic*, you will not find a wreck mark at the position you plotted, because the wreck has not been located in recent times.

When finding depths on a chart, always check to see if soundings are in fathoms or feet. A fathom equals six feet. Details on the availability of all charts are given in Appendix B, page 185. Most of the charts recommended for use in this book cost $1.00 each.

At right is a reproduction of a section of the Coast and Geodetic Survey Chart #1108 (approaches to New York Harbor) showing typical wrecks appearing in the chart.

(1) Best known position of the passenger liner REPUBLIC *(15,378 tons). (2) An unknown wreck. (3) The* ANDREA DORIA *(29,083 tons) which sank in 1956. (4) Doubtful position of the* REPUBLIC *reported in British Hydrographic Bulletin of 1909. (5) Location of freighter* STEPHANO *(3449 tons) which sank in 1916. (6) The freighter* ORE-GON *(6745 tons) went down in this position in 1941 with a cargo valued at $2,000,000. (7) The tanker* PENNSYLVANIA *(11,107 tons) sank at this location in 1944. (8) Position of the 4321-ton freighter* STRATHDENE *which went down in 1916. (9) Position of German Submarine U-5540 (740 tons) which sank in 1944.*

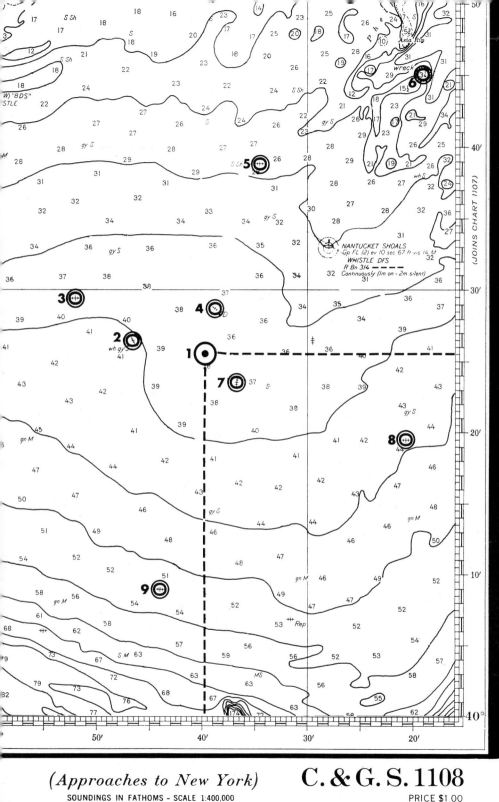

(Approaches to New York)   C. & G. S. 1108

SOUNDINGS IN FATHOMS - SCALE 1:400,000

PRICE $1.00

CHAPTER 1

Northeastern Coast

Maine, New Hampshire
Massachusetts, Rhode Island
Connecticut, and New York

THERE IS no more awe-inspiring chapter in the history of the
United States than the one that began on the bleak forbidding
shore of what is now Massachusetts. It was in 1620 that the Pilgrims established a beachhead, setting in motion forces which
would culminate in the United States of America. They left for all
time the indelible impress of their austere, striving spirit on the
nation.

Other voyagers had caught glimpses of the harsh, cruel, but
magnificent terrain that is known as the Northeast. But nearly all
were searching for a passage to the wealth of the Orient. With the
Pilgrims it was different. They were driven not by lust for gold
but by a fierce passion for freedom of conscience. So great was
this passion for liberty that they were willing to stake their lives
in a wild, strange country full of unknown terrors.

These first settlers were a shrewd and industrious folk. Within
a few generations after the landing at Plymouth, they had built
a trade empire stretching to all parts of the globe. In 1786, Samuel
Shaw established in Canton the first mercantile house in China.
A year later, the *Grand Turk* brought to Salem, Mass., the first
of many oriental cargoes which were to make that port famous.

Towards the end of the 18th century, Robert Gray's *Columbia*
carried the flag of the new Republic around the world for the

first time. That voyage laid the foundation for the United States' claim to Oregon as well as for a very profitable trade with the Northwest, where furs could be purchased to be exchanged in China for silks and tea. Salem, for a time, was the tea market of America and Europe. About this time, also, New England's first "merchant princes" came into being. New England had become the hub around which early America revolved.

During this same early period, the *Defense* was wrecked on Bartlett Reef in 1779, carrying a reported cargo in gold and silver valued at $200,000. Shortly thereafter, the *Lexington* sank in the East River off the harbor of New York with $1,800,000 in bullion on board. In the same year, another vessel, the *Hussar,* met her end in the East River off Brothers Island. According to reports, she was carrying gold and silver bullion estimated at $3,000,000. As far as can be determined, none of this cargo has ever been reclaimed. These shipwrecks testify to the opulence of the maritime trade of the Northeast in the early days of the Republic.

In the foundries and workshops of the Northeast, the fledgling nation developed its first industries. Some of America's finest craftsmen came from this area.

But it was in trade that New England's genius found its great expression. By the last half of the 19th century, this trade reached its zenith. The famous Yankee clippers were to be found in nearly all harbors of the world. From New Bedford and other bustling New England ports, the whaling ships set out on their long voyages to hunt for the sperm whale and its precious oil. Yankee boldness and enterprise had become bywords throughout the commercial world.

Time, however, was running out for this picturesque era. Already the Civil War was casting its shadow over the nation. Its outbreak dealt the whaling trade a mortal blow. The whaling fleet, once the pride of New Bedford and Nantucket, was broken up by Confederate raiders, and its monopoly of the illuminating-oil market was destroyed by the introduction of petroleum products. The change from wooden to iron and then to steel ships, and the rising costs of operation under the United States flag, stripped New England of its natural advantages in the construction and operation of ships.

As the nation continued to expand its frontiers, other harbors, notably in the Middle Atlantic area, became formidable competitors. Nevertheless, the Northeast remained a major factor in American commerce. In the pages to follow you will find many evidences of this activity. In 1866, the *City of Norwich* went down after a collision off Huntington, Long Island, with a cargo reported to be worth $1,000,000. In 1898, the *Portland*, with a small fortune aboard, was destroyed in a ferocious gale off the coast of Massachusetts. The same gale destroyed 11 other ships, including the steamer *Fairfax* which was wrecked on the Sow and Pigs Reef in Buzzards Bay, Mass., with a valuable cargo. In 1905, the steamer *Spartan* sank off the coast of Block Island, R.I., with a cargo estimated at $200,000.

The two World Wars added to the already tragically long list of ships lost off the Northeast coast. Many of these losses were due to the action of enemy submarines lurking in coastal waters. For anyone interested in shipwrecks and in the maritime history of the United States, the Northeast coast offers unrivalled possibilities. Data pertinent to the locations, reported values, and other known specifics about the wrecks discussed in this book are listed in the tabulations at the end of each chapter.

THE SAGA OF CAPE COD

Off the southeast coast of Massachusetts, jutting into the Atlantic for a distance of about 40 miles, is an odd-shaped piece of land known as Cape Cod. On the map it looks like a gigantic arm bent at right angles with fingers at its end, as if beckoning to the unwary sailor. Along these shores, vicious northeast winds have sent many a fine ship and brave sailor to his death. The Cape, with its story of human valor, provides an inspiring chapter of United States maritime history.

No one knows exactly how many men and ships have perished off Cape Cod. Very likely the figure runs to thousands of men and hundreds of ships. Many of these wrecks took place long before official records were kept, but their stories have been handed down from generation to generation. In its long history, the Cape has witnessed rescue efforts against desperate odds as well as scenes of human tragedy. The lifesavers of Cape Cod have won for themselves an honored place in the chronicle of human courage.

Only six years after the historic landing of the *Mayflower,* the first recorded shipwreck took place on the Cape. The ship was the *Sparrowhawk* from England, carrying colonists bound for Virginia. But she never reached her destination. Near what is now Orleans, she became stranded on the shoals and was lost. Her bones were discovered in a mud bank in 1863, when a washing away of the shore line uncovered her rotting timbers.

Then there was the *Somerset,* a British frigate, which stranded on Peaked Hill Bars on November 2 or 3, 1778. The vessel had been one of the fleet of British men-of-war whose guns had raked the heights of Bunker Hill and terrorized the commerce of the colonies. At the time of her disaster she was in pursuit of a fleet of French ships reported to be in Boston Harbor. While trying to round the Cape to enter the harbor at Provincetown, she struck Peaked Hill Bars in a northeast gale. The *Somerset* was a major vessel by 18th century standards with a complement of 480 men and 60 guns. She hit the bars with terrific force and almost instantly the seas began to pound her to pieces. Eventually, she was thrown up on the beach with Captain Aurey and a few of her crew who had managed to stay alive. They were taken prisoner and spent the rest of the war in Boston. The remains of the *Somerset* stayed buried for a century, until shifting sands exposed them to view. Relic hunters soon carried away much of the wreckage. Then the sands once again entombed what was left of the famous old frigate.

The list of wrecked vessels goes on and on and would probably take up many pages. But some of the most famous ones include the *Widdah, Josephus, White Squall, Clara Belle, Giovanni, Jason, Job H. Jackson, Daniel B. Fearing, Monte Tabor, Castagna,* and the *Portland.*

As early as 1790, the Massachusetts Humane Society, forerunner of the United States Lifesaving Service, attempted organized relief for shipwrecked seafarers on the Cape. In 1797, the town of Truro sold the Federal Government a tract of land on which to build the first lighthouse on Cape Cod—Highland Light.

Modern navigation instruments and better ships have greatly lessened the menace of Cape Cod. Today it no longer holds the same threat for seafarers as in the past. Nevertheless, the old Cape will always rate a chapter in any maritime history of the United States.

THE PORTLAND MYSTERY

Death in the form of a savage northeaster struck the Massachusetts coast on November 26, 1898. For two nights and a day the storm raged, destroying whole communities, and tearing away giant seawalls and piers of heavy granite blocks. When it was over, dozens of residents along the seashore were among its victims, and more than 40 vessels had been threatened. Of these, 10 were seriously damaged, and 11 were totally destroyed.

The outstanding casualty of the storm was the 2284-ton steamer *Portland*. At 7:00 p.m. on November 26, just before the storm struck, she had left Boston en route for Portland, Maine. On board were 65 passengers and 64 crewmen, as well as approximately $18,000 in cash and jewels, an unknown number of uncut diamonds, and a general cargo. The *Portland* was never seen again. The only indication of her fate came days later when bodies and debris, identified as coming from the *Portland,* began to wash up on the Cape Cod beaches.

Nothing further was heard about her until the early 1930's when a diver reported he had located what resembled the *Portland* nine miles northeast of Provincetown, Mass. But the currents were too dangerous and the hull too clogged with sand to permit further investigation. If the diver's report is correct, the *Portland* lies in 160 feet of water at the location given on page 14. A small fortune awaits the hardy treasure hunter who is willing to take the risk.

TRAGEDY OFF THE LONG ISLAND COAST

The 1534-ton sailing ship *Margaretha* of Bremerhaven, Germany, bound for New York, completed her trans-Atlantic crossing on January 27, 1882, only to ground on the rocks, 250 yards from shore, and a mile and a quarter east of Smith's Point, Long Island. Aboard were a crew of 22 and a cargo of merchandise valued at $20,000. The thunderous surf, pounding in from a strong thick-weather west gale, made survival in a surfboat impossible.

The first line fired by the U.S. Lifesavers fell short. A second line parted while being hauled aboard. A heavy braided line, fired on the third shot, held and was used to draw the whip-line aboard. A hawser was quickly set up and a breeches buoy rigged. With sand blasting their faces and burying every small article in sight, the surfmen painfully brought the crew ashore one by one from the stricken ship. The storm smashed at the ship for four more days, destroying it completely.

THE LARCHMONT DISASTER

On a freezing February 11, 1907, the passenger steamer *Larchmont* was fighting her way from Providence, R.I., to New York City. The temperature hovered near zero and a vicious nor'wester swept the seas over the vessel, leaving a coating of ice on everything above deck.

The *Larchmont* was a stout ship and had logged many miles since she was built by the Bath Iron Works in Maine in 1884. A 1605-ton, side wheel, single deck, two-masted vessel, she had proved her seaworthiness on numerous occasions. Her skipper, Captain George W. McVey, was a veteran sailor and his crew of about 40 men was competent. Yet under the cruel buffeting of icy wind and sea, even McVey's confidence was shaken. In these waters anything could happen. And trouble on a night such as this could be fatal. Nothing human could long survive in those freezing waters. Pious man though he was, McVey found the thought of Hell not unattractive. At least it was warm.

By ten o'clock, most of the *Larchmont's* passengers had retired to their cabins for the night. A skeleton crew was on watch. The men were rotated frequently to prevent their being frozen. As the minute hand crept toward 10:30, McVey began to feel a certain relief. Maybe they would weather this awful night without any more serious mishap than a few frostbitten hands and noses. It would be a very small price to pay.

Unknown to McVey, the schooner *Harry P. Knowlton* was passing through the same waters. The 317-ton ship was carrying a cargo of coal. She had been ice-bound at the head of Long Island Sound, but had gotten free early on the morning of the 11th. To make up for lost time she was carrying considerable canvas. Originally built for the South African trade, she was faster than the average vessel of her class. As the wind rose to gale force in the night, she was moving at a very good clip.

At 10:45 that evening, at a point approximately 10 miles west of the northern tip of Block Island, McVey saw the *Knowlton* loom up out of the darkness. So sudden was the encounter that there was no time to maneuver. The *Knowlton* smashed into the steamer on the port side forward of her paddle box, shearing away most of her headgear. The speed of the *Larchmont* carried her clear of the schooner.

Almost immediately after the collision, the *Larchmont* was filled with the screams and shouts of frightened people. Blind panic took over as passengers, routed from bed in night clothing, sought desperately for any means of escape. The *Larchmont* was sinking rapidly and it would be only a matter of minutes before she went under.

In the darkness and confusion it was almost impossible to reach the boats and life rafts. The crew was doing its best to lower boats and rafts over the side, but the savage onslaught of the sea and the crowding of the terrified passengers made their task nearly hopeless. In their anxiety to leave the sinking ship, many jumped or fell into the icy water and died in seconds. About half of the passengers, however, managed to get off the ship. Most of these were swept toward Block Island, the majority coming ashore near the Sandy Point Lifesaving Station. Many died from the exposure to the merciless cold. Twelve minutes after the collision, the *Larchmont* disappeared forever in the Atlantic.

Aboard the *Knowlton,* Captain Haley and his crew fared a little better. Shortly after smashing into the *Larchmont,* he signalled the unfortunate ship for help. But his signals went unanswered and, finding his ship rapidly filling, he decided to head for shore. The *Knowlton,* however, had been so badly damaged that the crew had to take to the ship's yawl while still a mile and a half from the beach.

Both the schooner and her small boat were discovered offshore about 1:30 a.m., February 12, by a surfman of the Quonochontaug Lifesaving Station. The men were half dead with cold but managed to regain their strength after several days at the station. It was obvious that they had no idea of the fate of the *Larchmont.*

It was on the forenoon of the 12th that the full extent of the **tragedy began to seep in.** The first indication came from the

Sandy Point Lighthouse keeper who phoned the lifesaving station that a half-frozen boy had appeared at the lighthouse. The surfman in charge, Charles A. Mitchell, sent one of his crew to the beach to investigate. Then he and the rest of his crew went to the lighthouse. They set to work at once to revive the boy. After he had recovered a little, he told them that he was one of several persons who had made it to shore in a *Larchmont* lifeboat.

Bit by bit the ghastly story began to take shape as the dead and dying of the *Larchmont* were recovered. Repeatedly, lifesavers waded shoulder deep into the freezing surf to recover bodies. During the entire day of February 12, several of them stayed on the open beach in the heavy gale, their clothing frozen stiff. According to an official report, they "resembled statues of ice more than human beings." Throughout the night of the 12th and until noon of the 13th they remained on the beach without sleep and with little refreshment.

Liferaft No. 6 of the *Larchmont* drifted to shore with one live man and nine frozen bodies. One of those on board had committed suicide while floating in the Sound. This was one of many similar instances. Vessels in the area of the collision picked up other victims of the tragedy. By the time the awful day was over, a stunned nation learned that only 17 of the approximately 200 on board the *Larchmont* had survived. It was a day that would be long remembered as one of the worst disasters in the maritime history of the United States.

Today, the remains of the stricken *Larchmont* and the valuables of her passengers still lie under 74 feet of water off Block Island. The exact location is given on page 17.

Aground, a four-masted is abandoned to the elements on the rocky coast of Massachusetts.

Chapter 1 — TABLES. The following listing gives the position (latitude and longitude); type, name of vessel, and tonnage; the Coast and Geodetic Survey charts covering the area; and general information concerning dates, cargo, and estimated value.

Lat/Long	Type, Name, Tonnage	Charts	Remarks
	COAST OF MAINE AND NEW HAMPSHIRE		
44-48.1 66-58.8	Bk. SCOTIA (1000)	1106 1201	Wrecked in 1882 when driven on rocks 250 yards offshore in easterly gale.
44-38.3 67-13.0	Shp. JOHN CLARK (1079)	1106 1201	Wrecked May 5, 1878, on Great Head.
44-37.1 67-14.3	Str. EDUARDO (2308)	1106 1201	Wrecked July 20, 1889, on Old Man Island
44-34.4 67-21.5	Ftr. D. M. MUNRO (1216)	1106 1201	Wrecked March 6, 1943, on shoals on east side between Libby Islands.
44-18.0 66-24.0	Ftr. EMPIRE STORY (7037)	1106	Sank May 4, 1942, in 60 feet, 2½ miles NW of Brier Island, Nova Scotia.
44-01.0 68-20.0	Ftr. CORNWALLIS (5458)	1106 1202	Torpedoed Dec. 3, 1944, in 260 feet.
——	ROYAL TAR	1106 1203	Wrecked Oct. 25, 1836, Penobscot Bay, Maine.
44-02.9 69-02.9	Str. CITY OF PORTLAND (1026)	1106 1203	Wrecked May 8, 1884, on NW Ledge, north end of Muscle Ridge Channel.
43-53.8 69-04.0	Str. CAROLYN (2241)	1106 1203	Wrecked Jan. 10, 1912, on Southern Triangles.
——	Pass. BOHEMIAN	1106 1204	Struck Alden Rock February 22, 1864 and sank before reaching Cape Elizabeth, Maine. 40 lives lost.
43-43.8 69-37.4	Coll. HARTWELSON (3078)	1106 1204	Wrecked March 5, 1943. Forward part on Bantam Rock, stern 150 yards to SW in 30 feet.

Lat/Long	Type, Name, Tonnage	Charts	Remarks
43-36.9 69-59.4	U.S. Submarine S-21	1106 1204	Sunk for experimental purposes in 150 feet.
43-36.0 66-00.0	Ftr. WEST JAFFREY (5663)	1106	Wrecked in 1942 in shoal water 2½ miles south of Frenchman Point, Nova Scotia.
43-33.3 70-13.0	Str. BAY STATE (2262)	1106 1205	Wrecked Sept. 23, 1916, in Hollicums Cove.
43-30.2 70-18.4	Sch. WASHINGTON B. THOMAS (2638)	1106 1205	Wrecked June 12, 1908, on rocks off Stratton Island. Cargo—coal.
43-20.0 66-20.0	Ftr. LIVERPOOL PACKET (1188)	1106	Torpedoed May 30, 1942, in 210 feet.
43-19.0 66-15.0	Ftr. THIRLEY (4887)	1106	Torpedoed Jan. 23, 1942, in 234 feet.
43-07.0 67-18.0	Ftr. SKOTTLAND (2117)	1106	Torpedoed May 17, 1942, in 520 feet.
43-07.0 70-25.7	Ftr. EMPIRE KNIGHT (7244)—part of wreck	1106 1205	Torpedoed Feb. 11, 1944, in 200 feet.
43-01.7 70-30.3	Ftr. EMPIRE KNIGHT (7244)—part of wreck	1106 1205	Torpedoed Feb. 11, 1944, in 150 feet.
43-00.5 70-36.0	Sch. SAMUEL J. GAUCHER (2547)	1106 1205	Wrecked Nov. 11, 1911, approximately 500 yards from Duck Island with cargo of coal.
42-57.0 70-30.0	Ftr. WILLIAM A. MACHEN (3922)	1106 1205	Sank July 7, 1942, in 200 feet.

COAST OF MASSACHUSETTS

Lat/Long	Type, Name, Tonnage	Charts	Remarks
42-40.6 70-35.1	Ftr. CHARLES S. HAIGHT (7198)	1106 1206	Foundered April 2, 1946, on rocks 1½ miles NE of Rockport Harbor.
42-33.0 68-58.0	Ftr. DAYTONA (3344)	1106	Sank Dec. 21, 1955, in 700 feet.
42-30.3 70-39.3	Ftr. MORITZ	1107 1207	Sank July 2, 1930, in 190 feet.
——	NORSEMAN	1107 1207	Wrecked March 20, 1899, near Marblehead.
42-26.4 70-40.3	Ftr. VAN	1107 1207	Sank May 16, 1935, in 215 feet.
42-24.4 70-39.0	Ftr. MASSOCOIT	1107 1207	Sank Jan. 22, 1931, in 240 feet.
42-23.7 70-51.8	Pass. ROMANCE (1240)	1107 1207	Sank Sept. 9, 1936. 41 feet over wreck 2¼ miles due east Nahant's East Point.

Lat/Long	Type, Name, Tonnage	Charts	Remarks
42-23.0 70-55.0	WINIFRED SHERIDAN (935)	1107 1207	Sank before World War II, 1800 yards north of Finns Ledge buoy. 31 feet over wreck.
42-22.8 70-39.5	Sch. ETHEL N.	1107 1207	Sank Dec. 31, 1930, in 210 feet.
42-22.4 70-51.6	CITY OF SALISBURY (397)	1107 1207	Broke in two and sank July, 1932, in 178 feet.
42-22.4 70-43.4	USS EAGLE BOAT NO. 42	1107 1207	Sank June 15, 1931, in 178 feet.
42-22.1 70-54.9	USS YMS-14 (207)	1107 1207	Sank Jan. 11, 1945, 4,025 yards, 275.5° from Graves Light. 33 feet over wreck.
——	VIRGINIAN	1205 1207	Wrecked in March 1895, near Boston.
42-22.1 70-43.1	Ftr. COYOTE	1107 1207	Sank Jan. 11, 1932, in 142 feet.
42-22.1 70-37.2	Pass. KING PHILLIP	1107 1207	Sank April 7, 1935, in 234 feet.
42-20.7 70-40.7	Yct. ROXANA	1107 1207	Sank Sept. 10, 1935, in 150 feet.
42-22 69-46	German Sub U-85	1107	Sank April 7, 1945, in 900 feet.
42-20.0 69-10.0	Ftr. TABORFJELL (1339)	1107	Torpedoed April 30, 1942, in 750 feet.
42-20.3 70-41.0	Bge. SAM MENGEL	1107 1207	Sank Oct. 16, 1935, in 84 feet.
42-19.3 70-53.1	Sch. ANNE PERRY	1107 1207	Sank in 1914, 1300 yards north of Point Allerton.
42-18.3 70-50.9	Sch. GLENWOOD (1649)	1107 1207	Wrecked Feb. 22, 1893, on Harding Ledge with cargo of coal.
42-16.6 70-36.4	Ftr. SOUTHLAND	1107 1207	Sank Dec. 2, 1930, in 162 feet.
42-12.0 69-07.0	Str. PORTLAND (2284)	1107 1207	Foundered Nov. 26, 1898, in 160 feet, 9 miles NNE of Provincetown. $18,000 in jewels and money reported on board.
42-09.3 70-34.0	PINTHIS	1107 1207	Sank after collision June 10, 1930. 58 feet over wreck.
42-09.3 70-33.8	Bge. WINSOR (1034)	1106 **1208**	Foundered Dec. 2, 1946.

Lat/Long	Type, Name, Tonnage	Charts	Remarks
42-09 70-34	USS C. W. CULLEN (703)	1107 1207	Sank Dec. 30, 1918, in 80 feet.
42-09 69-22.5	Ftr. PORT NOCHOLSON (8402)	1107	Collided and sank June 15, 1942, in 600 feet.
42-09 69-22.5	Pass. CHEROKEE (5896)	1107	Collided and sank June 15, 1942, in 600 feet.
42-04.4 70-19.8	Sch. GEORGINA M.	1107 1208	Sank Dec. 20, 1924, in 183 feet.
42-05 70-08.5	Bk. MONTE TABOR	1107 1208	Wrecked in 1896 on Peaked Hill Bars.
42-05 70-08.5	Bk. GIOVANNI	1107 1208	Wrecked in 1875 on Peaked Hill Bars.
42-05 70-08.5	Sch. JOB H. JACKSON	1107 1208	Wrecked in 1896 on Peaked Hill Bars.
42-05.0 70-08.5	JOSEPHUS	1107 1208	Stranded and broke up on Peaked Hill Bars in 1842.
42-04.6 70-19.8	Sch. GEORGINA M.	1107 1208	Sank Dec. 20, 1924, in 180 feet.
42-04.2 70-06.2	Sch. CLARA BELLE	1107 1208	Wrecked in 1872.
——	HMS SOMERSET	1107 1208	Wrecked in 1778, 2 miles east of Race Point, near Provincetown.
42-00.5 70-00.9	Shp. JASON (1512)	1107 1208	Wrecked Dec. 5, 1893, 800 yards offshore in 17 feet.
42-00.0 70-20.0	Twr. GLENSIDE (974)	1107 1208	Sank Nov. 20, 1944, in 155 feet.
42-00.0 70-00.0	Twr. OSCEALA (1621)	1107 1208	Sank April 2, 1942, in 40 feet.
42-00.0 69-00.0	Sch. WILMINGTON (1371)	1107	Sank Jan. 2, 1945, in 480 feet.
41-57.2 69-58.9	WHITE SQUALL	1107 1208	Wrecked in 1866 with block tin cargo.
41-56.5 69-58.5	Sch. DANIEL B. FEARING	1107 1208	Wrecked in 1896.
41-56.5 69-58.5	Shp. FRANKLIN	1107 1208	Intentionally run aground in 1849. Most of crew perished.
41-56.5 69-58.5	Sch VIRGINIA	1107 1208	Wrecked in 1929.

Lat/Long	Type, Name, Tonnage	Charts	Remarks
41-54.4 70-29.6	Bge. HENRY ENDICOTE	1107 1208	Sank Sept. 18, 1939, in 67 feet with locomotive on board.
41-53.8 69-57.5	Bk. CASTAGNA (843)	1107 1208	Wrecked Feb. 1914.
41-53.0 69-57.0	WIDDAH (300)	1107 1208	Wrecked in 1717. Gold, silver and ivory valued at $100,000 reported on board.
41-49.8 70-02.9	Ftr. JAMES LONGSTREET (7176)	1107 1208	Wrecked Oct. 26, 1943, in 14 feet in restricted area.
41-48 66-38	German Sub U-215 (500)	1107	Sank July 3, 1942, in 210 feet.
41-47.1 70-29.1	Ftr. EXMINSTER (4985)	1107 1208	Sank April 20, 1942, 890 yards, 38.5° from Cape Cod Canal Breakwater in 31 feet.
41-46.5 70-27.8	Bge. POTTSTOWN (974)	1107 1208	Sank Nov. 20, 1944.
41-39.0 66-32.0	Ftr. ALEX MACOMB (9172)	1107	Torpedoed July 3, 1942, in 240 feet. 9,000 tons of general cargo.
41-38.5 60-54.8	CONNECTICUT	1107 1208	Sank in 1904 in 49 feet.
41-35.1 69-57.8	Tkr. PENDLETON (10,000)	1107 1209	Broke up Feb. 18, 1952. (See facing page.)
41-33.0 69-57.8	Ftr. DIXIE SWORD (3283)	1107 1209	Wrecked Feb. 12, 1942.
41-32.0 69-59.9	SS WINIFRED MARTIN	1107 1209	49 feet over wreck.
—	JOHN	1107 1209	Wrecked May 3, 1855, Falmouth.
—	Sch. STORM KING (1262)	1107 1209	Wrecked Nov. 16, 1892, Pollock Rip Shoal. Main cargo—coal.
—	Ftr. PORT HUNTER	1107 1209	Sank in 1918 after collision off Hedge Fence Shoal 3 miles from East Chop Light, Nantucket Sound. In 70 feet with $250,000 in steel billets reported aboard.
—	Sch. FOWNES	1107 1209	Foundered Dec. 16, 1910, on Nantucket Shoals 5 to 6 miles SE of Monomoy Island.
41-24 70-07.6	Bge. MARIE HOOPER (2190)	1107 1209	Sank Dec. 28, 1944, in 40 feet.
—	Sch. MILDRED M. FOLEY	1107 1209	Burned and sank in 1910 off Great Point, Nantucket Island.

The bow of the SS Pendelton lies awash off North Beach, Mass. On February 18, 1952, the tanker broke up in a severe snow storm which was accompanied by winds varying between 35 and 70 knots. No survivors were found in this section of the tanker but Coast Guardsmen rescued 32 crewmen from the stern section which was located in the vicinity of Chatham Bar.

15

Lat/Long	Type, Name, Tonnage	Charts	Remarks
—	LYONNAIS	1107 1209	Sank in collision Nov. 2, 1856, Nantucket Island.
—	GLASGOW	1107 1209	Burned July 31, 1865, Nantucket Island.
41-18.0 70-16.7	Shp. ANTOINETTE (1118)	1107 1209	Wrecked Jan. 27, 1889, 350 yards from beach.
—	SS CANONBURY (1676)	1107 1209	Wrecked March 28, 1887, on Old Man Shoal SE of Nantucket.
41-40.1 70-41.7	Bge. MANOKIN (1289)	1107 1210	Collided with WALTER D. NOYES on Aug. 23, 1944, near Wings Neck.
41-31.0 70-42.0	Ftr. WINNEGANCE (1327)	1107 1210	Wrecked Oct. 14, 1943, in Woods Hole Passage.
41-30.7 70-54.5	Bge. SHERWOOD (1281)	1107 1210	Stranded June 21, 1947, on Wilkes Ledge. Wreck in 20 feet.
41-30.0 70-54.0	Wreck 185 feet long	1107 1210	Sank in 53 feet.
41-29.1 70-55.1	Ftr. CORWIN	1107 1210	Sank Dec. 20, 1927, in 81 feet.
41-28.2 70-58.3	COWEN	1107 1210	Sank Dec. 29, 1944.
—	Str. JUANITA (2537)	1107 1210	Wrecked Feb. 23, 1916, on Middle Ground Shoal, Vineyard Sound, with miscellaneous cargo.
—	Str. ARDANDHU (2091)	1107 1210	Sank Jan. 23, 1900, Vineyard Sound.
41-27.8 70-45.4	Sch. LUNET	1107 1210	Wrecked in 1898, 192° magnetic from Tarpaulin Cove Light, Naushon Island, on steep sand bank in 40 feet.
41-25.4 70-50.7	Sch. GEORGE P. DAVENPORT (1461)	1107 1210	Wrecked Jan. 19, 1901, in south side of Nashawena Island, with cargo of coal.
41-24.6 70-00.4	SEA CONNET (3372)	1107 1210	Sank March 10, 1945.
—	Str. FAIRFAX (2551)	1107 1210	Wrecked Nov. 27, 1898, on Sow and Pigs Reef, Cuttyhunk Island, with cargo of merchandise. Loss estimated at $275,000.
41-24.6 70-56.0	Sch. DOUGLAS DEERBORN (1024)	1107 1210	Wrecked Feb. 20, 1893, with cargo of coal.
41-24.2 70-58.5	SS SILVIA (1708)	1107 1210	Wrecked March 14, 1908, on Sow and Pigs Reef with cargo valued at $222,285.

Lat/Long	Type, Name, Tonnage	Charts	Remarks
41-23.8 71-01.0	Lightship VINEYARD SOUND	1107 1210	Sank Sept. 14, 1944. 40 feet over wreck.
——	Str. CITY OF COLUMBUS (1992)	1107	Wrecked Jan. 18, 1884, on Devils Bridge, Gayhead. Cargo of general merchandise. 109 lives were lost.
41-20.2 70-55.0	Ftr. HERMAN WINTER (2625)	1107 1210	Sank March 7, 1944.
41-27.7 71-06.4	HMCS SAINT CLAIR	1108 1210	Sank in 1945 in 60 feet with 14 feet over wreck. Four stack Canadian destroyer, 315 feet long.

COAST OF RHODE ISLAND

Lat/Long	Type, Name, Tonnage	Charts	Remarks
——	GEM	1108 1210	Wrecked in 1850 in 8-10 feet on west side (center) of Brenton Cove alongside Fort Adams, Newport.
——	Ftr. BELVILLE	1108 1210	Wrecked in 1958 on Seal Ledge ¼ mile south of 12 Mile Drive, Newport.
——	Shp. LYDIA SKOLFIELD (1264)	1108 1210	Wrecked April 19, 1891, on Butter Ball Rock off Brenton Point, Newport.
41-19.7 71-25.8	Ftr. BLACK POINT (5353)	1108 1210	Torpedoed May 5, 1945. 44 feet over wreck. Bears 129°, 5,910 yards from Point Judith Light. 7,759 tons of coal on board.
41-19.1 71-26.0	Sch. LUTHER HOOPER (2190)	1108 1210	Sank March 2, 1927, in 70 feet.
41-13.0 71-25.0	German Submarine U-853	1108 1210	Sank May 5, 1945, in 130 feet. $1,000,000 in mercury reported on board.
41-19.8 71-43.2	Sch. JOHN PAUL (1509)	1108 1211	Wrecked Feb. 10, 1893, off Greenhill Point. Cargo—coal.
41-17.6 71-51.4	Str. ONONDAGA (2667)	1108 1211	Wrecked June 28, 1918. In 50 feet. Ship and miscellaneous cargo valued at $1,775,000.
41-16.1 71-49.3	Str. LARCHMONT (1605)	1108 1211	Foundered Feb. 11, 1907 3¼ miles 142° T. from Watch Hill Light. 74 feet over wreck. 183 lives lost.
41-17.0 71-38.0	Bge. ANNAPOLIS (1371)	1108 1211	Collided with a submarine Feb. 17, 1945, and sank in 120 feet.
——	PRINCESS AUGUSTA	1108 1211	Wrecked on N tip of Sandy Point, Block Island, in 1738. Loss reported at $100,000 including gold, silverplate and specie.
41-10.6 71-32.4	Str. SPARTAN (1596)	1108 1211	Sank March 19, 1905, with general cargo. Loss estimated at $265,000.

Lat/Long	Type, Name, Tonnage	Charts	Remarks
——	SS EDWARD LUCKENBACK	1108 1211	Stranded in 1930 on Southwest Point, Block Island.
41-04.3 71-32.3	Tkr. LIGHTBURN (6429)	1108 1211	Sank Feb. 10, 1939. 55 feet over wreck.
41-08.8 71-33.2	Ftr. ESSEX (2155)	1108 1211	Sank Sept. 26, 1941.
41-08.7 71-33.3	Sch. TEXAS (1627)	1108 1211	Sank April 6, 1905, carrying 2,500 tons of coal.
41-07.2 71-34.2	Sch. POCAHONTAS (1382)	1108 1211	Sank Jan. 12, 1890, with cargo of coal.
41-05.8 71-33.3	GRECIAN (2827)	1108 1211	Sank before World War II in 80 feet.
41-01.2 71-32.8	U.S. Submarine BASS	1108 1211	Sank in 1925 in 150 feet.
40-52.8 71-13.2	Ftr. SUFFOLK (4607)	1108	Sank Dec. 11, 1943.

COAST OF CONNECTICUT AND NEW YORK

Lat/Long	Type, Name, Tonnage	Charts	Remarks
41-18.0 72-08.9	U.S. Submarine G-2 (450)	1108 1211	Sank in 1919 in 75 feet in Twotree Channel.
41-18.0 72-05.0	MASSACHUSETTS	1108 1211	Sank Jan. 31, 1913.
——	Frg. SAN JOSE	1108 1211	Wrecked in rocks off New London, Conn., in 1752. $500,000 in silver reported on board.
41-17.7 71-52.0	Ftr. GEORGE HUDSON	1108 1211	Wrecked in 1918 on Watch Hill Reef.
——	Bge. OLINDA (1479)	1108 1211	Wrecked June 11, 1895, on Fishers Island, N.Y.
——	ATLANTIC	1108 1211	Wrecked Nov. 28, 1846, on Fishers Island. 42 lives lost.
——	DEFENSE	1108 1211	Wrecked on Bartlett Reef, Niantic, Conn., in 1779 in 30 feet. Loss reported at $200,000, including gold and silver.
41-05.9 71-46.5	SNUG HARBOR (2388)	1108 1211	Sank in 1920 in 40 feet.
41-05.8 71-52.4	MALDEN (5054)	1108 1211	Sank in 1921 in 35 feet.
41-05.5 71-45.7	VERMILLION	1108 1211	Sank in 1920 in 58 feet.

Lat/Long	Type, Name, Tonnage	Charts	Remarks
41-04.8 71-52.4	Str. ONTARIO (3082)	1108 1211	Wrecked April 8, 1912, with general cargo. Loss estimated at $395,000.
——	Bge. VENTURA	1108 1211	Lost Dec. 7, 1906, off Montauk Point, Long Island. Cargo—coal.
41-03.0 71-52.5	Str. GEORGE APPOLD (1456)	1108 1211	Wrecked Jan. 9, 1889, with a miscellaneous cargo valued at $133,000.
41-02.7 71-53.5	Coll. HARRY BOWEN (3522)	1108 1211	Stranded Dec. 1930.
41-57.7 72-07.9	Shp. CIRCASSIAN (1741)	1108 1211	Wrecked Dec. 11, 1876, with general cargo valued at $45,000.
——	Bge. LAKE HEMLOCK (2015)	1108 1212	Foundered Dec. 13, 1957, in Long Island Sound about 2 miles north of 28 Foot Lump, 25 miles west of New London.
41-14.0 72-55.0	Ftr. BUR (4343)	1108 1212	Sank Aug. 28, 1942, in entrance to New Haven Harbor.
——	Ferryboat PRISCILLA ALDEN	1108 1212	Sank in Port Jefferson, Long Island, Harbor off Mount Misery Point.
——	U.S. Submarine S-48	1108 1213	Sank off Bridgeport, Conn., in 1922.
——	LEXINGTON	1108 1213	Burned and sank off Bridgeport, Conn., in 1840. $60,000 in specie reported aboard.
41-00 73-30	Ftr. GARRETT (2301)	1108 1213	Sank Sept. 8, 1944.
——	CITY OF NORWICH	1108 1213	Sank April 18, 1866, in 80 feet, after collision, 3 miles off Huntington, Long Island. $1,000,000 cargo reported aboard.
40-52.7 73-44.4	Pass. Ferry	1108 1213	Wrecked about 1915, 100 yards west of Execution Light.
40-48.0 73-54.0	Pass. GENERAL SLOCUM	1108 1213	Burned in 1904 on North Brother Island, N.Y. 1,000 lives lost.
40-50.8 72-26.8	Shp. M. P. GRACE (1928)	1108 1214	Wrecked Nov. 13, 1906, 400 yards offshore. cargo—coal.
——	VINEYARD	1108 1214	Sank 2 miles SE of Southampton Light, L.I., 1836, in 36 feet. Loss reported at $54,000 including gold and silver specie.
40-45.9 72-44.6	Str. CATE CITY (1997)	1108 1214	Wrecked Feb. 8, 1900, 200 yards offshore. Loss estimated at $221,555.
40-45 69-19	Ftr. OREGON (6745)	1108	Sank after collision Dec. 10, 1941, in 20 feet. Cargo valued at $2,000,000.

Lat/Long	Type, Name, Tonnage	Charts	Remarks
40-44.5 72-48.8	Sch. MILES M. MERRY (1589)	1108 1214	Wrecked Feb. 17, 1909. Loss valued at $45,000.
40-44.1 72-50.7	Shp. MARGARETHA (1534)	1108 1214	Wrecked Jan. 27, 1882. Cargo—merchandise. Loss estimated at $47,000.
40-44.0 72-48.9	Sch. WILLIAM C. CARNEGIE (2663)	1108 1214	Wrecked May 1, 1908. Cargo—coal.
40-43.7 72-51.4	Sch. LOUISE H. RANDLE (1502)	1108 1214	Wrecked Nov. 28, 1893, 650 yards from shore in 30 feet. Cargo—coal.
40-43.3 72-53.9	SS VINDICATOR (1021)	1108 1214	Sank Jan. 4, 1879, with a general cargo. Loss valued at $140,000.
40-41.6 72-58.0	Str. GREAT WESTERN (2000)	1108 1214	Wrecked March 26, 1876.
40-40.6 73-01.0	Str. GLUCKAUF (2306)	1108 1214	Wrecked March 29, 1893. Loss valued at $125,000.
40-38.8 69-34.5	Ftr. STEPHANO (3449)	1108	Sank Oct. 8, 1916.
40-33.3 73-01.3	USS SAN DIEGO (13,400)	1108 1214	Torpedoed July 19, 1918, in 90 feet. 50 lives lost.
——	LEXINGTON	369	Sank in East River off 138th Street, N.Y.C., 1780, in 66 feet. Loss reported at $1,800,000.
——	HUSSAR	369	Sank in East River off Brother Island, N.Y.C., 1780. Loss reported — $3,000,000.
——	M/V EMPRESS BAY (531)	369	Collided with NEBRASKA, June 25, 1958, in the East River, foot of Manhattan Bridge, New York.
——	Str. FINANCE (2603)	1108 1215	Sank in New York Bay in 1908 with a general cargo.
——	Str. MANDALAY (1120)	369	Collided with ACADIA, May 28, 1939, in New York Harbor.
——	Str. SANCRAFT (2054)	1108 369	Collided with MELROSE, July 2, 1959, in Narrows, New York Harbor.
40-38.2 73-18.4	Bk. JOSIE T. MARSHALL (1072)	1108 1215	Wrecked Jan. 7, 1881, on west end of Oak Island.
——	MYSTERY	1108 1215	Capsized July 10, 1887, in Jamaica Bay, L.I. 25 lives lost.
40-37.2 73-17.2	Str. DRUMELZIER (3625)	1108 1215	Wrecked Dec. 26, 1904, on Fire Island bar with general cargo. Loss valued at $544,000.
40-37.2 73-17.3	Paddle Wheel Steamer	1108 1215	200 yards south of Fire Island Light in 20 feet.

Lat/Long	Type, Name, Tonnage	Charts	Remarks
40-36.3 73-25.6	Str. RODA (2516)	1108 1215	Wrecked Feb. 13, 1908, with cargo of copper ore. Loss valued at $102,680.
40-35.3 73-26.5	ELIZABETH	1108 1215	Wrecked in 1850 with cargo of stone from Italy. $16,000 reported on board.
——	BRISTOL	1108 1215	Wrecked Nov. 21, 1836, off Far Rockaway L.I., 77 lives lost.
40-35.1 70-31.5	Str. PETER RICKMERS (2958)	1108 1215	Wrecked April 30, 1908, 600 yards offshore.
——	Str. ACARA (4193)	1108 1215	Wrecked March 1, 1902, on Jones Inlet Bars, L.I. Loss estimated at $700,000. Cargo—general.
——	BLACK WARRIOR	1108 1215	Sank in 30 feet off Rockaway Beach, L.I., in 1858.
——	Str. PORT PHILLIP (4060)	1108 1215	Sank after collision, 1919, in Ambrose Channel, N.Y., carrying general cargo.
40-30 74-00	Str. AYURUOCA (6872) Ftr. TURNER (1630)	1108 1215	Sank in 1940.
40-30 72-00	Tkr. SUNOCO (1214)	1108	Sank Jan. 2, 1945.

U.S. Coast and Geodetic Survey Charts Covering Northeastern States Atlantic Coastal Waters — Chapter 1

Maine, New Hampshire, Massachusetts,
Rhode Island, Connecticut and New York.

Chart	Price	Title	Scale	Size
369	$1.00	New York Harbor	1:40,000	35x46
1106	$1.00	Bay of Fundy to Cape Cod	1:378,838	36x46
1107	1.00	Georges Bank and Nantucket Shoals	1:400,000	34x48
1108	1.00	Approaches to New York—Nantucket Shoals to Five Fathom Bank	1:400,000	34x48
1201	1.00	Quoddy Roads to Petit Manan Island	1:80,000	33x42
1202	1.00	Frenchman and Blue Hill Bays and approaches	1:80,000	34x44
1203	1.00	Penobscot Bay and approaches	1:80,000	33x44
1204	1.00	Monhegan Island to Cape Elizabeth	1:80,000	35x45
1205	1.00	Cape Elizabeth to Portsmouth	1:80,000	34x43
1206	1.00	Portsmouth to Cape Ann	1:80,000	34x40
1208	1.00	Cape Cod Bay	1:80,000	35x43
1209	1.00	Nantucket Sound and approaches	1:80,000	35x43
1210	1.00	Martha's Vineyard to Block Island, including Buzzards and Narragansett Bays	1:80,000	36x43
1211	1.00	Block Island Sound and approaches	1:80,000	35x43
1212	1.00	Long Island Sound — eastern part	1:80,000	30x46
1213	1.00	Long Island Sound — western part	1:80,000	33x42
1214	1.00	Shinnecock Light to Fire Island Light	1:80,000	34x44
1215	1.00	Approaches to New York — Fire Island to Sea Girt Light	1:80,000	35x43

CHAPTER 2

Middle Atlantic Coast

New Jersey, Delaware,
Maryland, Virginia,
and North Carolina

NO SECTION of the country has contributed more to the mercantile development of the United States than the Middle Atlantic area. Our richest and most flourishing seaports are to be found in this vital stretch of coastline, extending from New York to South Carolina. Today, the bulk of America's commerce is transacted at New York, Philadelphia, Baltimore, Hampton Roads, and other major seaports of this region. Vessels flying the flags of all nations ride at anchor in its harbors. Through them flows the lifeblood of United States foreign trade.

The pattern of development for the Middle Atlantic area was very much the same as in the Northeast. Most of its first settlers came to the New World to escape religious persecution in the Old. They were a much more varied lot than their northerly neighbors. They included Quakers, Huguenots, Congregationalists, Baptists, Presbyterians, and other dissenters from the established Church of England. To this mixture were added German Lutherans, Irish Catholics, and Jews. Like their brethren to the north, they burned with a fierce passion for independence, both religious and political. They were deeply involved in the political ferment which would one day erupt into Revolution.

Long before the fateful shots were fired at Bunker Hill, New York had become a focal point of resistance to the British Crown. In 1774, a group of New Yorkers calling themselves "The Sons of Liberty" held a "tea party" of their own. After refusing a British cargo ship permission to land, they dumped a few chests of tea into the harbor.

The profit motive played an important part in the development of Middle Atlantic commerce. To promote passenger traffic, ships' captains in the early 1600's offered to transport to America emigrants who had no money for passage. They collected the costs, with a profit, by selling their passengers' skills and labor to employers for a term of years. The prospective employers were much more interested in the brains and muscles of their future employees than in their theology.

Nature was also kinder to the Middle Atlantic region than to the Northeast. Its fertile soil, good climate, and abundant natural resources speeded its economic development. It was inevitable that the same ships which carried emigrants to the colonies should also carry their products back to Europe. That was the start of a trans-Atlantic commerce which ultimately made Middle Atlantic ports the principal gateways to the wealth of America.

With the gradual dwindling of New England trade, New York and other Middle Atlantic harbors gained steadily in importance. By the early 20th Century, New York had become the principal port of arrival for immigrants from Europe. To oppressed peoples all over the world it had become the symbol of the new life for which they hungered. Ellis Island, long since abandoned as a quarantine station for immigrants, became famous as the portal to the fabled land towards which they had traveled so many weary miles.

Two world conflicts and an expansion of port facilities to meet the increased demands of modern shipping made New York America's most important seaport. In recent years, New York has handled nearly one-quarter of our ship traffic. Cargo worth hundreds of millions of dollars has passed through its facilities.

Equally dramatic was the rise of Philadelphia as a seaport. In the early 1700's, it already had an active trans-Atlantic, coastal, and West Indian trade. Philadelphia's importance increased during the Revolution when it became an interstate port. By imposing import taxes on goods brought in for transshipment, the shrewd Philadelphians derived a tidy profit. Marine construction mushroomed and Philadelphia ships and sailors won high praise. Its Humphrey model revolutionized frigate building and its old Navy yard was the forerunner of the present naval base.

But it was in the era of fast clippers, from 1775 to 1831, that Philadelphia really came into its own. After the Fisk-Fulton-Rumsey-Evans period of steamboat experimentation came the Liverpool packet service of Thomas P. Cope. Pilot service was established in October, 1788.

United States involvement in World War II speeded the development of Philadelphia as a great port. In 1942, the 40-foot Philadelphia-to-sea channel was completed, permitting access to deep-draft vessels. Today, the Philadelphia port complex includes railroad tracks with sidings, a 1500-foot tidewater terminal, a large grain elevator, electrically operated ore-loading machinery, and coal-loading facilities.

Development of the Atlantic seaboard was by no means confined to New York and Philadelphia. Farther south, in Virginia, the port of Norfolk came into existence in the early 17th century to meet foreign demands for locally grown tobacco and other native products.

America's foothold along the Atlantic coast was gradually being broadened and deepened as the nation expanded its frontiers. Other harbors felt the impact of this steady industrial and commercial growth. The nation was on the march to the conquest of the continent and nothing could stop it.

Part of the price paid for trade expansion was in the loss of many vessels in coastal waters. The shores and waters of the Atlantic seaboard are littered with the bones of wrecked merchant ships.

There was the Norwegian bark *Dictator* which on March 27, 1891, met a tragic end off the Virginia coast. Going down with her were the captain's wife and infant son.

Other tragedies include the *Republic, Merida, Nuphar,* and *Delaware.* During World War I, the British freighter *Mirlo,* with a cargo of oil, was turned into a flaming torch by a German torpedo. The rescue of her men from the blazing inferno is one of the great stories of courage on the sea. In the "Battle of the Atlantic" in World War II, many other ships and their crews met their deaths through enemy action. The list is long and tragic and much of it is given in the following pages. There is no question that a large part of the chronicle of America's rise to greatness was written in the enterprising area known as the Middle Atlantic.

THE TREASURE OF THE REPUBLIC

Riches beyond most men's wildest dreams — $3,000,000 in the American ten dollar gold pieces known as "Eagles" — reportedly lie in the hulk of the liner *Republic*, about 12 miles southwest of Nantucket Lightship.

If it hadn't been for the wireless which had just come into use, the *Republic* would probably have gone down without a trace as had many ships before her. News of her sinking wouldn't have reached the world for days or weeks. But through the wireless, her call for help went out over the water even while she was reeling from a collision with the *Florida*, and with water pouring into her hull.

Her anguished cries were heard by the *Baltic, Lorraine, Lucania,* and half a dozen other ships within a 100-mile radius. From all directions they sped through the fog, giving hope that she would not sink before help arrived.

The ill-starred *Republic* had hauled anchor at New York on Friday afternoon, January 22, 1909. She carried a gay, fashionable crowd bound for a winter cruise in the Mediterranean. Many of her 231 first-class passengers were wealthy and socially prominent. As the ship pulled out of New York harbor, private celebrations were held in staterooms, and the pop of champagne corks echoed throughout the vessel. For the next several weeks, they would cruise the warm Mediterranean, absorbing the wonders of its ancient cities.

But the sounds of revelry could not be heard by the other 211 passengers huddled in the dark steerage. About 160 were Italians returning to the homeland to visit relatives who had suffered in recent earthquakes in Sicily and Calabria. For many, it was a sad journey undertaken to learn whether mothers, fathers, sisters or brothers were still alive.

There was no reason to doubt the seaworthiness of the *Republic.* She had made the journey many times before without mishap.

She was a stoutly built vessel of 15,378 tons, driven by twin screws at speeds up to 16 knots with a single funnel and four masts. She was valued at $1,500,000, and such records as are available indicate that she was carrying $3,000,000 in American gold Eagles on the fatal voyage.

From the moment the *Republic* stuck her stern into the North River, she was in the grip of pea-soup fog. Once outside Sandy Hook, she took the common path of outbound liners, a course that swings northeasterly to a point just south of Nantucket Shoals Lightship. From there starts the long stretch across the Atlantic. Steaming at 7 to 11 knots, she held to her course.

Thirty miles off the prescribed course for inbound ships, the new 381-foot Italian liner *Florida*, with 900 returning Italians, steamed towards New York.

Aboard the *Republic*, at 6:30 a.m. Saturday morning, the four to eight watch nervously peered into the white nothingness. Suddenly from the fog-shrouded bow the lookout screamed, "Ship ahead, just off the starboard bow!"

"Left full rudder, all engines back full!"

It was too late! The *Florida* knifed deep into the *Republic's* side. The massive steel plates and framing of both ships ripped as if made of tin foil. The *Republic* heeled far to port as she absorbed the *Florida's* momentum.

Four persons on the *Republic*, caught in the Gargantuan grinder, were instantly killed. Passengers on both ships were jolted out of their bunks. The *Republic*, divided into 16 watertight compartments, had a longitudinal watertight bulkhead separating her two enginerooms. Both enginerooms were immediately flooded, indicating that the *Florida* had cut more than half way through the 68-foot beam. The ships remained locked together like feuding monsters.

Captain Sealby of the *Republic* gave the call to quarters. It was obeyed with the discipline of a man-of-war. Every man from the first officer to the stewards jumped to his place. Boats were lowered and the men told to guard them. Panic-stricken passengers were led immediately out of their cabins and assembled on deck with little confusion. Most had on only night clothes and robes.

There had been no time to dress or bring their possessions with them. Some of the frightened passengers, sure that the ship would sink under them momentarily, threaded their way across the jagged, shredded metal of both ships to the *Florida*.

On orders from Captain Sealby, the *Republic's* radio operator, 25-year-old Jack Binns, switched over to batteries. He began pounding out the distress signal of that time. "C Q D, C Q D, C Q D — This is the *Republic* — Rammed by unknown vessel —40-17 N, 70-00 W. — Need immediate assistance."

This was Binn's 41st trip between Europe and America. On the long lonely watches he had practiced the signal over and over. Now he was sending it in earnest. Calmly, deliberately, he repeated his distress message over and over.

At Siasconset, on the south shore of Nantucket, in a little room crowded with wire coils and choked with dusty battery cases, A. H. Ginman fingered his key. Eerie flashes of blue jumped between the hammock of wires over his head. He was engaged in his usual business of handling routine traffic for ships at sea. Abruptly, his measured cadence of finger tapping stopped. He strained to hear a new, an ominous, sound coming out of the rubber disk clamped over his ear by the harness around his head.

"Dah Dit Dah Dit Dah Dah Dit Dah Dah Dit Dit."

To Ginman these simple sounds meant the same as three nines to a fire chief or the sound of a general alarm aboard a battle ship. They were absolutely imperative. Instinctively he sent back "C Q D. Here Sc G," which meant "Distress signal received at Siasconset. Go ahead."

Binns quickly replied, "We were struck by an unknown ship —engine rooms filled — passengers safe — can stay afloat — Lat. 40-17 N, 70-00 W. — *Republic*."

Automatically, Ginman scribbled out the message being tapped into his ear. The stern regulations of the Marconi Wireless Telegraph Company of America prescribed that: "Whenever an operator shall receive the C Q D signal, he shall immediately ascertain the locality and damage and send to every ship and station within 200 miles word of the distress."

Ginman prefaced his message with the alarm, "C Q D", carefully repeated the message, and then sat back and waited. Ten minutes had elapsed from the time of the collision.

Ginman did not have long to wait. His powerful signals ignited the airways. The French liner *La Lorraine,* which was nearing New York, whirled about. The Cunard liner *Lucania* and the White Star liner *Baltic,* both heading toward the Nantucket Lightship from east and west respectively, responded immediately by dangerously increasing speed in the blinding fog.

Four Coast Guard cutters scrambled to get underway. The *Gresham* lifted its anchor and started from Provincetown, and the *Seneca* left New London. The *Mohawk* got underway from New Bedford but ran into a reef in the zero visibility. The *Acushnet* probed the fog from Woods Hole, but was diverted to another distress case before reaching the scene. A sizeable flotilla was now speeding to the rescue of the stricken vessels.

Captain Voltolin of the *Florida* was in a terrible dilemma. He couldn't stay locked to a sinking ship, yet he might sink if he backed off. Reports from his crew told him that the bulkheads abaft the *Florida's* shattered bow were leaking but holding. He ordered his carpenters to shore the bulkheads with timbers as best they could. When this was done, he gambled and backed off. Precariously, the steel bulkheads forward held out the water. Captain Voltolin maneuvered to stay close to the *Republic.*

Later in the morning, the rest of the *Republic's* passengers and most of its crew were ferried by lifeboats to the *Florida.* Only Captain Sealby and a salvage crew of 30 remained on board. Theoretically, the *Republic* would float with six to seven of its compartments flooded.

The *Baltic* was the first ship to arrive at the scene, about 1:00 p.m., Saturday. By now, the *Republic's* batteries had given out, and the *Florida* had no radio. There was no way to communicate except through submarine signals. An hour later, the *Lorraine* arrived.

The new arrivals groped about in the white blanket of fog in deadly fear of colliding. With four Goliaths of the sea in such a small area, invisible to one another, the possibility of further disaster weighed heavily on each skipper's mind. At 4:00 p.m. they were still searching with the added help and hazard of the *Lucania* which had now joined the crowd. At 6:00 p.m., the *Baltic*, under Captain Ransom, hove to within megaphoning distance of both the *Florida* and the *Republic*. The *Lorraine* and *Lucania* stayed within easy calling distance. The *Baltic* took over the burden of all the communications.

During a council of war between Captains Voltolin, Sealby, and Ransom, it was decided that they would remain this way until the fog cleared. The *Florida* could then leave for New York trailed by the *Lorraine*. The *Baltic* would remain with the *Republic* until salvage vessels arrived. This plan crumbled when, at 11:00 p.m., the fog did lift slightly, but was accompanied by a fresh easterly breeze. Captain Voltolin of the *Florida*, with over 2,000 persons on board—more than twice what he normally carried — became understandly concerned. It was therefore decided that the passengers would be transferred to the *Baltic*.

Since the *Baltic* was the larger vessel, she moved to the windward of the *Florida* and as near as she could safely lie. Then came the order to man the boats. Each of the crew went promptly to his station. Quickly, the *Baltic's* ten boats were lowered, each manned by a crew of seamen and coxswained by an officer. The falls were cast off and the flotilla pulled to the stricken *Florida*. The *Baltic's* gangways were lowered, made rigid with lifelines and manned by sailors ready to assist the passengers from the boats as they were brought over.

The *Baltic's* big searchlight burned through the light drizzle. Captain Ransom tensely superintended operations from high on the *Baltic's* bridge. Each little change in the weather took on heightened significance. Fortunately, the sea remained smooth. The lives of 2,000 humans on the *Florida* hung on the strength of the inner bulkheads of steel in the forward part of the ship.

The first boat, in the charge of the *Baltic's* first officer, pulled alongside the *Florida*. The sailors held her steady under the ladder. Women and children were helped down first until 20 filled the boat. It shoved off and was replaced by the next boat and so on. When the passengers reached the *Baltic*, they were given hot food and a bed to sleep in if they wished it. Passengers on the *Baltic* lined the rail to watch and assist when they could. It was 10 o'clock Sunday morning before the transfer was complete. It had taken more than ten hours and 83 boatloads to transfer 1,650 passengers, one of the biggest at-sea transfers of passengers on record.

The *Florida* headed for New York trailed by the *Lorraine*. The *Baltic* again began searching for the *Republic* which had drifted out of sight during the night. Hardly had she started searching when orders from White Star officials told her to proceed to New York without regard to the *Republic*. By now the American liner *New York* and the Anchor liner *Furnessia* were on the scene, so the *Baltic*, laden with the passengers of two other ships besides her own, departed for a hero's welcome in New York.

The night before, Captain Sealby and his crew of 30 stayed alongside the *Republic* in lifeboats so as not to be caught aboard if she sank. In the morning they reboarded the vessel. Binns jury-rigged other ships' batteries to his radio and was soon back on the air. Contact was established with the *Gresham* and *Seneca* who found the vessel in the afternoon. Attaching 12-inch circumference hawsers, the cutters began tugging their awesome burden westward.

Shortly after 8:00 p.m. Sunday, the *Republic* began to settle. The hawsers got tauter and tauter as the big ship slowly filled and became harder to pull. She began to lurch and then steady as the inner bulkheads gave way one at a time. Captain Sealby did not want to give up. He urged the cutters to keep pulling towards shallow water. To Captain Perry on the *Gresham*, which was the closer, it was obvious that the *Republic* would last only a short while. He ordered his hawser let go and the *Gresham's* boats launched to pick up survivors.

The *Republic* lurched again, this time deeper than before. The crew began to leap overboard. The *Gresham's* boats picked them up as fast as they fell in the water. The sound of exploding bulkheads and escaping air broke the silence of the still fog-bound seas. Suddenly, the bow arced high into the air. There was a loud clattering sound as innards broke loose and tumbled sternward. With a tremendous shudder and the hiss of escaping air, the once-proud *Republic* shot to the bottom stern first.

As the water rushed in to fill the void where she had been, mountainous waves nearly swamped the boats witnessing the cataclysm. Under the powerful blue pencils of light from the *Gresham's* searchlights, the boats continued the grim business of picking up the flailing men screaming for help in the debris. Second to last rescued was Binns, the radio operator. He had continued pounding out news of the saga to the last minute.

The boats had started back to the cutter before Captain Sealby was discovered missing. Frantically, the rescuers circled through the flotsam again. They found the captain alive on a piece of grating. He had been last to leave in accordance with tradition of the sea.

SHIPWRECK FOR PROFIT

One of the most ghoulish chapters in United States naval history was written in the early and middle years of the past century. Along the New England and Middle Atlantic coasts, organized bands of men followed the barbaric profession of ship plundering. To lure unsuspecting vessels ashore, they would show false lights and draw them into disaster. Once ashore, the ships would be methodically looted and all valuables taken from the passengers and crew. Sometimes, the pirates, in their impatience to obtain the loot, would cut off the fingers of the hapless seafarers for their rings or other jewelry.

Perhaps the most enterprising of these gangs operated off the Jersey shore and were not inappropriately known as the "Jersey wreckers." Barnegat Bay was the frequent scene of their depredations. It was because of these and other outrages that the Federal Government in 1871 built its lifesaving stations along this stretch of coast. This was also the year in which Congress set up a centrally supervised lifesaving system to replace the loosely administered volunteer system.

"Mooncussers," as they were sometimes called because of their abhorrence of moonlight, were not limited to the Jersey coast. As one of these pirates pointed out in a Congressional inquiry into piratical practices in Barnegat Bay: "Well, Sir, them stories is onjust, the men as is called Barnegat pirates are not us fishermen —never were; they're from the main-colliers and sech—as come down to a wrack. And they will have something to kerry home when they're kept up all night. They do their share of stealin'. I'll confess; but from Sandy Hook to Cape May, it's innocent to what is done on Long Island. No man or woman was ever robbed on this beach till they was dead. Of course, I don't mean their trunks and sech, but not the body. The Long Islanders cut off fingers of living people for rings, but the Barnegat men never touch the body till it's dead, no, sir." Obviously, he was a man of great sensitivity.

Another haunt of the ship plunderers was Nag's Head Beach, N.C. Its name came from the quaint practice of putting a lantern on a "nag's head" and then heading it in a direction opposite to that in which the ship was moving. These deceptive lights would sometimes cause a ship to beach where it would be despoiled by the wreckers.

Progress, however, finally put the "mooncussers" out of business. As sailing vessels gradually gave way to engine-powered ships, and as more advanced navigation instruments came into use, wrecks became less frequent. It was no longer so easy to lure an unwary skipper to his doom. That was the beginning of the end for these human vultures. Today, no one remembers them with pleasure, but they make an interesting footnote to history.

HATTERAS, CAPE OF STORMS

If the god of winds were searching for a dwelling place, he couldn't find a better one than Cape Hatteras. On this lonely spur of land off the coast of North Carolina, he could survey his vast domain with satisfaction.

To sailing men everywhere, the waters surrounding the Cape are known as among the most treacherous in the world. Out of clear blue skies, storms can, and often do, strike with sudden and demoniac intensity. One could probably devote a life-long search for shipwrecks to this area alone and not run out of vessels. It is for no trifling reason that Cape Hatteras is known as the "Graveyard of the Atlantic."

It was, in fact, Alexander Hamilton who gave it that name. He saw it first in 1773, when, as a youth of 17, he sailed by the Cape en route to the colonies. His memory of the vicious storm they encountered never left him. Many years later as Secretary of the

Treasury, he wrote a long letter to his First Assistant instructing him to buy land on which to build a lighthouse. The present light is maintained by the U. S. Coast Guard.

But then, as now, the Government did not always permit itself to be hurried. There was considerable difficulty in purchasing the land. Nine years went by before the lighthouse was finally built. In that time, plans were drawn by Hamilton's friend, Major General Henry Dearborn, and submitted with a bid for construction. Hamilton then took the plan to President Adams for his signature. After that, it was turned over to Tenche Coxe, first Commissioner of Revenue, for action. A part of the old tower still stands on the Cape. If it could speak it would tell some fascinating stories of goings on in these turbulent waters.

Over the years, Hatteras has bred a special breed of men. Winds and stormy seas are their natural element and many of them have won heroes' medals. Outstanding among this is the Midgett family which has produced some of the most valiant and skillful lifesavers in the world. For generations, this distinguished family has been contributing its skill and courage, first to the Lifesaving Service and then to the Coast Guard which absorbed it in 1915. Since 1884, four Midgetts have won the coveted Gold Lifesaving Medal and three others have received the silver medal. One of the recipients of the Gold Lifesaving Medal was John Allen Midgett who carried out an extraordinarily hazardous rescue of British seamen from the torpedoed tanker *Mirlo*.

Except for a modern lighthouse operated by the Coast Guard, the Cape is pretty much the same as in the days of Hamilton. Its windswept beaches look out on the deceptively beautiful Atlantic. On calm sunny days, it's hard to believe that so many ships have been the victims of its cruel caprice. Yet any sailor who has seen a vicious storm come up out of nowhere knows that the waters of Hatteras cannot be trusted. So far as he is concerned, Hatteras is still the abode of the god of winds.

The 656-foot Italian liner SS ANDREA DORIA *goes down following a collision with the Swedish liner* SS STOCKHOLM *in heavy fog approximately 205 miles east of New York.*

(Official U.S. Coast Guard Photograph)

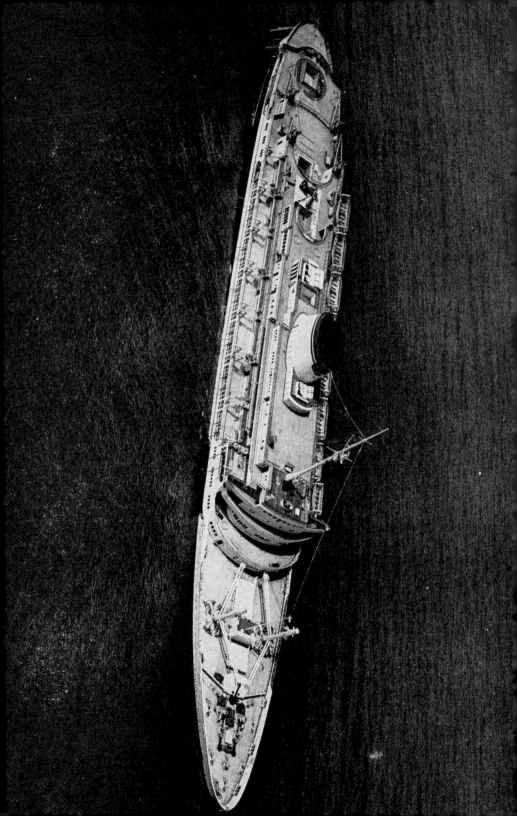

CHAPTER 2 — TABLES. The following listing gives the position (latitude and longitude); type, name of vessel, and tonnage; the Coast and Geodetic Survey charts covering the area; and, general information concerning dates, cargo, and estimated value.

Lat/Long	Type, Name, Tonnage	Charts	Remarks
		COAST OF NEW JERSEY	
——	Shp. CALEDONIA	1108	Wrecked in 1715 on S shore of Raritan River, between Edison and Victory Bridges.
40-29.5 69-50.6	Pass. ANDREA DORIA (29,083)	1108	Sank July 26, 1956, after collision with liner STOCKHOLM. In 200 feet. Passenger valuables, rich tableware, ship's furnishings, and proba-bly unopened safes still on board.
40-28.6 73-53.2	FORT VICTORIA	1108 1215	Sank in 1925. 42 feet over wreck.
40-27.5 73-27.0	Bge. BARDNESS (1295)	1108 1215	Sank November 10, 1910, in 75 feet.
40-27.0 71-50.0	Sch. EDWARD B. WINSLOW (2046)	1108	Sank December 12, 1928, in 265 feet.
40-16.0 70-50.0	Tkr. NORNESS (9577)	1108	Sank January 14, 1942, in 270 feet.
40-25.7 73-51.2	HMS PENTLAND FIRST (900)	1108 1215	Torpedoed September 19, 1942. 45 feet over wreck.
40-25.5 69-40.0	Pass. REPUBLIC (15,378)	1108	Sank Jan. 23, 1909, while in tow of Coast Guard cutters, GRESHAM and SENECA, after colliding with liner FLORIDA. In approximately 240 feet. $3,000,000 in American gold Eagles reported on board.
40-25.5 73-54.1	RAMOS (1208)	1108 1215	Sank in 1933. 54 feet over wreck.
40-24.0 73-55.1	CECILIA M. DUNLAP (835)	1108 1215	Sank before World War II in 60 feet.

Lat/Long	Type, Name, Tonnage	Charts	Remarks
40-23.3 69-36.5	Tkr. PAN PENNSYLVANIA (11,017)	1108	Torpedoed April 16, 1944, in 220 feet.
40-22.0 72-20.0	Tkr. COIMBRA (6768)	1108	Torpedoed January 15, 1942, in 180 feet.
——	Shp. HANNA (996)	1108 1215	Wrecked Feb. 18, 1879, off Monmouth Beach Coast Guard Station.
40-20.0 73-16.5	Ftr. YANKEE (2418)	1108 1215	Sank June 11, 1919, in 100 feet.
40-19.5 69-20.7	Ftr. STRATHDENE (4321)	1108	Sank Oct. 8, 1916, in 265 feet.
40-18.8 73-58.4	Bge. CORNELIUS GRINNELL (1001)	1108 1215	Wrecked Nov. 23, 1885. Cargo—coal.
40-17.2 73-58.2	Bk. W. J. STAIRS (1062)	1108 1215	Sank March 2, 1882. 24 feet over wreck.
40-16.5 73-11.4	Sch. BURNSIDE (855)	1108 1215	Sank March 20, 1913, in 125 feet.
40-15.9 73-47.5	Ftr. IOANNIS P. GOULANDRIS (3750)	1108 1215	Sank December 1, 1942, in 128 feet.
—— ——	Pass. RUSLAND (3000) Bk. ADONIS	1108 1215	Wrecked March 17, 1877, carrying passengers and general cargo. Loss valued at $416,000. Lies about 200 yards from beach at Long Branch, behind the present site of St. Alphonzo Priest Retreat. Next to it lies the ADONIS, wrecked in 1859. Cargo—lead ingots and millstones.
40-14.2 73-59.5	Str. PLINY (1060)	1108 1215	Wrecked on May 13, 1882, 200 yards off beach opposite Phillips Ave., Deal. Carried a general cargo. Loss estimated at $443,000.
40-13.8 73-50.1	Ftr. PINTA (195 feet long)	1108 1215	Sank April 20, 1963, after colliding with CITY OF PERTH.
40-13.3 73-59.8	NEW ERA (1828)	1108 1215	Wrecked November 13, 1854, off Asbury Park between 6th and 7th Ave. 300 lives lost.
40-13.0 73-44.5	Ftr. CHOAPA (1700)	1108 1215	Sank Sept. 21, 1944, after collision with Tanker VOCO. 95 feet over wreck.
40-10.9 74-00.5	Shp. MALTA (1611)	1108 1215	Wrecked Nov. 24, 1885, 250 yards from shore. Cargo of silver sand, stone & barrels. Loss valued at $75,362.
40-10.5 73-57.4	Bge. DRUIDHILL	1108 1215	Sank in 1940 in 46 feet.
40-10.4 73-41.0	Ftr. ARUNDO (5163)	1108 1215	Sank April 28, 1942. 73 feet over wreck.

Lat/Long	Type, Name, Tonnage	Charts	Remarks
40-10.0 72-02.0	Ftr. MAIDEN CREEK (5031)	1108	Sank Dec. 31, 1942, in 210 feet.
40-09.0 69-44.0	German Submarine U-550 (740)	1108	Sank April 16, 1944, in 310 feet.
40-09.0 74-01.2	AYRESHIRE	1108 1215	400 feet from shore and 300 feet south of the new jetty in Spring Lake, N.J.
40-08.3 74-01.3	Shp. TSERNOGORA (1252)	1108 1216	Wrecked March 28, 1886, 200 yards from beach.
40-08.0 73-53.0	Ftr. SAMMERSTAD (3875)	1108 1216	Sank Aug. 12, 1918, in 80 feet.
40-07.3 73-57.3	Bge. MARION	1108 1216	Sank Oct. 29, 1938.
——	LIVE OAK	1108 1216	Stranded in Squam Beach, Manasquan, in 1769. $20,000 in specie was reported lost with wreck.
40-06.5 74-01.8	Merchantship—150 feet long	1108 1216	Wreck is 800 feet from shore in 25 feet.
40-06 73-58.7	Shp. CADET	1108 1216	In 75 feet.
——	CIVITA CARRARA	1108 1216	Stranded a few hundred feet from Squam Inlet, Manasquan, in 1888 with a cargo of Italian marble.
40-06.0 71-00.0	FILLET (535)	1108	Sank before World War II.
40-04.6 73-58.5	Ftr. VALPARAISO (4979)	1108 1216	Sank Dec. 20, 1940. Also reported 1/3 mile south of this position.
40-03.7 74-00.5	Ftr. CADWALADER (1478)	1108 1216	Sank Aug. 29, 1942, in 65 feet.
40-02.5 74-02.7	Shp. META (1812)	1108 1216	Wrecked Oct. 14, 1883, 250 yards from beach.
40-01.5 73-31.7	Ftr. LILLIAN	1108 1216	Sank Feb. 27, 1939. 114 feet over wreck.
40-01.4 73-54.3	Ftr. MOHAWK (5896)	1108 1216	Sank Jan. 24, 1945, after colliding with TALIS-MAN. 51 feet over wreck.
39-57.0 73-55.0	Ftr. ANASTASIA (1313)	1108 1216	Sank before 1939. 63 feet over wreck.
39-53.8 73-48.2	Ftr. TOLTEN (1858)	1108 1216	Sank March 14, 1942. 51 feet over wreck.

Lat/Long	Type, Name, Tonnage	Charts	Remarks
39-53.3 73-58.7	Ftr. MAURICE TRACY (2468)	1108 1216	Collided with JESSE BILLINGSLEY June 17, 1944. 47 feet over wreck.
39-51.3 74-04.3	Str. CHARLEMAGNE TOWER (1825)	1108 1216	Sank March 6, 1914, 3/4 mile offshore with a cargo of coal.
39-51.1 74-03.3	Str. DELAWARE (1646)	1108 1216	Most of the possessions of 70 passengers and a general cargo valued at $150,000 went to the bottom with the Clyde Line steamer, at 4:30 a.m., July 9, 1898, 1½ miles offshore, NE of Barnegat Inlet. Bound for Charlestown, S.C., from New York, the ship had burst into a blazing inferno the previous night. Passengers and crew were forced to hastily abandon ship in boats and jury-rig rafts. All on board were rescued.
39-50.0 72-10.3	Sch. SAGUN (1585)	1108	Sank March 1, 1914, in 290 feet.
39-49.5 73-50.0	Tkr. GULFTRADE (6776) (stern)	1108 1216	Torpedoed March 10, 1942. 48 feet over wreck. 81,223 barrels bunker "c" oil aboard.
39-49.2 74-04.7	Sch. UNDAUNTED (1768)	1108 1216	Wrecked Dec. 26, 1913, ½ mile from shore with cargo of coal.
39-49.2 74-04.7	Sch. A. G. RAPES (2436)	1108 1216	Wrecked Dec. 26, 1913, ½ mile from shore with cargo of coal.
39-48.8 74-05.0	Shp. J. W. WENDT (2369)	1108 1216	Wrecked March 21, 1889, with cargo of iron. Loss valued at $32,000.
39-48.5 72-49.0	Ftr. BIDEVIND (4906)	1108 1216	Sank April 30, 1942. 143 feet over wreck.
39-48.3 73-55.7	Ftr. F. F. CLAIN (963)	1108 1216	Sank Feb. 17, 1943. 57 feet over wreck.
39-46.6 73-25.3	Tkr. R. P. RESOR (7451)	1108	Sank Feb. 27, 1942, with 105,025 barrels of fuel oil. 60 feet over wreck.
39-47.0 74-05.0	Bone wreck	1108 1216	½ mile offshore in 30 feet.
39-46.2 74-02.0	Tkr. PERSEPHONE (8426)—stern	1108 1216	Sank May 25, 1942. 39 feet over wreck.
39-37.0 73-39.0	Ftr. LILLIAN (3482)	1108	Collided with SS WIEGARD Feb. 6, 1939.
——	Str. GUADALOUPE (2839)	1108 1216	Wrecked Nov. 19, 1884, on outer edge of Barnegat Shoals on the northern side of the inlet channel. Carried a general cargo. Loss valued at $345,000.

Lat/Long	Type, Name, Tonnage	Charts	Remarks
39-45.4 73-50.8	Str. VISCAYA (2458)	1108 1216	Collided and sank Oct. 30, 1890, 12 miles east of Barnegat. A cargo of general merchandise and 70 lives were lost.
——	Sch. JOHN A. BRIGGS (2965)	1108 1216	Foundered Dec. 26, 1909, near Barnegat.
——	Str. CAROLINA (3125)	1108 1216	Lost June 14, 1918, near south side of Barnegat Inlet.
——	USS SUMNER (3524)	1108 1216	Lost Dec. 12, 1916, near south side of Barnegat Inlet with a cargo of scrap iron.
39-43.8 73-56.7	Tkr. SAN SABA (2458)	1108 1216	Torpedoed Oct. 4, 1918. 68 feet over wreck.
39-43.8 73-56.7	Ftr. HARRY RUSH (965)	1108 1216	Sank Feb. 17, 1943. 68 feet over wreck.
39-43.7 74-01.3	Tkr. GULFTRADE (6776) (bow)	1108 1216	Sank March 10, 1942. 44 feet over wreck.
39-42.2 74-07.8	Sch. HENRY FINCH (1976)	1108 1216	Wrecked Nov. 28, 1897.
39-40.8 73-55.0	Tug GREAT ISAAC (1117)	1108 1216	Collided with M/V BANDEIRANTE April 16, 1947, in 85 feet.
39-40.4 74-08.6	Shp. SIMILA (1110)	1108 1216	Wrecked Jan. 6, 1877.
39-39.4 73-56.8	Ftr. CHAPARRO (1505)	1108 1216	Torpedoed Oct. 27, 1918. 60 feet over wreck.
39-39.3 73-13.0	Ftr. CORVALLIS (2922)	1108	Sank in 130 feet before World War II.
39-37.0 73-39.0	LILLIAN (3482)	1108	Sank in 102 feet before World War II.
39-36.0 73-01.5	Sch. JACOB HASKELL (1778)	1108	Torpedoed June 2, 1918, in 210 feet.
39-35.7 74-12.2	Sch. HELEN J. SEITZ (2547)	1108 1216	Wrecked Feb. 9, 1906, with cargo of coal.
39-31.5 74-15.7	Shp. ONTARIO (1500)	1108 1216	Wrecked March 8, 1876.
39-30.0 74-00.0	Ftr. OKLAHOMA (5853)	1108 1216	Sank Jan. 4, 1914 in 80 feet.
39-29.3 74-15.6	Shp. FRANCIS (2077)	1108 1217	Wrecked April 8, 1897 with a general cargo. Loss valued at $262,000. 24 feet over wreck.

Lat/Long	Type, Name, Tonnage	Charts	Remarks
39-27.8 74-17.2	Sch. ANN HOOPER (1900)	1108 1217	Wrecked Feb. 7, 1942. 9 feet over wreck.
39-27.5 74-16.2	Shp. PARKFIELD (1397)	1108 1217	Sank Feb. 4, 1883, 2½ miles offshore. 28 feet over wreck.
39-26.0 72-50.0	Ftr. WINNECONNE (1869)	1108	Torpedoed June 2, 1918, in 220 feet.
39-26.0 73-07.0	SS KENNEBECK (2183)	1108	Sank June 17, 1921, with cargo of iron plates.
39-22.5 74-23.5	Str. MONTGOMERY (1100)	1108 1217	Lost Jan. 7, 1877, with a general cargo.
39-22.5 73-59.5	M/V VALCHEM (10,416)	1108 1217	Collided with SANTA ROSA Mar. 26, 1959, 20 miles east of Atlantic City.
39-21.2 74-17.2	Pig iron wreck	1108 1217	Barge loaded with pig iron with 44 feet over wreck. Sank before World War II.
39-21.2 74-12.8	Ftr. ALMIRANTE (5010)	1108 1217	Known as the "Flour Wreck," it sank Sept. 6, 1918. 42 feet over wreck.
39-20.8 74-27.0	Shp. GEESTEMUNDE (1098)	1108 1217	Wrecked Sept. 12, 1889.
39-20.5 74-11.4	Ftr. ASTRA	1108 1217	Sank in 1951 in 60 feet.
39-19.6 74-13.2	FALL RIVER (1759)	1108 1217	Sank before World War II. 63 feet over wreck.
39-18.2 74-15.9	Ftr. LEMUEL BURROWS (7610)	1108 1217	Sank March 14, 1942. 40 feet over wreck. 12,450 tons of coal on board.
39-17.5 74-21.4	Bge. DARIEN (924)	1108 1217	Sank May 2, 1948. 39 feet over wreck.
39-15.9 74-32.6	Bk. SINDIA (3068)	1108 1217	Sank Dec. 15, 1901, with a general cargo. Loss valued at $249,000.
39-15.0 72-30.0	Ftr. RIO TERCERO (4864)	1108	Sank June 22, 1942, in 470 feet.
39-14.8 74-09.1	Ftr. SAN JOSE (3358)	1108 1217	Sank Jan. 17, 1942. 69 feet over wreck.
39-10.3 73-20.5	Sch. EDWARD H. COLE (1791)	1108	Sank June 20, 1918, in 186 feet.
39-10.0 73-07.0	Sch. ISABEL B. WILE (776)	1108	Sank June 2, 1918, in 230 feet.

Lat/Long	Type, Name, Tonnage	Charts	Remarks
39-06.8 74-32.9	SALEM (703)	1108 1217	43 feet over wreck.
39-06.3 74-40.6	Str. NUPHAR (1279)	1108 1217	With a cargo of pig iron aboard, the British steamer lies 1½ miles offshore and 2 miles SE of the north side of Townsend's Inlet. The iron vessel stranded there at 4:00 a.m., Sept. 23, 1882, while enroute to Philadelphia from New Castle, England. Salvors, boarding that morning, were forced to abandon ship in the afternoon when a savage storm blew in. The ship and its $150,000 cargo were completely lost.
39-05.0 74-37.8	Bge. WAYNE	1108 1217	Sank in 1932. 33 feet over wreck.
39-05.0 73-47.0	Ftr. CAYRU (5152)	1108	Sank March 8, 1942. 102 feet over wreck.
39-00.4 74-04.9	Ftr. VARANGER (9305)	1108 1217	Sank Jan. 25, 1942. 76 feet over wreck.
——	Sch. ALEX GIBSON (2154)	1108 1217	Lost Nov. 29, 1915, near Hereford Inlet Light.
——	BAY RIDGE	1108 1217	Lost in 1928 near Hereford Inlet.
39-00 74-10	Sch. AZUA (664)	1108 1217	Sank May 14, 1930.
38-57.0 73-06.0	Ftr. CAROLINA (5093)	1108	Torpedoed June 2, 1918, in 245 feet.
38-56.5 74-41.9	Ftr. WILLIAM B. DIGGS (1034)	1109 1219	Sank in 1934. 33 feet over wreck.
38-56.0 74-51.5	IRMA PAULINE	1109 1219	Sank in 30 feet in entrance to Cape May Harbor.
38-54.9 74-23.0	Bge. L. B. SHAW (967)	1108 1219	Sank July 1, 1939. 82 feet over wreck.
38-54.0 74-34.0	Sch. DOR B. BARRETTUS (2088)	1108 1219	Sank Aug. 14, 1918, in 70 feet.
38-53.1 74-51.2	F. H. BECKWITH	1109 1219	Sank in 37 feet.
38-51.1 74-36.1	SS EVENING STAR	1108 1219	Sank in 1942.
38-50.0 73-12.2	Ftr. TEXEL (3210)	1108	Sunk by German sub June 2, 1918, in 270 feet.

Lat/Long	Type, Name, Tonnage	Charts	Remarks
——	M/V FAIR MOON (1327)	295	Foundered Mar. 24, 1958, in Delaware River approximately 1000 feet off Thompson's Point.
—— ——	MERLIN AUGUSTA		Both the MERLIN and the AUGUSTA (below) reported sunk by gunfire from Forts Mercer and Nassau in the Delaware Channel. The MERLIN, reported sunk in 108 feet, was carrying gold and silver bullion, estimated loss—$2,000,000. The AUGUSTA, carrying gold specie, reported sunk in 96 feet. Loss estimated at $1,000,000.

COAST OF DELAWARE

Lat/Long	Type, Name, Tonnage	Charts	Remarks
——	M/V A. C. DODGE (1147)	294	Collided with MICHAEL, May 25, 1952, in Delaware River off Reedy Is.
38-58.8 75-09.7	Tkr. CHINA ARROW (8403)	1219	Sank Feb. 5, 1942, in Delaware Bay in 35 feet.
——	Sch. WHITE BAND (1816)	1219	Foundered in Delaware Bay, Jan. 24, 1908.
38-52.0 75-07.9	Shp. ADOLPHUS (1319)	1109 1219	Sank Jan. 4, 1886 in 60 feet with cargo of chalk.
38-52.0 75-02.0	Shp. SUNRISE (1181)	1109 1219	Sank April 6, 1889, with cargo of coal.
——	DE BRAAK	1109 1219	Sank in 1798, 3½ miles off Lewes, in 84 feet. Gold and silver bullion reported on board. Loss estimated at $15,000,000.
38-49.2 74-31.3	HAMSHIRE	1109 1219	60 feet over wreck.
38-48.3 75-04.1	Ftr. GYPSUM PRINCE (3915)	1109 1219	Sank May 2, 1942, in 68 feet.
38-47.1 74-33.8	CITY OF GEORGETOWN	1109 1219	59 feet over wreck.
——	Bge. NIPHON	1109 1219	Sank off Cape Henlopen, in 1891.
——	FAITHFUL STEWARD	1109 1219	Said to have sunk in 90 feet 2 miles NE of Rehoboth Beach in 1785 with silver bullion and specie on board. Loss estimated at $500,-000.
38-42.6 74-59.8	Sch. HARRY K. FOOKS	1109 1219	Sank Sept. 10, 1941, in 33 feet.
38-42.0 75-04.0	Ftr. THOMAS TRACY (2443)	1109 1219	Lost Sept. 14, 1944, in 30 feet; 700 yards off Rehoboth Beach.

Lat/Long	Type, Name, Tonnage	Charts	Remarks
38-41.0 74-51.0	Ftr. NEW ORLEANS (1564)	1109 1219	Sank Oct. 11, 1917, in 65 feet.
38-40.3 74-28.7	USS JACOB JONES (bow) (1090)	1109 1219	Sank Feb. 28, 1942. 91 feet over wreck.
38-40.0 74-08.0	U.S. Submarine S-5	1109	Sank in 1920 in 150 feet.
38-38.3 74-24.0	USS JACOB JONES (stern) (1090)	1109 1219	Sank Feb. 28, 1942. 89 feet over wreck.
38-36.0 74-58.3	Bge. SOUTHERN SWORD (2180)	1109 1219	Sank March 18, 1946, in 45 feet.
38-35.5 75-03.4	Sch. ANNA MURRY (1534)	1109 1219	Wrecked Feb. 17, 1902.
38-33.5 73-50.6	Tkr. INDIA ARROW (8327)	1109	Torpedoed Feb. 4, 1942, in 180 feet with 88,369 barrels of diesel fuel.
38-29.5 74-33.3	Yct. MOONSTONE	1109 1219	Sank Oct. 15, 1943. 90 feet over wreck.
—	Str. CHAMPION (1418)	1109 1219	Sank Nov. 7, 1879, 15 miles from Delaware Lightship with a general cargo.
38-28.0 74-58.8	Bge. JOSEPH E. HOOPER (2233)	1109 1219	Sank Nov. 15, 1943. 25 feet over wreck.
38-27.4 74-47.2	Ftr. WASHINGTONIAN (7000)	1109 1219	Sank in 1915. 61 feet over wreck.

COAST OF MARYLAND

Lat/Long	Type, Name, Tonnage	Charts	Remarks
38-33.7 76-25.6	Bge. BRIGHT (2176)	1225	Sank Sept. 17, 1940, in 50 feet in Chesapeake Bay.
38-27.0 75-03.0	Sch. RELIANCE	1109 1220	Wrecked Aug. 17, 1944.
38-26.1 74-23.7	T. J. HOOPER (2197)	1109	Sank in 1935. 120 feet over wreck.
38-25.8 74-46.1	Tkr. W. L. STEED (3798)	1109 1220	Torpedoed Feb. 2, 1942. 57 feet over wreck. Carried 65,936 barrels of crude oil aboard.
38-25.0 74-42.0	Ftr. HVOSLEF (1630)	1109	Sank March 11, 1942, in 100 feet.
—	SS MANHATTAN (1525)	1109 1220	Lost Nov. 20, 1889, near Fenwick Island with a general cargo.
—	Sch. TECUMSEH (1658)	1109 1220	Lost March 2, 1892, on Fenwick Island Shoals.

Lat/Long	Type, Name, Tonnage	Charts	Remarks
38-24.7 74-50.2	Sch. ELIZABETH PAL	1109 1220	Sank in 1915. 54 feet over wreck.
38-22.7 74-58.8	CARPENDER	1109 1220	
38-21.0 74-40.0	Sch. ESTER ANN (753)	1109	Sank Oct. 9, 1920, in 108 feet.
38-18.0 74-00.0	Ftr. HARPATHIAN (4588)	1109	Sank June 5, 1918, in 220 feet.
38-17.6 75-00.0	Bge. JONES PORT (1322)	1109 1220	Sank Feb. 18, 1937.
37-17.0 74-08.0	Ftr. ALTAIR (6933)	1109	Sank Nov. 21, 1943, in 192 feet.
38-15.9 85-02.1	ESTHER ANN	1109 1220	
38-14.3 74-44.7	S. G. WILBUR (604)	1109 1220	Sank before World War II. 75 feet over wreck.
38-13.4 74-45.8	Ftr. SAITA (2873) (part of wreck)	1109 1220	Sank Nov. 9, 1918. 62 feet over wreck.
38-13.4 74-45.4	Ftr. SAITA (2873) (part of wreck)	1109 1220	Sank Nov. 9, 1918. 72 feet over wreck.
38-10.0 73-58.0	Tkr. ROCHESTER	1109	Sank Jan. 20, 1942.
38-06.1 74-37.0	Ftr. SAN GIL (3598)	1109	Sank Feb. 3, 1942. 90 feet over wreck.
38-05.4 74-48.6	Bge. GORDON S. COOK (2030)	1109 1220	Sank April 12, 1947. 50 feet over wreck.
38-04.0 74-06.0	USS ST. AUGUSTINE (1535)	1109	Sank Jan. 6, 1944, in 260 feet.
38-12.8 76-11.8	HUSTLER	1224	Sank in 1950.

COAST OF VIRGINIA

37-58.6 75-10.1	Tkr. CHINA ARROW (8403)	1109 1220	Torpedoed Feb. 5, 1942. 40 feet over wreck. 81,773 barrels of fuel oil aboard.
37-58.0 75-08.7	Bge. BARNSTABLE	1109 1220	Foundered before World War II on Winter Quarter Shoal. 14 feet over wreck.
37-57.2 75-06.3	Ftr. DAVID ATWATER (1468)	1109 1220	Sank April 3, 1942. 40 feet over wreck. 3911 tons of coal on board.

Lat/Long	Type, Name, Tonnage	Charts	Remarks
——	Str. SAGINAW (1835)	1109 1220	Sank May 5, 1903, near Winter Quarter Shoal with a cargo of merchandise.
37-55.0 75-03.0	Str. HERMOD (1928)	1109 1220	Sank April 12, 1918.
37-55.0 74-00.0	Ftr. OLINDA (4053)	1109	Torpedoed Feb. 18, 1942, in 600 feet.
37-54.0 75-19.7	Str. OAKDENE (1594)	1109 1220	Wrecked Feb. 2, 1895.
37-51.2 75-16.0	Str. TRECARRELL (3874)	1109 1220	Foundered Feb. 25, 1916, on Blackfish Shoal with a cargo of pyrites.
37-49.0 75-22.0	Ftr. E. R. SMITH (565)	1109 **1220**	Sank Dec. 5, 1943.
37-50.0 74-55.0	Ftr. MADRUGADA (1613)	1109 1220	Sank Aug. 15, 1918.
37-45.0 74-53.0	Tkr. FRANCIS E. POWELL (7096) part of wreck	1109	Torpedoed Jan. 27, 1942, with 81,024 barrels furnace oil mid-ships and gasoline in ends.
37-41.8 75-25.8	Sch. A. McDONALD (2218)	1109 1221	Sank Feb. 20, 1937, in 50 feet.
37-38.4 76-09.9	Sch. FANNY INSLEY	1223	Sank Aug. 1940 in Chesapeake Bay.
37-33.5 74-56.0	Sch. HANOVER No. 1 (915)	1109 1221	Sank Sept. 28, 1935.
37-33.3 75-34.2	Str. AMY DORA (1708)	1109 1221	Wrecked Oct. 5, 1889.
37-32.2 75-24.6	Bge. ALLEGHANNY (914)	1109 1221	Sunk March 31, 1942, by submarine shellfire while in tow of MENOMINEE. 56 feet over wreck. Cargo—coal.
37-32.1 75-13.8	Bge. BARNEGAT (914)	1109 1221	Sunk March 31, 1942, by submarine shellfire while in tow of MENOMINEE. 60 feet over wreck. Cargo—coal.
37-32.0 75-26.0	Tug MENOMINEE (441)	1109 1221	Sunk March 31, 1942, by submarine shellfire. 40 feet over wreck. 16 lives lost.
37-27.8 75-16.7	Tkr. FRANCIS POWELL (7096) part of wreck	1109 1221	Torpedoed Jan. 27, 1942. 60 feet over wreck.
37-27.0 **75**-09.0	Ftr. HAUPPAUGE (1446)	1109 1221	Torpedoed May 25, 1918.
37-26.3 75-37.2	SS SAN ALBANO (1291)	1109 **1221**	Wrecked Feb. 22, 1892.

Lat/Long	Type, Name, Tonnage	Charts	Remarks
37-23.5 74-42.0	Pass. MERIDA (6207)	1109	Two positions are given for this wreck. For description and other position, see MERIDA at 37-07.0.
——	Sch. INDEPENDENT (2253)	1109 1222	Foundered Nov. 14, 1908, off Hog Island. Cargo—coal.
37-17.0 75-39.0	Ftr. MERIDIAN	1109 1222	Sank in 1933 in 55 feet.
37-15.3 75-44.4	Sch. GASTON (1442)	1109 1222	Sank March 25, 1912.
37-15.3 75-44.4	Sch. S. D. CARLETON (1874)	1109 1222	Sank March 25, 1912.
37-15.4 75-37.3	Bge. BIRCH LAKE	1109 1222	Sank April 7, 1943. 41 feet over wreck.
37-14.6 76-02.3	PECOMIC	1222	Wrecked July 15, 1950, in Chesapeake Bay.
37-10.0 75-45.0	Shp. NORWOOD (1718)	1109 1222	Sank Feb. 18, 1910.
37-07.0 74-45.5	Pass. MERIDA (6207)	1109	$5,000,000 in gold and jewels reportedly went down with the MERIDA when she sank 60 miles off the Virginia Capes, May 11, 1911. Although millions have been spent in salvage attempts, there is no indication that any treasure has ever been recovered from the hulk.
37-06.4 76-15.1	Tkr. MARGARET	1222	Sank Feb. 11, 1950, in Chesapeake Bay.
37-03.6 74-55.3	Ftr. OCEAN VENTURE (7174)	1109	Torpedoed Feb. 8, 1942, in 150 feet.
37-03.4 75-54.0	SS ANGLO-AFRICAN (4186)	1109 1222	Sank Jan. 6, 1909, with a cargo of nitrate of soda. Loss valued at $700,000. 11 feet over wreck.
37-03.3 75-51.3	Sch. FRANCIS O. BOY	1109 1222	Sank in 1924. 24 feet over wreck.
37-03.3 75-51.1	Ftr. BRAZIL (2388)	1109 1222	Sank April 9, 1942. 23 feet over wreck.
37-03.5 76-10.7	ATKINSON	1222	Sank in 1949 in Chesapeake Bay.
37-02.0 76-14.0	Ftr. DRUID HILL (1281)	1222	Sank Sept. 21, 1942, in Chesapeake Bay in 15 feet.
——	Sch. MARY E. H. G. DOW (1139)	1222	Sank Dec. 20, 1892, on Middle Ground Shoal, Chesapeake Bay, with a cargo of coal.

Lat/Long	Type, Name, Tonnage	Charts	Remarks
37-01.4 76-12.9	Ftr. SEMINOLE	1222	Sank April 26, 1947, in Chesapeake Bay.
37-00.9 76-14.4	MARGARET ATKINSON	1222	Sank in Chesapeake Bay in 1947.
——	Str. PAWHATAN (2898)	1222	Sank Dec. 19, 1916, after a collision off Thimble Shoals, Chesapeake Bay, with a cargo of general merchandise.
37-00.1 75-24.4	Ftr. JOHN MORGAN (7176)	1109	Sank June 1, 1943. 55 feet over wreck.
37-00.0 73-25.0	Ftr. TREPCA (5042)	1109	Sank March 13, 1942, in 84 feet.
36-58.7 75-58.1	Sch. CHARMER (1885)	1109 1222	Sank Dec. 3, 1912, with cargo of coal. 21 feet over wreck.
36-58.6 75-25.1	Ftr. LILLIAN LUCKENBACK (6369)	1109	Sank March 27, 1943. 51 feet over wreck.
36-58.0 76-13.8	M/V WANDERER	1222	Sank in Chesapeake Bay in 1946. 16 feet over wreck.
36-57.6 76-00.7	Ftr. CHILORE (9310)	1222	Sank July 15, 1942, in Chesapeake Bay. 37 feet over wreck.
36-57.6 76-21.0	MARY HOOPER	1222	Sank April 19, 1927, in Hampton Roads.
36-57.0 76-01.3	Examination Vessel	1222	Sank July 29, 1944, in Chesapeake Bay. 49 feet over wreck.
36-56.8 75-57.6	Bge. WESTMORELAND	1109 1222	Foundered Oct. 3, 1939. 50 feet over wreck.
36-56.6 76-20.0	Schooner	1222	Sank in Hampton Roads in 1942.
36-55.2 74-43.0	Sch. B. A. VAN BRUNT (1191)	1109	Sank Sept. 20, 1925, in 260 feet.
36-55.0 75-00.0	Ftr. EIDSVOLD (1570)	1109	Sank April 6, 1918, in 115 feet.
36-54.0 75-58.0	Sch. OCEAN BELLE (1591)	1109 1222	Sank Oct. 10, 1903, in 23 feet with 2,605 tons of coal on board.
36-53.9 75-46.9	Ftr. SANTORE (7117)	1109 1222	Sank June 17, 1942. 37 feet over wreck.
36-53.5 75-58.9	Bk. JOANNA H. CANN (1169)	1109 1222	Wrecked Feb. 10, 1881, 250 yards from shore.

Lat/Long	Type, Name, Tonnage	Charts	Remarks
36.53.0 74-45.0	Sch. ISABELLA PARMENTER (979)	1109	Sank Oct. 30, 1925, in 245 feet.
36-52.7 75-58.7	Shp. A. S. DAVIS (1399)	1109 1222	Wrecked Oct. 23, 1881.
36-52.2 85-58.5	Bk. DICTATOR (1242)	1109 1222	Wrecked March 27, 1891.
36-51.5 75-58.5	Sch. GEORGIA	1109 1222	Wrecked Oct. 10, 1903, with cargo of coal.
36-51.1 76-18.8	Bge. HARRY F. HOOPER	1222	Sank July 23, 1941, in Scott Creek.
36-49.6 75-23.0	Tkr. FRANCIS E. POWELL (7076) stern	1109	Torpedoed in 1942. 56 feet over wreck.
36-49.7 75-52.1	KINGSTON CEYLONITE (500)	1109 1227	Sank June 17, 1942. 43 feet over wreck.
36-46.0 75-46.2	Tkr. TIGER (5992)	1109 1227	Torpedoed April 1, 1942, with 64,321 barrels of Navy #1 fuel. 39 feet over wreck.
36-45.5 75-43.9	Bk. FIGOGNA (843)	1109 1227	Sank in 1883 in 48 feet of water with 1,000 tons of iron ore on board.
36-44.6 75-56.7	Shp. ELIZABETH (1239)	1109 1227	Wrecked Jan. 8, 1887, with cargo of kainite.
36-37.5 75-53.2	Str. METROPOLIS (878)	1109 1227	Wrecked Jan. 29, 1878, with cargo of railroad iron.
36-33.9 75-50.4	Str. STAFFA (2146)	1109 1227	Wrecked Jan. 16, 1897, on Pebble Shoal, 1½ miles offshore.
36-33.7 75-52.1	Bk. CLYTHIA (1140)	1107 1227	Wrecked Jan. 22, 1894, 300 yards from head of Pebble Shoal with a cargo of marble on board. Loss estimated at $78,000.

COAST OF NORTH CAROLINA

Lat/Long	Type, Name, Tonnage	Charts	Remarks
36-32.4 75-51.9	Sch. WILLIAM H. MACY (2163)	1109 1227	Wrecked April 3, 1915.
36-31.3 75-51.7	Str. KIMBERLEY (2464)	1109 1227	Wrecked Nov. 29, 1887.
36-30.0 74-47.0	Sch. NORDHAV (2846)	1109	Sank Aug. 17, 1918, in 290 feet.
36-29.7 75-51.0	USS HURON (541)	1109 1227	Wrecked Nov. 24, 1877. 160 lives lost.
36-27.6 74-56.6	Pass. CHENANGO (3106)	1109	Torpedoed April 20, 1942, in 96 feet.

Lat/Long	Type, Name, Tonnage	Charts	Remarks
36-23.0 75-49.0	Sch. A. ERNEST MILL (1800)	1109 1227	Sank before World War II.
36-22.5 75-27.0	Str. CONSOLS (2300)	1109 1229	Foundered Feb. 3, 1912, while being towed by Revenue Cutter ONONDAGO.
36-20.1 75-48.6	Bk. N. BOYNTON (1065)	1109 1229	Wrecked April 17, 1889.
36-18.0 75-03.0	Ftr. BAURQUE (5152)	1109	Torpedoed Feb. 15, 1942. 102 feet over wreck.
36-16.2 75-47.0	Str. ELLIN (4000)	1109 1229	Wrecked Dec. 15, 1919.
36-15.6 74-51.6	Pass. EQUIPOSE (6210)	1109	Torpedoed March 27, 1942.
36-08.9 75-14.7	Tkr. B. D. BENSON (7952)	1109	Torpedoed May 4, 1942, with 91,500 barrels crude oil aboard. 54 feet over wreck.
36-04.0 75-13.7	Ftr. YORK (1600)	1109	Torpedoed in 1942. 72 feet over wreck.
36-02.3 75-40.0	Tkr. PARAQUAY	1109 1229	Wrecked before 1928, 300 yards from shore.
36-01.0 75-30.0	Tkr. OLYMPIC (5335)	1109 1229	Torpedoed Jan. 22, 1942. 60 feet over wreck.
36-00.0 76-00.0	Ftr. WRIGHT I (2693)	1109 1228	Lost Jan. 5, 1944.
35-56.7 76-41.5	WINTHROP wreck	1228	Sank March 29, 1939.
35-53.2 75-17.0	German Submarine U-85 (500)	1109	Sunk April 15, 1942. 54 feet over wreck.
35-50.5 75-33.3	Sch. FLORENCE C. MEGEE (1081)	1109 1229	Wrecked Feb. 26, 1894, with cargo of phosphate rock.
35-42.0 75-25.5	Tkr. MIRLO (6978)	1109 1229	Torpedoed Aug. 16, 1918, in 75 feet.
35-37.8 75-53.4	Tkr. SAN DELFINO (8072)	1109	Torpedoed April 9, 1942. 100 feet over wreck.
35-36.7 75-27.6	Str. PLYMOUTH	1109 1229	Wrecked in 1853. Boiler still visible in 1928.
35-35.9 75-27.6	Bk. JOSIE TROOP (1099)	1109 1229	Wrecked Feb. 22, 1889, with cargo of chalk.
35-35.4 75-27.5	Str. STRATHAIRLY (1919)	1109 1229	Wrecked March 24, 1891, with cargo of iron ore.

Lat/Long	Type, Name, Tonnage	Charts	Remarks
35-32.6 75-15.0	Ftr. MARORE (8251)	1109 1232	Torpedoed Feb. 26, 1942, with 22,000 tons of iron ore. 69 feet over wreck.
——	Sch. GOVERNOR AMES (1778)	1109 1232	Stranded Dec. 13, 1909, on Wimble Shoals.
35-24.0 75-21.0	Ftr. CILTVAIRA (3779)	1109 1232	Torpedoed Jan. 19, 1942, in 84 feet.
35-23.5 75-20.2	Ftr. CITY OF ATLANTA (5269)	1109 1232	Torpedoed Jan. 19, 1942. 57 feet over wreck.
35-13.7 75-12.1	Ftr. MERAK (3024)	1109 1232	Torpedoed Aug. 6, 1918. 70 feet over wreck.
35-13.6 75-26.9	CENTRAL AMERICA	1109 1232	Sank Sept. 12, 1857. Gold bullion & nuggets reported on board. Loss estimated at $2,400,000 (wreck has never been found).
35-13.4 75-37.9	Sch. GEORGE W. WELLS (2970)	1109 1232	Stranded Sept. 3, 1913, 450 yards off of beach.
——	Sch. VENTURA (3529)	1109 1232	Lost Feb. 20, 1918, on Hatteras Shoals, with cargo of nitrate.
——	Str. CIBAO	1109 1232	Lost on Hatteras Shoals before 1928, 2 miles from shore.
35-11.8 75-15.3	Ftr. EMPIRE THRUSH (6160)	1109 1232	Torpedoed April 14, 1942. 42 feet over wreck.
35-11.0 75-45.0	Ftr. A. R. HEIDRITTEUS (694)	1109 1232	Sank March 3, 1945, in Hatteras Inlet.
35-10.9 75-21.2	Str. VIRGINIA (2314)	1109 1232	Lost May 2, 1900, with cargo of iron ore.
——	Str. ISLE OF IONA (3789)	1109 1232	Lost Dec. 13, 1914, in Hatteras Inlet, with cargo of iron ore.
35-10.3 75-47.9	Str. ARIOSTO (2919)	1109 1232	Stranded Dec. 24, 1899, 400 yards from beach.
35-10.3 75-21.5	Ftr. K. LOULOUDIS (5106)	1109 1232	Torpedoed March 19, 1942. 36 feet over wreck.
35-10.2 75-19.8	Iron Vessel	1109 1232	75 feet of forefoot of capsized iron vessel reported showing in 1918.
——	Sch. CARROLL DEERING (1000)	1109 1232	Sailed onto Diamond Shoals in 1921 with no one aboard.
——	Sch. ROBERT H. STEVENSON (1290)	1109 1232	Stranded Jan. 13, 1906, on Diamond Shoals. Cargo—coal.
——	Str. SANTAGO	1109 1232	Foundered on Diamond Shoals in March 1924.

Lat/Long	Type, Name, Tonnage	Charts	Remarks
——	Ftr. VENORE (8016)	1109 1232	Torpedoed Jan. 1942, 5 miles from Diamond Shoals. 8,000 tons of iron ore on board.
35-09.4 75-18.2	Tkr. BRITISH SPLENDOR (7138)	1109 1232	Torpedoed April 6, 1942. 52 feet over wreck.
——	Str. HESPERIDES (2404)	1109 1232	Lost Oct. 9, 1897, on Outer Diamond Shoals, with cargo of iron ore.
——	Str. PALESTRA (2410)	1109 1232	Lost August 9, 1900, on Outer Diamond Shoals.
35-09.0 75-31.9	Ftr. LIBERATOR (7720)	1109 1232	Torpedoed March 19, 1942, with 11,000 tons of sulfur on board, in 45 feet.
35-08.0 75-22.0	Tkr. LANCING (7866)	1109 1232	Torpedoed April 7, 1942, in 60 feet.
35-07.9 75-28.0	Str. BREWSTER (1517)	1109 12_2	Lost Nov. 28, 1909.
35-07.3 75-22.1	Tkr. AUSTRALIA (11,628)	1109 1232	Torpedoed March 17, 1942, in 70 feet.
35-07.0 75-07.0	Tkr. W. ROCKEFELLER (14,054)	1109	Torpedoed June 28, 1942, with 125,000 barrels of fuel oil on board in 650 feet.
——	Str. WETHERBY (2129)	1109 1232	Lost Dec. 12, 1893, on Outer Diamond Shoals, 12 miles offshore with cargo of phosphate rock.
——	HOME	1109 1232	Wrecked Oct. 9, 1837, off Ocracoke. 100 lives lost.
35-06.0 75-27.1	Str. GIANAYRON (1631)	1109 1232	Lost May 22, 1896, with cargo of phosphate.
35-05.5 75-33.5	Str. NORTHEASTERN (2206)	1109 1232	Lost Dec. 27, 1904, with cargo of crude oil.
35-05.5 75-35.0	Schooner	1109 1232	Sank before World War II.
35-05.0 75-20.0	Ftr. NORLAVORE (2713)	1109 1232	Torpedoed Feb. 26, 1942. 3,335 tons of general cargo on board. 28 lives lost. In 198 feet.
35-04.9 75-23.4	Ftr. TENAS (2212)	1109 1232	Sank March 17, 1942. 77 feet over wreck.
35-04.8 75-20.0	Lightship DIAMOND SHOAL	1109 1232	Torpedoed August 6, 1918.
35-04.7 75-23.7	Large Vessel	1109 1232	Large vessel lies on its side in 95 feet.
35-03.3 76-00.3	Twr. ALBATROSS	1109 1232	Sank before World War II in Ocracoke Inlet.

Lat/Long	Type, Name, Tonnage	Charts	Remarks
35-01.8 75-28.6	Tkr. EMPIRE GEM (9139)	1109 1232	Torpedoed Jan. 24, 1942. 101 feet over wreck.
34-59.4 75-48.1	Tkr. F. W. ABRAMS (14,500)	1110	Torpedoed June 10, 1942, with 101,500 barrels of fuel oil on board. 54 feet over wreck.
34-59.0 76-03.1	Str. ARRAYO (3564)	1110 1233	Sank Feb. 20, 1910, with cargo of iron ore.
34-57.0 75-40.0	Sch. MERAK (7024)	1110	Torpedoed Aug. 6, 1918, in 100 feet.
34-54.0 75-45.0	Tkr. DIXIE ARROW (8046)	1110	Torpedoed March 26, 1942, with 88,136 barrels of crude oil on board. 54 feet over wreck.
34-51.0 75-22.0	German Submarine U-576 (500)	1110	Sunk July 15, 1942, in 700 feet.
34-49.5 75-33.0	Tkr. E. M. CLARK (9647)	1110	Torpedoed March 18, 1942, with 114,000 barrels of diesel oil on board, in 270 feet.
34-49.1 75-54.3	Ftr. PROTEUS (4836)	1110	Sank August 19, 1918. 66 feet over wreck.
34-45.0 75-29.0	SS CHILORE (8310)	1110	Torpedoed July 15, 1942.
34-44.0 75-35.0	Ftr. POWELL (1218)	1110	Sank April 6, 1920.
34-41.5 75-35.1	Ftr. NORDAL (3848)	1110	Torpedoed June 24, 1942.
34-41.0 75-49.0	U.S. Submarine TARPON (1135)	1110	Sank August 26, 1957, in 270 feet.
34-39.0 75-47.8	Ftr. MANUELA (4772)	1110	Torpedoed June 24, 1942, in 240 feet.
34-37.8 76-19.8	Tkr. ARIO (6952)	1110 1233	Torpedoed March 15, 1942. 63 feet over wreck.
34-36.5 76-18.9	Ftr. CARIBSEA (2609)	1110 1233	Torpedoed March 11, 1942, with 3600 tons of manganese ore. 49 feet over wreck.
34-33.0 76-36.0	HMS SENATEUR DUHA (913)	1110 1233	Sank May 6, 1942. 39 feet over wreck.
34-32.8 76-00.8	Tkr. TAMAULIPAS (6943)	1110 1233	Torpedoed April 10, 1942, with 77,782 barrels of heating oil on board. 96 feet over wreck.
34-32.4 76-31.2	Str. THISTLEROY (4027)	1110 1233	Sank Dec. 28, 1911, on Cape Lookout Shoals.
34-31.7 76-14.6	Tkr. ATLAS (7137)	1110 1233	Torpedoed April 9, 1942, with 87,000 barrels of gasoline. 66 feet over wreck.

Lat/Long	Type, Name, Tonnage	Charts	Remarks
34-30.0 75-40.0	Ftr. L. MATKOVIC (3289)	1110	Torpedoed June 24, 1942.
34-29.6 76-25.8	Ftr. PORTLAND (2648)	1110 1233	Torpedoed Feb. 11, 1943. 18 feet over wreck.
34-26.0 76-28.2	Str. EA (2632)	1110 1233	Sank March 15, 1902, with a cargo of phosphate and rosin.
34-22.8 76-21.9	Ftr. ASHKABAD (5284)	1110 1233	Torpedoed April 29, 1942. 39 feet over wreck.
34-32.8 76-53.7	Ftr. SULOID (3235)	1110 1234	Sank March 26, 1943. 39 feet over wreck.
34-30.1 76-54.3	Tkr. W. E. HUTTON (7076)	1110 1234	Torpedoed March 19, 1942, with 64,000 barrels of fuel oil on board. 42 feet over wreck.
34-13.7 76-34.0	German Submarine U-352 (500)	1110	Sunk May 9, 1942. 84 feet over wreck.
34-09.0 75-47.0	USS SHURZ (1657)	1110	Sank June 21, 1918.
34-08.6 76-39.2	Tkr. PAPOOSE (5939)	1110	Torpedoed March 18, 1942. 60 feet over wreck.
34-08.1 76-07.0	Tkr. PANAN (7277)	1110	Torpedoed May 4, 1943.
34-07.8 77-56.3	BLANCHI	1110 1235	Sank Nov. 27, 1947, in Cape Fear River.
34-03.6 76-34.1	Tkr. NAECO (5373)	1110	Torpedoed March 23, 1942. 96 feet over wreck.
33-59.0 76-40.0	Tkr. NAECO (5373)	1110	In 132 feet. 72,000 barrels of kerosene on board.
33-58.5 77-39.5	Wreck	1110 1235	Approximately 375 feet long. In 60 feet.
33-57.8 77-36.0	Wreck	1110 1235	Approximately 185 feet long. In 66 feet.
33-57.3 77-39.0	Wreck	1110 1235	Approximately 220 feet long. 54 feet over wreck.
33-56.0 76-22.3	Sch. W. H. WALKER (592)	1110 1235	Sank Oct. 29, 1927, in 150 feet.
33-51.0 77-28.8	Wreck	1110 1235	Approximately 385 feet long. 16 feet over wreck.
33-51.3 77-26.5	Wreck	1110 1235	Approximately 180 feet long. 78 feet over wreck.

Lat/Long	Type, Name, Tonnage	Charts	Remarks
33-50.5 77-27.5	Tkr. JOHN D. GILL (11,641)	1110 1235	Torpedoed March 12, 1942, with 141,981 barrels of crude oil. 72 feet over wreck.
33-54.1 77-49.0	Tkr. CASSIMER (5030)	1110 1236	Sank Feb. 26, 1942. 38 feet over wreck.
33-45.5 77-13.3	Tkr. ESSO NASHVILLE (4697)	1110	Torpedoed March 23, 1942.
———	Bk. LAUNBERGA (1302	1110 1236	Lost Sept. 21, 1906, on Frying Pan Shoals.
33-37.8 77-54.2	Sch. MARIE PALMER (1904)	1110 1236	Lost Dec. 1, 1909.
33-36.7 77-51.4	Ftr. MOUNT DIRFYS	1110 1236	Sank Dec. 29, 1936.
33-36.0 77-28.0	Wreck	1110	Approximately 381 feet long. 60 feet over wreck.
33-31.0 77-57.0	Ftr. RARITAN (2649)	1110 1236	Sank Feb. 25, 1942, in 78 feet.
33-17.0 77-49.5	U. S. YDS 68	1110	Sank Sept. 24, 1952, in 100 feet.

U.S. Coast and Geodetic Survey Charts Covering
Middle Atlantic States Coastal Waters — Chapter 2

New Jersey, Delaware, Maryland, Virginia and North Carolina

Chart	Price	Title	Scale	Size
294	$1.00	Delaware River — Smyrna River to Wilmington	1:40,000	31x47
295	1.00	Delaware River — Wilmington to Philadelphia	1:40,000	34x44
1108	1.00	Approaches to New York	1:400,000	34x48
1109	1.00	Cape May to Cape Hatteras	1:416,944	33x52
1110	1.00	Cape Hatteras to Charleston	1:432,720	34x46
1215	1.00	Approaches to New York — Fire Island Light to Sea Girt Light	1,80,000	35x43
1216	1.00	Sea Girt to Little Egg Inlet	1:80,000	35x42
1217	1.00	Little Egg Inlet to Hereford Inlet	1:80,000	35x43
1219	1.00	Cape May to Fenwick Island Light	1:80,000	35x49
1220	1.00	Fenwick Island Light to Chincoteague Inlet	1:80,000	35x42
1221	1.00	Chincoteague Inlet to Great Machipongo Inlet	1:80,000	38x43
1222	1.00	Chesapeake Bay Entrance	1:80,000	35x45
1223	1.00	Chesapeake Bay — Wolf Trap to Smith Point	1:80,000	34x41
1224	1.00	Chesapeake Bay — South Point to Cove Point	1:80,000	32x43
1225	1.00	Chesapeake Bay — Cove Point to Sandy Point	1:80,000	36x40
1227	1.00	Cape Henry to Currituck Beach Light	1:80,000	35x43
1228	1.00	Albemarle Sound	1:80,000	34x44
1229	1.00	Currituck Beach Light to Wimble Shoals	1:80,000	34x48
1232	1.00	Cape Hatteras — Wimble Shoals to Ocracoke Inlet	1:80,000	36x44
1233	1.00	Portsmouth Island to Beaufort, including Cape Lookout Shoals	1:80,000	35x44
1234	1.00	Cape Lookout to New River	1:80,000	34x41
1235	1.00	New River Inlet to Cape Fear	1:80,000	35x44
1236	1.00	Approaches to Cape Fear River	1:80,000	35x45

CHAPTER 3

Southeastern Coast

South Carolina

Georgia, Florida

JUST BELOW the border between North and South Carolina, where the coast bends sharply inward, the Atlantic becomes a brilliant aquamarine. This is the storied Southeast. To its blue-green waters have come ships of many nations. They started coming more than four and a half centuries ago when North America was a trackless wilderness inhabited by Indians. The first explorers to sight the new continent probably anchored at one of the many islands off the southern tip of Florida.

Only a few years after Columbus had made his epochal discovery, Spanish vessels were already plying the South Atlantic. Mostly, the Spaniards came to find the fabled wealth of the New World. They were hard, ruthless men from all classes of society. Some were jailbirds who had been given the hard option of signing on for a voyage of exploration or languishing in a Spanish prison. Others were ne'er do wells, seeking to escape from their frustrations and failures. Many were unemployed veterans of the terrible religious wars then devastating Europe. And there were also a few improverished aristocrats, hoping by one bold stroke of fortune to replenish their empty coffers and restore lustre to the family name. But whatever their social position, these men all shared a common hunger for the gleaming yellow metal that held, and still holds, the key to wealth and power.

For many, the quest would end in an unmarked grave, far from the orange groves of Spain. Only a few would find the riches for which they yearned. The great majority would return as empty-handed as they had come. But they had glimpsed a new land of unimaginable potential. And that vision would change their lives forever.

Yet not all of the voyages were motivated by greed. A spirit of adventure was stirring in the world. Men were curious to know more about this planet which was evidently a great deal larger and more varied than they had been led to believe. Foremost in this era of exploration was Spain, whose galleons were probing the limits of the known world. In an unending stream they carried the wealth of the new continent homeward for the enrichment of Spain and her monarch.

The opulence of Spanish trade with the new world colonies is evidenced by the wreck of the *Santa Margarita* in 1595 off the coast of Florida. She carried a cargo of gold and silver bullion valued at approximately $3,000,000. More than a century later, in 1733, another Spanish treasure ship, the *Almiranta*, was wrecked off the Florida Keys with a cargo estimated at $1,500,000. That same unlucky year the *San Ignacio* and the *San Fernando* were also wrecked off the Keys with valuable cargoes.

As English seapower grew, a great and deadly game of empire building developed between Spain and Britain. Bold English sea captains like Sir Francis Drake took special delight in "singeing King Philip's beard" with quick hit and run raids on Spanish outposts in the South Atlantic and Carribbean. The English, however, did not escape without scars of their own. In 1695, a British frigate, *HMS Winchester* was sunk off Key Largo. In 1744, *HMS Loo* was wrecked on Loo Reef.

In developing their new possessions, the Spanish employed trade routes which took their slow moving galleons through the Bahama Channel and along the coast of Florida into the South Atlantic. The ships were loaded with such exotic cargoes as gold, emeralds, pearls, indigo, tobacco, and coffee. Some carried bricks of Mexican silver stacked in their holds. It was inevitable that such rich prizes would sooner or later attract pirates. Useful to the sea robbers were the many small islands off the Southeast coast which made ideal pirate headquarters. Soon these nautical brigands were swarming throughout the area. No one knows exactly how much treasure was transported from the colonies to Spain, but it has been estimated at billions of dollars. Of this huge total, approximately a quarter of a billion dollars in treasure was lost through pirate raids or through sudden storms, coming up from that mother of storms, the Caribbean.

Piracy along the Atlantic coast had become such big business by the start of the 18th century that it had almost attained respectability. Some of the pirates' names became legend: Thomas Tew, Blackbeard, Captain Kidd, John Quelch, Ned Low, Major Stede Bonnet, to mention just a few of the ruffianly crews. Even today, their names read like a litany of terror.

Piracy continued to plague the Atlantic coast long after the colonies had joined to form the United States of America. By the 1820's their depredations were so feared that many merchant captains refused to leave port unless their vessels were heavily armed with cannon manned by trained crews. In the United States, mounting public indignation caused Congress to grant President Monroe extraordinary powers to protect American shipping. The Navy was given the right to halt and search all suspicious vessels. To put teeth into the law, Congress in 1822, appropriated $5,000,000 to equip a special naval squadron for the task. The squadron proved highly successful in eradicating piracy from the waters of the New World.

But all the drama wasn't confined to the peninsula of Florida. Farther up the coast, in the colonies of South Carolina and Georgia, the English were laying the foundations for successful colonization. A beneficent climate and good soil produced a thriving agricultural economy in both colonies. In South Carolina, the port of Charleston became the center of southern colonial trade, while in Georgia, Savannah was developing into one of the principal seaports on the southeast Atlantic coast.

In the great War Between the States, the waters of the Southeast were a major theater of conflict as Union naval units established a blockade to strangle the hard pressed Confederacy by shutting off supplies from abroad. One of the most unusual episodes of this turbulent period took place on February 17, 1864.

Peering through the morning mists on Charleston harbor, J. K. Crosby, Officer of the Deck of the *USS Housatonic,* sighted an object resembling a porpoise, running about 100 yards to starboard. As he looked more closely, he could see that the object was moving too swiftly towards the *Housatonic's* wooden hull to be a porpoise. He recalled that previously the Rebels had tried to attack Union vessels with semi-submersible craft. Immediately he sounded the alarm, ordering the 1240-ton Union vessel to swing away from the missile's course.

His action was too late. Lieutenant George E. Dixon, commander of the Confederate submarine *Hunley,* had brought his vessel too close under the *Housatonic's* guns for them to be trained effectively on his small cigar-shaped craft. On board the *Housatonic* all hands dashed to battle stations. Pistols and rifles were emptied futilely at the oncoming submarine. In a daring maneuver, Dixon thrust the submarine's spar torpedo (a copper cylinder with 90 pounds of explosive) at the *Housatonic's* stern. Detonated by contact, the cylinder smashed a huge hole in the wooden hull.

It was a costly victory. The blow proved fatal to both ships. As the *Housatonic* went down, the *Hunley* was swamped through its insecure hatch. Neither the intrepid commander of the first successful submarine attack in the world nor his eight-man volunteer crew survived. A few of the *Housatonic's* men managed to get away. The location of the *Housatonic* is given on page 70.

World Wars I and II added many new names to the already long list of vessels lost in the South Atlantic. In both conflicts, the ports of the Southeast were essential to the Allied effort to supply its armies in Europe. Raiding German U-boats, lying off the Atlantic coast, exacted a heavy price in blood and materials. Especially hard hit in World War II was the southeast coast of Florida. During the climactic year of 1942, sinkings in this area

The ss overbrook *with a cargo of fuel oil caught fire in position Latitude 30-40 N., Longitude 79-38 W. The cutter* tampa *and Destroyer* wilkins *proceeded to the scene on April 26, 1928. The crew had been taken off and were later transferred to the* tampa. *The* overbrook *sank while being towed to port.*

included the *Lubrafol, Leslie, Laertes, Pan Massachusetts, Cities Service Empire, Ocean Venus, Korsholm, Elizabeth Massey, Norlavore, Amazone, Halsey, W. D. Anderson, Republic, Carabulle, Untata, J. A. Moffet, Onondaga, Santiago,* and *Manzanillo.* This is only a partial listing, but it's enough to suggest the ferocity of the submarine attacks.

WRECK OF THE VALENTINE

It had been an uneventful voyage for the Italian bark *Georges Valentine.* Heavily laden, the 822-ton vessel was on her way from Pensacola, Fla., to Buenos Aires, Argentina. Her 11-man crew was looking forward to liberty in the colorful Argentine capital where they could rest and buy some trinkets for the homeward trip to Italy.

On October 13, 1904, while still off the Florida coast, the *Valentine's* luck ran out. A vicious gale suddenly darkened the skies to unbroken blackness. With the terrible force of a West Indian hurricane, it turned the calm sea into a white-capped maelstrom. Under scant canvas, plunging, tossing, the heavy seas pounding over her bow and breaking over the weather bulwarks, the *Valentine* held stubbornly to her course, northward through the coral-fringed strait of Florida. Threatening shifts in the wind and numerous counter currents made this a dangerous body of water at best. In a sea whipped to madness by the gale, the prospect was dim.

The wind by this time had become a screaming, vengeful demon bent on destruction. Against this awful force of nature, the frail *Valentine* seemed pathetically inadequate. To make her more seaworthy, the captain ordered the deck load thrown overboard.

For three days, the storm battered the *Valentine* without mercy. At one time a terrific squall accompanied by torrents of rain knocked her down broadside to the sea. There she wallowed helplessly as crashing seas swept over her, dragging her leeward. Her captain tried desperately to get his vessel by the wind, but her sails would not stand. With the heavy sea throwing her bow off in the trough of the sea, she continued to drift until after nightfall.

Then, for the first time in several terror-filled days, it seemed as though the storm might be subsiding. The crew hauled out the

Valentine's storm sails, hoping to head her offshore. In spite of their efforts, she continued to drift to leeward. By 8:00 p.m., October 16, the *Valentine* had drifted periously close to shore, about 25 miles north of Palm Beach. The roar of the breakers was deafening. The end could not be far off.

Their faces haggard with lack of sleep and the ceaseless toil of the past days, the crew waited for the final moment of tragedy. Under smashing breakers, the *Valentine's* stern pounded heavily on the bottom in the shoal water. Her bow swung off as the crashing surf drove her straight for shore. Decks rolling under the breakers, she hit the shore with terrible force, her three masts falling simultaneously. Heard above the storm was the terrible sound of grinding and crunching metal, the parting of wire rigging and gear, and of slatting sails torn by the wind.

All pretense at discipline was abandoned on the breaking ship. It was now every man for himself. But the trapped men could find no refuge. The *Valentine's* hull had broken open and the sea was rushing through her gaping sides with awful force. It lifted the deck house, boats, and decks clear out of the ship. Like a maddened giant it flung the terrified crew into the breakers amid the mass of wreckage and floating timber piling up on the edge of the surf. One man was killed instantly, struck on the head by a falling spar. The others made a desperate bid for life by striking out for shore. Bruised and bleeding, more dead than alive, seven of the crew were thrown up on the beach. The remainder struggled vainly to reach the shore which they could make out dimly in the distance. They were never seen again. One crewman, Victor Erickson, a powerful swimmer, made it to shore against unbelievable odds. Nearly naked, chilled and exhausted, he groped his way along the beach for help.

During the storm, the keeper of the nearby Gilberts Bar Station had been keeping a watchful eye to sea. But in the driving rain and wind, it was almost impossible to see to any distance. His first knowledge of the shipwreck came when Erickson reached the station, carrying a helpless shipmate whom he had discovered in the debris. The keeper quickly gave the exhausted men stimulants and put them to bed before setting out for the scene of the disaster.

Throughout the long night, the keeper searched for the ship-wrecked sailors. By daybreak, five of the crew had been rescued while clinging to floating timbers and rocks on the shore. Almost dead with fatigue, they were taken to the station where they were given dry clothing and medical treatment.

By his valor, the keeper of the Gilberts Bar Station had cheated the South Atlantic of its intended victims. As long as they lived, they would remember him with gratitude. That was reward enough for many man.

As for the ill-fated *Valentine*, she was soon pounded to pieces by the surf. Her position is given on page 72.

Her position is given on page 72.

THE KEY WEST STORY

Like lonely sentinels, the islands of Key West stand watch over the southeasterly approaches to the United States. Lying off the southernmost point of Florida, they thrust their narrow length far into the Straits of Florida.

Death and violence seem strangely out of place in this lush tropical setting where the warm waters of the South Atlantic murmur softly as they break upon the islands' shores. Yet on and around these seemingly peaceful islands has unfolded a pageant of history unmatched in modern times. By some odd quirk of fate, Key West has been in the path of history. Repeatedly, the islands of the Keys have been caught up in world movements, originating far from their coral reefs.

The world first learned of the Keys when the famed Spanish explorer, Ponce de Leon, passed them in 1513, after his unsuccessful search for the "fountain of youth". According to Herreira, de Leon's chronicler: "On Sunday, the day of the feast of the Holy Spirit, the 15 of May, 1513, they ran along the coast of rocky islets ten leagues, as far as the two white rock inlets. To all this line of islands and rocky islets they gave the name of *Los Martires* because, seen from a distance, the rocks, as they rose to view, appeared like men who were suffering, and the name remained fitting, because of the many that have been lost there since."

Obviously, the islands depressed de Leon, and it isn't likely that he explored them. However, more than 40 years later, in 1566,

Pedro Menendez de Aviles, Governor of Florida, searched the island maze to find a channel for the Spanish treasure fleet along whose trade route the Keys lay. He probably visited Key West, but his inadequate knowledge of geography prevented him from realizing the strategic potential of the Keys.

For nearly two centuries after de Leon's visit, the islands were inhabited by a motley assortment of aborigines, pirates, and fishermen. Savage Indian wars were fought between tribes on the mainland and those on the Keys. In the course of the bloody fighting, the mainlanders invaded the Keys, forcing the defenders from island to island until they reached Key West. With their backs to the sea, the defending tribes made a last desperate stand—which could account for the many human bones found on the island by the Spanish explorers. Appropriately, the Spaniards named the island "*Cayo Hueso*" or "Bone Key." This was later corrupted by the English into Key West.

Very little more was heard of the islands until 1815 when Juan Pablo Salas, a young Spanish artillery officer, was given the island of *Cayo Hueso* for services to the Spanish crown. Salas, however, did very little with his newly acquired real estate. In 1822, he sold it to John W. Simonton, a merchant of Mobile, Ala. The transaction was concluded in Havana.

But Simonton wasn't fated to enjoy his property long either. A few days after his purchase, the Federal Government ordered Lieutenant M. C. Perry, later Admiral Perry of North Pole fame, to take formal possession of the Keys from Spain. Perry was also directed to establish a depot and supply center for the war against piracy which had become a serious threat to shipping. Later in the year, Commodore David Porter, another famous name in U.S. naval history, arrived with his West Indies Squadron to step up the campaign against the "brethren of the coast" as the pirates styled themselves.

Porter decided on a bold new plan of attack. Since former expeditions against the pirates had been unsuccessful, he replaced his large frigates with a fleet of eight light-draft schooners and five 20-oared barges. He used an old New York ferry boat, the *Sea Gull*, to tow the barges until they fell in with the sea robbers.

According to sea historians, this was the first use of a steam-propelled vessel in the U.S. Navy.

Porter did a thorough job, and by 1823, piracy had been largely stamped out. A few pirate ships, however, escaped to the port of Fajardo, Puerto Rico. Here the buccaneers paid tribute to the Spanish government in return for protection. When Porter demanded the surrender of the remaining pirate ships, Spanish authorities refused. Porter countered by sending a punitive expedition ashore. That broke the back of piracy forever.

Porter was not well rewarded for his successful exploit. Following a diplomatic protest by Spain, he was court-martialed and suspended for six months. Understandably bitter, he resigned his commission and took service in the Mexican Navy, and later in the Turkish. In his final years, he was appointed Consular Agent of the United States in Turkey where he died in 1843, far from his native country. The Jolly Roger and the bewhiskered brigands who flew it were no more.

During the 1820's, the most lucrative occupation on the Keys was the legitimate, if slightly ghoulish, shipwreck business. Contributing to the prosperity of this new enterprise were the frequent shipwrecks on the treacherous reefs of the Florida Keys. Often the vessels carried silks from China, wine and liquors from Spain, silverware from England, and gowns from France.

So many vessels foundered and sank on the reefs that in 1828 Congress set up a special Territorial Court at Key West to settle salvage questions. This move was also intended to prevent wrecking crews from taking salvaged ships and goods to Nassau and Havana. Henceforth, any wrecked ship and its cargo had to be sold in Key West under the Court's direction, and the proceeds properly distributed.

Auctions at Key West became famous. Valuable cargoes were bid on by speculators and underwriters' agents from all parts of the United States. In years of severe storms, receipts reached as high as $1,500,000—a lot of money by the standards of the early 1800's. Wrecked vessels not only provided rich prizes but often brought new residents to the islands for often stranded shipmasters chose to remain there. Today, many outstanding Key West families are descended from those wrecked on the reefs.

During the heyday of the shipwreck business, salvage vessels would sometimes lay at night in safe anchorage, cruising by day on the watch for ships in distress. In 1835, more than 20 Key West ships were engaged in the business. The first to arrive on the scene became wrecking master, according to rules laid down by the United States court. He also had charge of salvage operations for which he received extra compensation.

One of the most colorful characters of the time was Brother Egan, parson, and owner-master of a wrecking vessel. For his text one Sunday he chose "Know ye not that which run in a race run all, but one receiveth the prize? So run that ye may obtain."

While delivering this edifying discourse, the good brother sighted a ship in distress. He had to make an agonizing decision. If he announced the news, the congregation to a man would rush out and probably some one would reach the wreck before him. But the brother was more than equal to the occasion. Striding to the door still preaching, he turned and gave the familiar cry "Wreck ashore! Now we will all run a race to see who receiveth the prize." A very canny soul, Brother Egan.

But Key West's golden days were numbered. In 1852, the Federal Government began to install a system of reef lights which sharply diminished the number of wrecks. Twenty years later, masters of wrecking ships had to be licensed by the judge of the Federal Court in the Southern District of Florida, and establish to the satisfaction of the judge that their crafts were seaworthy and suitably equipped for rescue operations.

Lean days followed the end of the shipwreck era. During the War with Mexico in 1846-48, the Government sought to make Key West a "Gibraltar of America." Construction of Fort Taylor was begun, but the grandiose plans were never completed. Then in 1856 the Navy Department began the building of a depot and storehouse which remained unfinished until the War Between the States in 1861. During that terrible conflict, Key West was filled with men in the blue uniforms of the Union, and a large number of United States vessels were stationed there. Approximately 300 captured blockade runners were brought into Key West and disposed of in Admiralty Court.

Although the people of Key West were strongly sympathetic to the Southern cause, the city, like other port towns of Florida, remained in Federal hands throughout the war. As one of the most strategic points in the southern States, Key West in Union hands turned out to be one of the determining factors in Federal victory.

Four years after the end of the Civil War, Key West was involved in another drama, originating on the island of Cuba. In 1869, Carlos Manuel de Cespedes began a movement for freedom from Spain. Key West became the center for the revolutionists. Most of the plotters were cigar makers and they brought their skills to Key West. Before long, Key West was the cigar center of the world, producing as many as 100,000,000 cigars annually. By 1886, it is estimated that about 15,000 Cubans had settled there. By this time, machine methods of cigar making were replacing the old fashioned techniques employed by the Cubans, and the center of the cigar industry shifted to the more industrialized north. The Key West industry never regained its former economic status.

During the Spanish American War of 1898, the Keys figured prominently in the headlines. As troops and newspapermen flooded the islands, the Keys became the news center of the world. Buildings were turned into hospitals and most military operations were planned there.

World War I restored Key West's prestige as a major naval base. It served as an important submarine base and as a harbor for large naval units. Patrol vessels, planes, dirigibles, and observation balloons were stationed there to halt enemy efforts to obtain oil from Mexican ports. It was there that Thomas A. Edison experimented with naval depth bombs.

Then as if to prove that history does repeat itself, another era of piracy began for the Keys. The time was the early 1920's, and the United States had embarked on the "noble experiment" otherwise known as Prohibition. Because of their closeness to such important sources of liquor supplies as Cuba and the Bahamas, the islands of the Keys became important links in the chain of "rum-runners" extending along the entire Atlantic coast. "Rummies" who knew every channel, bayou, and sand bar made life a nightmare for Federal law enforcement officials. Sometimes running naval gunfights would take place within sight of the islands.

The Keys themselves were the headquarters for many of the liquor-smuggling barons and their henchmen. They were a colorful if disreputable lot, and Key West was considered a "wide open" city.

The repeal of Prohibition brought less than a decade of peace before the Keys were once more caught up in the holocaust of war. When the United States entered World War II in 1941, Key West quickly became a strategic defense center. Its geographic position made it an important point for conducting operations against German U-boats, then carrying out deadly raids against Allied shipping. During this crucial phase of the "Battle of the Atlantic," Key West served as a base for forming convoys and supplying escorts, making a significant contribution towards curbing this threat to the vital Allied supply line to Europe.

Today, the Keys are mainly a deep-sea fisherman's paradise. Sportsmen from all over the world come to these warm tropical waters to pursue the marlin, swordfish, sailfish, and other deep-sea beauties. Skin divers in growing numbers also find the translucent waters of the Keys irresistible. The crystal clear waters are ideally suited to this popular sport.

Yet not all of the activity here revolves about sport. Time and again, forces hostile to the United States have used these waters for unfriendly purposes. Less than 90 miles from Key West is the unhappy island of Cuba in the grip of a Communist tyranny. Thousands of Cubans, desperate for freedom, have braved death to escape to the free soil of the United States. In their bid for liberty, many put to sea in almost anything that will float, hoping sheer faith will take them to the Keys and the chance for a new life. Many never make it. Some who do are often picked up from small boats by the U.S. Coast Guard's Cuban Patrol, half dead from thirst and exposure, but happy to have escaped Communist Cuba.

The hand of history is still writing. No one knows what the next chapter will be. But if the past is any indication of the future, it's highly likely that Key West will figure prominently in events that lie ahead.

CHAPTER 3 — TABLES. The following listing gives the position (latitude and longitude); type, name of vessel, and tonnage; the Coast and Geodetic Survey charts covering the area; and general information concerning dates, cargo, and estimated value.

Lat/Long	Type, Name, Tonnage	Charts	Remarks
	COAST OF SOUTH CAROLINA		
33-15.0 79-00.0	Ftr. TORUNGEN (1948)	1110 1237	Torpedoed Feb. 26, 1942, in 42 feet.
33-08.7 78-15.0	Ftr. HEBE (1140)	1110	Sank April 11, 1942. 47 feet over wreck.
32-59.8 79-05.8	Ftr. HECKTOR	1110 1238	Sank in 1936. 11 feet over wreck.
32-45.3 79-53.1	Str. ETIWAN	1110 1239	Sank before 1865.
32-45.2 79-51.8	PATAPSCO	1110 1239	Sank before 1865.
32-44.5 79-49.9	GEORGIANA	1111 1239	Sank before 1865.
32-43.5 79-48.7	Sch. KARSNAES	1110 1239	Sank Feb. 7, 1941.
32-43.1 79-46.5	USS HOUSATONIC (1240)	1110 1239	Torpedoed Feb. 17, 1864, in Charleston Harbor by the Confederate Ship H. L. HUNLEY. The first recorded sinking of a warship by a submarine.
32-43.0 79-50.9	WEEHAWKIN	1111 1239	Sank before 1865.
32-41.6 79-51.6	KEOKUK	1111 1239	Sank before 1865.
32-41.8 79-49.2	Str. DAVENTRY (2455)	1111 1239	Sank Dec. 27, 1900, with cargo of kainite.

Lat/Long	Type, Name, Tonnage	Charts	Remarks
32-39.0 79-52.4	Sch. FRED W. CHASE (625)	1111 1239	Foundered Feb. 4, 1887, in breakers, with cargo of granite.
32-36.0 79-40.1	FRED W. DAY	1111 1239	Sank in 1914. 36 feet over wreck.
32-11.0 80-38.0	BARNSTABLE	1111 1240	Sank before World War II.

COAST OF GEORGIA

30-50.8 81-10.0	Ftr. ESPARTA (3365)	1111 1242	Torpedoed April 9, 1942, with 1450 tons of general cargo. 36 feet over wreck.
30-74.0 81-24.0	CAROLINE	1111 1242	Sank in 1949 in 24 feet.

COAST OF FLORIDA

30-16.6 81-13.7	Tkr. GULF AMERICA (8081)	1111 1243	Torpedoed April 11, 1942, in 60 feet with 101,505 barrels of furnace oil on board.
29-34.0 81-09.0	NORTH WESTERN	1111 1244	Sank before World War II in 56 feet.
29-14.0 80-10.0	Tkr. LUBRAFOL (7138)	1111	Torpedoed May 9, 1942, in 300 feet.
28-34.2 80-18.9	Ftr. LESLIE (2609)	1112	Torpedoed June 13, 1942. 54 feet over wreck.
28-28.7 80-22.0	Ftr. LAERTES (5825)	1112 1245	Torpedoed May 3, 1942. 42 feet over wreck.
28-27.0 80-08.0	Tkr. PAN MASSACHUSETTS (8201)	1112	Torpedoed Feb. 19, 1942 in 150 feet.
28-23.9 80-32.2	Ftr. MOHICAN (2255)	1112 1246	Sank in 1934. 30 feet over wreck.
28-23.5 80-02.5	Tkr. CITIES SERVICE EMPIRE (8103)	1112	Torpedoed Feb. 22, 1942, with 95,000 barrels of crude oil. 150 feet over wreck.
28-23.3 80-17.7	Ftr. OCEAN VENUS (7174)	1112 1246	Torpedoed May 3, 1942. 42 feet over wreck.
28-12.2 80-29.4	Ftr. KORSHOIM (2647)	1112 1246	Torpedoed April 13, 1942. 50 feet over wreck.
28-11.2 80-19.7	Sch. DUNHAM WHEELER (1926)	1112 1246	Sank before World War II. 63 feet over wreck.
28-09.2 80-00.7	Ftr. ELIZABETH MASSEY (2598)	1112	Torpedoed July 19, 1942, in 240 feet.

Lat/Long	Type, Name, Tonnage	Charts	Remarks
28-00.0 80-00.0	NORLAVORE (2713)	1112	Sank Feb. 24, 1942.
27-39.1 80-20.9	Str. BEACONSHIRE (2544)	1112 1247	Foundered April 30, 1894.
27-23.7 80-03.2	Ftr. AMAZONE (1294)	1112 1247	Torpedoed May 7, 1942. 42 feet over wreck.
27-23.0 80-08.0	Tkr. HALSEY (7088)	1112 1247	Torpedoed May 6, 1942, in 48 feet, with 78,000 barrels of gasoline.
27-20.4 80-09.8	Str. AMERICA (782)	1112 1247	Foundered Feb. 11, 1885, on St. Lucie Rocks.
27-11.9 80-09.8	Bk. GEORGES VALENTINE (882)	1112 1247	Wrecked Oct. 16, 1904, 150 yards from shore. 5 lives lost.
27-09.0 79-56.0	Tkr. W. D. ANDERSON (10,227)	1112 1247	Torpedoed Feb. 22, 1942, with 133,360 barrels of crude oil.
27-07.0 27-07.0	Brig. J. H. LANE (391)	1112 1247	Sank April 19, 1886.
27-00.6 80-02.7	Tkr. REPUBLIC (5287)	1112 1247	Torpedoed Feb. 22, 1942. 31 feet over wreck.
27-00.3 80-05.2	Tkr. GULFLAND (5277)	1112 1247	Stranded Oct. 21, 1943, 400 yards from beach in 15 feet.
26-45.0 79-51.0	Bge. ARIZONA SWORD (3161)	1112	Foundered in 1961 with 5000 tons of sulphur on board. 7 lives lost.
——	SANTA MARGARITA	1112 1248	Reportedly sank in 1595 off Palm Beach, in 180 feet with $3,000,000 in silver and gold bullion.
26-31.0 79-59.0	Ftr. OHIOAN (6078)	1112 1248	Torpedoed May 8, 1942, in 600 feet with 7800 tons of ore and general cargo on board.
26-19.1 80-04.0	Shp. PROTECTOR (851)	1112 1248	Stranded in 1877.
26-14.8 80-04.7	Str. COPENHAGEN (3297)	1112 1248	Stranded May 26, 1900, with cargo of coal.
26-12.3 80-05.1	CUMBERLAND	1112 1248	900 yards off Pompano Beach.
26-10.0 80-00.0	Tkr. CARRABULLE (5030)	1112 1248	Torpedoed in 1942.
25-59.0 79-11.0	MONSTER	1112	Lost in 1955 on Great Bahama Bank in 30 feet. Another part of vessel is at 25-54.0 and 79-15.8.

Lat/Long	Type, Name, Tonnage	Charts	Remarks
25-48.6 80-05.2	Ftr. ELIZABETH (3482)	1112 1248	Sank Nov. 4, 1935.
25-36.0 80-04.0	MASSACHUSETTS	1112 1248	Sank before World War II.
25-35.0 80-02.0	Ftr. UNTATA (8141)	1112 1249	Torpedoed July 7, 1942.
25-33.6 80-05.7	Unidentified	1112 1249	An unidentified ship reportedly sank in this vicinity in 1829 in 72 feet. $2,000,000 in silver bullion reported on board.
25-35.0 80-05.0	ATHENE	1112 1249	Collided and sank May 31, 1943. In 350 feet.
——	EL POPULO	1112 1249	Reportedly lost near Triumph Reef in 1733 with $250,000 on board.
25-12.0 80-13.1	HMS WINCHESTER	1112 1249	This 60 gun British frigate sank in 1695 in 30 feet. Now in Key Largo Coral Reef Preserve.
25-03.1 80-20.0	Ftr. BENWOOD (3931)	1112 1249	Sank April 9, 1942. Now in Key Largo Coral Reef Preserve.

The freighter EMPIRE THRUST, torpedoed on April 14, 1942, lies off the coast of North Carolina under 42 feet of water.

(Official U.S. Coast Guard Photograph)

Lat/Long	Type, Name, Tonnage	Charts	Remarks
25-03.0 80-13.0	Sch. NORTHERN LIGHT (2351)	1112 1249	Sank Nov. 8, 1930.
24-58.0 80-19.0	Ftr. VITRIC (765)	1112 1249	Sank March 29, 1944, in 350 feet.
——	FLY	1112 1249	Sank in 1805 on Little Conch Reef with $100,000 in gold and silver specie reported on board.
24-56.1 80-28.1	EL INFANTE	1112 1249	Wrecked in 1733.
24-55.1 80-31.1	SAN JOSEY LAS ANIMAS	1112 1249	Wrecked in 1733 in 20 feet.
24-51.1 80-37.0	Shp. ALLIGATOR	1112 1250	Sank 200 yards ENE of Alligator Reef Light.
——	SANTA MARGARITA	1112 1250	Said to have foundered on Alligator Reef between Upper Matecumbe Key and Long Key with $1,500,000 on board.
24-49.0 80-42.0	EL PODER DE DIOS	1112 1250	Broke up on reef in 1733.
——	ALMIRANTA	1112 1250	Lost in 1733 with $1,500,000 on board. Variously reported off Alligator Reef, Long Key and Coffins Patch in 60-72 feet.
24-47.0 80-42.0	Tkr. J. A. MOFFET (9788)	1112 1250	Torpedoed July 8, 1942.
——	SAN FERNANDO	1112 1250	Wrecked in 1733 off Grassy Key in 40 feet.
——	SAN IGNACIO	1112 1250	Wrecked in 1733 off Vaca Key. $50,000 reported on board.
24-41.0 81-05.0	MARIA	1112 1250	Sank April 29, 1944.
24-40.0 78-44.0	Ftr. ONONDAGA (1440)	1112	Torpedoed July 24, 1942, on Great Bahama Bank in 12 feet.
——	HMS LOO	1112 1251	Wrecked in 1744 against Loo Reef in 25 feet.
24-30.0 81-29.0	Ftr. LAKE CITY (2485)	1112 1251	Torpedoed Oct. 3, 1918. 30 lives lost.
24-52.0 83-19.0	German Submarine U-2513 (500)	1113	In 210 feet.
24-45.0 82-01.0	USS STURTEVANT (1190)	1113 1252	Sank April 26, 1942.

Lat/Long	Type, Name, Tonnage	Charts	Remarks
24-38.4 82-06.5	USS EAGLE BOAT (800)	1113 1252	In 25 feet.
24-36.0 83-32.0	Ftr. HERMIS (5234)	1113	Torpedoed June 7, 1942, in 300 feet.
24-35.6 82-53.6	MARIA LOUISA	1113	Sank before World War II.
24-34.5 82-14.0	LST (1000)	1113 1252	In target area.
24-25.2 82-02.4	S-16 U. S. Submarine (700)	1113 1252	Sunk March 2, 1945, for experimental purposes.
24-22.0 81-55.0	Ftr. SANTIAGO DE CUBA (1685)	1113 1252	Torpedoed Aug. 12, 1942, in 700 feet.
24-16.0 81-52.0	Ftr. MANZANILLO (1025)	1113	Torpedoed Aug. 12, 1942, in 700 feet.
——	Str. E. J. BULLOCK (6630)	1113 1351	Foundered Sept. 17, 1938, off SW Dry Tortugas.

U.S. Coast and Geodetic Survey Charts Covering
Southeastern States Atlantic Coastal Waters — Chapter 3

South Carolina, Georgia, Florida

Chart	Price	Title	Scale	Size
1110	$1.00	Cape Hatteras to Charleston	1:432,720	34x46
1111	1.00	Charleston Light to Cape Canaveral	1:449,659	33x45
1112	1.00	Cape Canaveral to Key West	1:466,940	31x47
1113	1.00	Habana to Tampa Bay	1:470,940	31x45
1237	1.00	Little River Inlet To Winyah Bay Entrance	1:80,000	35x44
1238	1.00	Winyah Bay Entrance to Isle of Palms	1:80,000	35x44
1239	1.00	Charleston Harbor and approaches	1:80,000	34x44
1240	1.00	St. Helena Sound to Savannah River	1:80,000	35x43
1242	1.00	Doboy Sound to Fernandina	1:80,000	34x44
1243	1.00	Amelia Island to St. Augustine	1:80,000	34x47
1244	1.00	St. Augustine Light to Ponce de Leon Inlet Light	1:80,000	34x47
1245	1.00	Ponce de Leon Inlet to Cape Canaveral	1:80,000	36x45
1246	1.00	Cape Canaveral to Bethel Shoal	1:80,000	35x45
1247	1.00	Bethel Shoal to Jupiter Inlet	1:80,000	34x48
1248	1.00	Jupiter Inlet to Fowey Rocks	1:80,000	35x42
1249	1.00	Fowey Rocks to Alligator Reef	1:80,000	35x47
1250	1.00	Florida Keys — Alligator Reef to Sombrero Key	1:80,000	35x43
1251	1.00	Florida Keys — Sombrero Key to Sand Key	1:80,000	35x44
1252	1.00	Sand Key to Rebecca Shoal	1:80,000	34x43
1351	.75	Florida Keys — Sombrero Key to Dry Tortugas	1:180,000	30x48

CHAPTER 4

Gulf of Mexico

Florida, Alabama,
Mississippi, Louisiana,
Texas

WITHIN A VAST semicircle, extending from western Florida to Brownsville, Texas, lies a great inland sea known as the Gulf of Mexico. For 2,028 miles it stretches along our southern coast, touching Florida, Alabama, Mississippi, Louisiana, and Texas. Then it points down towards Mexico's remote Yucatan peninsula where it forms that country's oil rich east coast.

The Gulf covers about 700,000 square miles, comparing in size with the western Mediterranean. But size alone tells little about this fabulous southern sea. Its oil resources are among the richest in the world. It is the heart of a mammoth chemical industry, and thousands of ships from all over the world crowd the great ports of Galveston, Mobile, New Orleans, and Corpus Christi. The teeming marine life in the warm Gulf waters provides the world's finest crabs, oysters, red snappers, spotted sea trout, Spanish mackerel and many other delicacies of the sea.

The colorful story of the Gulf goes back to the Spanish conquistadors and includes some of the most interesting characters ever to set foot in North America. Both culturally and economically, the Gulf is an indispensable national asset.

In many ways, the people who live along the Gulf coast reflect their exotic heritage in which French and Spanish strains comingle. Nowhere else in the United States can you find that same combination of shrewdness and amused tolerance for human frailties. It's an attitude which could be summed up by a shrug of the shoulders as if to say: "That's the way people are, and you might just as well accept it."

The sophistication of Gulf people is the product of over four and a half centuries of stormy history during which virtually every foot of the Gulf was fought over by succeeding waves of Spanish, French, English and American invaders. Each wave left behind it grisly mementoes, including scores of wrecked ships which dot the waters of the Gulf.

A brief review of some of the events which have shaped the development of the Gulf region would logically begin with Hernando de Soto, one of the most famous Spanish adventurers who visited the Gulf in 1541. By all accounts, he was the classic conquistador: avaricious, lecherous, and brave. He enjoyed royal license to kill and plunder to his heart's content, provided that a part of the loot was reserved for the Spanish crown. It was a handsome arrangement while it lasted.

De Soto's first demonstration of the superiority of western civilization took place at Mavila, now called Mobile. As a gesture of friendship, the local Indian chieftain had entertained de Soto and his men at a feast attended by 20 dancing girls. As de Soto's historian, Louis Fernandez de Biedma put it: "because the Indians had not heard of the Christians, they were a little careless." Just how careless they were was shown by subsequent events.

During the festivities, one of de Soto's men learned of the presence of five to six thousand Indian braves — very probably an exaggerated figure. He brought this intelligence to de Soto who took the following action: "De Soto ordered 60 or 80 horsemen to arrange themselves into four platoons and attack the village in four different places. He directed the first who should enter the village to set fire to the houses while the rest of the soldiers were ordered not to let any escape. We fought from morning until night without asking any quarter. When night came only three Indians were found left guarding the 20 women who had danced before us. Two of these were killed and the other, climbing a tree, took the string of his bow and hung himself from one of the limbs. We lost 20 men killed and had 250 wounded. During the night we dressed the wounded with the fat of the slain Indians because our medicine was burnt with baggage. We remained there 27 or 28 days until the wounded could recover. We then departed, taking with us the women, whom we distributed among the wounded to nurse them". Thus did de Soto bring the blessings of civilization to the benighted Indian savages.

As Spain's empire began to wither on the vine, the French came down from Canada to help speed the disintegration. Under the leadership of such outstanding men as de la Salle, and Pierre d'Iberville, they eventually took possession of the entire Mississippi Valley for France. They were scarcely less cruel in their treatment of the Indians, who by now had been introduced to such additional white man's blessings as venereal disease, tuberculosis, and alcoholism. In a century, their numbers had declined shockingly. The French, however, did succeed in establishing permanent colonies on the Gulf Coast.

By the end of the 18th century, France's hold on her North American colonies began to weaken. Napoleon was finding out that the price of glory was exorbitantly high. The *Grande Armee* had an insatiable appetite for supplies and munitions. Also, an expanding United States was beginning to push westward. In 1803, Napoleon decided to sell the vast Louisiana territory for a little over eleven million dollars. For the United States, that was probably the best real estate buy of all time. Subsequently, Florida was ceded to the United States by Spain, and later, Texas was annexed, putting the entire Gulf coast in the possession of the United States.

Sad to say, American rule in the Gulf was not a great deal more enlightened than that which preceded it. In 1815, not too long after the Louisiana Purchase, Andrew Jackson and his army of frontiersmen defeated Sir Edward Packingham's highly trained British troops.

In the 1820's, a force of Revenue Cutters, ancestors of today's Coast Guard, destroyed the pirate fleets that roamed these waters. One of these marauders was the notorious Jean Lafitte, who, among other things, joined the American forces in repulsing the British attack on New Orleans. His name is legend in the Gulf country.

At one time, the desolate Dry Tortugas, lying well to the southeast of Florida, were fortified by the United States to defend the Gulf ports. They were also used as a penal colony, coaling base, and wireless station. In the Civil War, deserters and Federal prisoners were confined there, among them Dr. Samuel A. Mudd of Maryland, the innocent country doctor who had had the misfortune to treat the wounded leg of John Wilkes Booth, Lincoln's crazed assassin. Earlier, the islands were a favorite rendezvous for pirates. All that remains now are the old moats, massive brick walls, powder magazines, and marble stones marking the graves of men who died of the "black vomit." Today the islands belong to the National Park Service and are once again a breeding place for birds and big turtles.

The Gulf is still of great military importance. In World Wars I and II, the Naval Air Training Station at Pensacola, Florida, turned out great numbers of naval aviators. It is still a major training base for Navy and Coast Guard fliers. During the Second World War, Navy and Air Force bombers patrolled the Gulf constantly for prowling enemy submarines. In spite of their vigil, enemy U-boats sent many allied merchant ships to the bottom. A partial listing includes the *Empire, Mica, Vamar, Tulsa, Bayard, Rawleigh, Warner, Virginia, Halo, Parker, Gallagher, Sheherozada, Hamlet, City of Toledo,* and the *Oaxaca.* These and other shipping losses are listed in this chapter.

The Gulf's involvement in World War II is dramatically illustrated by events which took place in May, 1942. On May 14, the 6820-ton tanker *David McKelvy,* was torpedoed and sunk off the Mississippi River Delta. A Coast Guard plane proceeded to its reported position, located an oil slick 15 miles to the eastward, and discovered that the tanker was afloat but on fire. The tanker *Norsol* was approaching, and its captain was told that some of the crew were still on the burning vessel. Twenty-five of the 42 crew members were saved. Two days later, the same plane proceeded to almost the same position, where the American tanker *William C. McTarnahan,* 7305 tons, had been struck by two torpedoes. Two lifeboats and four rafts carrying 28 persons were three miles away. The plane flew five miles to give the news to fishing boats which carried out the rescue.

Five days later, the 4732-ton United States freighter *Heredia* was torpedoed south of Atchafalaya Bay, Louisiana. About a mile

to the west, eight men and a small boy were found clinging to a
raft made from a hatch cover. Four other men were a half-mile to
the eastward. Some distance away, still more men as well as a
small frightened girl were near the mast. Five men were clinging
to bits of wreckage. One body was supported by a life preserver.
A Coast Guard plane from Biloxi Air Station flew out to the
scene of the disaster and requested immediate aid from his station. After dropping message blocks to the survivors, telling them
of approaching aid, he proceeded to six fishing boats, five miles to
the northwest. They went to the scene and took all survivors on
board.

The damage was not all one-sided however. On August 1, 1942,
Coast Guard pilot Henry C. White and his crewman, Radioman
First Class George H. Boggs, were patrolling an area near the
sunken *Heredia* in a small Coast Guard amphibian. At 1:30 p.m.,
White sighted a submarine on the surface. He ordered Boggs to
send an emergency message indicating the position.

White circled to attack the vulnerable stern of the submarine.
Before he could get behind the U-boat, it started to submerge.
Without pausing he started his attack from the submarine's beam
at an altitude of 1500 feet. The submarine was going down fast.
White nosed over into a 50 degree dive keeping the submarine in
sight. At 250 feet, he released his bomb. It exploded in the water
directly over the still barely visible submarine.

White circled back but could only see patches of oil coming to
the surface. He flew over the spot until two Army planes took
over the patrol an hour later. Soundings later showed that White
had made a direct hit and destroyed the German submarine U-166.
For this action, White was awarded the Distinguished Flying
Cross and Boggs received the Air Medal.

Not only do Gulf ports handle hundreds of millions of tons of
foreign shipping, but also they serve as points of distribution for
river-borne freight. Down the winding Mississippi and its tributaries come thousands of barges and towboats, carrying the products of America's heartland, the Midwest. For many, the end of
the journey is New Orleans, near the mouth of this great river
which winds like a silver thread through our past. Through the
Straits of Florida, from the North Atlantic, and up through the
Caribbean from South and Central American ports, ships of all

nations spin a network of ocean routes through the Gulf. Major airline routes also criscross this thriving, vital area. The Gulf may be steeped in history, but it is very much a part of today's world.

Some of the world's most fabulous fishing is to be found in the Gulf with its infinite variety of marine life. Because its waters are a warm 72° to 75°, nearly every sea creature grows to an incredible size. For generations, scientists have been investigating the many species of sea organisms found here, yet they have barely scratched the surface. Fish seeking food move about the Gulf in uncounted millions. Vast schools of mackerel, some as large as five miles by three miles wide, swim up the Texas Gulf coast every Spring. Shrimp come in by heavy boatloads. If for any reason, the United States should face a food shortage, the waters of the Gulf could probably provide a large part of the answer. It is in fact, a huge sea food factory whose resources are almost limitless.

This, then, is the Gulf of Mexico — colorful and exotic, yet excitingly alive and full of promise. In its ancient waters lie treasures waiting to be discovered by shipwreck hunters.

THE LEGEND OF JEAN LAFITTE

Who was Jean Lafitte? Was he a pirate or a patriot? Was he a liar, betrayer and double agent, or a suave and charming gentleman? Probably he was all of these and more. Good and evil were so mixed in him that it is difficult to tell where one left off and the other began. Which is another way of saying he was human. Except that in Lafitte, everything was a little larger than life size. Yet for all his renown, Lafitte remains an enigma. Only one thing is certain: He must have been a remarkable personality to have inspired so many legends.

According to Lafitte's own journal, which is open to question, he was the son of a prosperous Spanish-Jewish merchant in Santo Domingo. His family had suffered under the Spanish Inquisition. Lafitte, père, apparently was affluent enough to give both his sons, Jean and Pierre, a good education and training in the amenities.

A four-masted schooner lies helpless in the rough surf off Santa Rosa Island, Florida. Her crew was rescued by a U.S. Coast Guard breeches buoy.

(Official U.S. Coast Guard Photograph)

Pierre was later overshadowed by his more spectacular younger brother. Hovering vaguely in the background is a third Lafitte, Alexandre. Some say that Alexandre was the redoubtable Dominique who later joined Jean's privateer fleet. Whether he was a brother or just a trusted lieutenant is uncertain.

Jean's grandmother had great influence in shaping his personality. In his journal, he pays warm tribute to her strong character and determined will. Jean also refers to his father as a "free-thinking Jew with neither Catholic faith nor traditional adherence to the Jewish synagogues". He had manufactured Morocco leather in both Spain and France before coming to Santo Domingo. Later he would die in a Spanish dungeon, a victim of the Inquisition.

Lafitte first appeared in New Orleans in the early 1800's. He and his brother Pierre operated a modest blacksmith shop in St. Phillip Street. Their slaves produced the intricate grill work still so much in evidence in the *vieux carré*. Actually, they were agents for a well-organized smugglers' ring. During the Spanish occupation of Louisiana smuggling had become a regular facet of commerce. In the amoral atmosphere of early New Orleans, merchants didn't question the sources of their goods so long as they were cheap.

The smugglers also handled slaves, who were in very short supply after the ban on their importation after 1809. The going price for a slave at the time was "a dollar a pound."

It wasn't long before the gentry of Barataria, as the smugglers' headquarters was known, offered the Lafittes leadership of their organization. The lure of easy riches was too tempting to refuse and they become privateers. At his own expense, Jean fitted out a vessel and sailed to Carthagena for Venezuelan letters of marque. These amounted to licenses to plunder under cover of legality.

In the summer of 1810 his brother Pierre suffered a stroke which paralyzed the left side of his face. Although Pierre recovered, Jean from this time on was boss of the Barataria smuggling trade.

In the spring of 1811, Jean built a house near the slave warehouse on Grand Terre island off the mouth of the Mississippi. For the next several years he operated with practically no interference from the authorities. During this interval, Dominique You joined Lafitte. He had been part of the unsuccessful French expedition against the rebellious Haitians in 1802. Now he became Lafitte's "favorite lieutenant".

Flying the Bolivian flag, Dominique brought shipload after shipload of slaves into Barataria. Heavily weighted with chains, the terrified captives were herded into the *barracoon*.

Then Lafitte decided that he could obtain slaves even more cheaply by hijacking slavers off the Cuban coasts as they came from Africa. The cargoes would be stolen and the ships burned or scuttled. It was plain piracy, but it paid off handsomely, and Lafitte accumulated a sizable fortune. He moved in the highest circles of New Orleans where he cut a dashing figure. One of his friends was Auguste Davezac, a wealthy merchant and brother-in-law of Governor William Claiborne, first U. S. Governor of the Territory.

Lafitte's organization numbered more than 1,000 men and his operations extended throughout the Gulf. His rising success, however, was offset by growing public resentment for the Baratarians. Merchants feared to travel by water because of their depredations. The U.S. Customs Office also frowned on Lafitte's operations which had brought commerce almost to a standstill.

To counteract this hostility, Lafitte called a conference of his lieutenants, ordering that, in the future, American ships were not to be attacked. When an unruly follower defied him, Lafitte shot him on the spot. After that he was unquestioned king of Barataria.

But Jean's troubles were only beginning. Increasingly, the Baratarians were turning the streets of New Orleans into places of terror. On Grand Terre, there were drunken orgies which are still whispered about in the Gulf Country. Finally on March 15, 1813, Claiborne proclaimed Jean Lafitte and his brother Pierre outlaws in the Territory. This was followed a few months later by another proclamation naming "John Lafitte" as the principal malefactor and asking public cooperation in his capture. It also offered a reward of $500. Claiborne had declared war on the pirate king.

Undaunted, Lafitte continued his illegal traffic in open defiance of the Governor. Claiborne retaliated by impaneling a grand jury which returned indictments against the Lafittes and their henchmen. He then dispatched a platoon of dragoons to search the usual pirate haunts. His persistence was rewarded when Pierre was surprised in the Place d'Armes and jailed in the Calaboose. Jean hurried to New Orleans to effect his brother's release. His attempts at bribery failed. The trap had snapped shut.

At this low ebb in his fortunes, history came to Lafitte's aid. On a morning in early September, a party of British officers arrived in a small boat at Barataria. They had come to offer the buccaneer a captain's commission in the Royal Navy and about $150,000 for his cooperation in the capture of New Orleans. They also implied that if Lafitte did not cooperate the British forces would smash Barataria.

The wily Lafitte was in a difficult position. He had no special love for the English, the Spanish, or for that matter, the Americans. But brother Pierre was in the Calaboose awaiting execution. Also this was an opportunity to regain public favor. He decided to play a skillful stalling game. With great finesse, he sent a melodramatic letter to his friend John Blanque in the Legislature and to Governor Claiborne, telling of his decision to decline the offer. Simultaneously, he sent a letter to Captain Lockyer of the Royal Navy, asking for time to consider the proposal further. (During these negotiations, Pierre somehow managed to escape from jail.)

Claiborne couldn't bring himself to accept Lafitte's offer of help against the British. Instead he sent a naval force against Barataria, destroying it. Although Lafitte's fleet escaped intact, Barataria never again would serve as a pirates' headquarters.

Meanwhile the British were closing in on New Orleans and Claiborne began to have some sober second thoughts. Then General Andrew Jackson arrived in the city fresh from his Florida triumphs. "Old Hickory" would have welcomed the devil himself as an ally if it served his purpose. He needed all the help he could get to offset his losses in Florida. He also knew that he had to move swiftly against the British before they could entrench themselves. Grudgingly, Claiborne accepted Jackson's advice. As skilled gunners, Lafitte and his men took their places behind United States artillery pieces.

What followed is history. The Battle of New Orleans may have been an unnecessary action, but it was nevertheless decisive. Militarily, it sounded the death knell of formal 18th century warfare. As the British, resplendent in battle dress, marched in parade-ground fashion against American artillery, Jackson's uncouth army of backwoodsmen and pirates opened point blank fire. The British were cut down like wheat. The ground was stained red with their blood. It was Britain's last stand in North America.

Once again Lafitte was the darling of New Orleans. Everyone was more than willing to forgive and forget. Friends speculated that he would settle down with a well-bred belle of New Orleans. But Lafitte's sharp instinct told him that, in time, public favor would turn to bitter hostility as former foes remembered old scores. Accordingly, he and his fleet set sail for Galveston, his last headquarters.

The rest of the Lafitte story is downhill. The once daring sea robber was growing cautious with age. He was also increasingly hard pressed for money. Pickings had become lean ever since the U.S. Government had sent Commodore Porter to rid the Caribbean of freebooters. Porter was smashing the major pirate rings and many of the leaders were in jail awaiting execution.

Pressed by circumstance, Lafitte sank so low as to become a Spanish spy on the payroll of the Governor of Cuba. His unsavory task was to report developments among Spanish-Americans in Texas, then preparing to set up an independent republic. It was the act of a scoundrel, ready to sell out his comrades for money.

The Lafitte story was nearly over. Exasperated by his attacks on American shipping, the U.S. Government ordered Lafitte to abandon Galveston. Lafitte complied, and his men burned the stronghold at Campeachy. American sailors on the *Enterprise* saw three vessels, their sails filled, heading for the sea. Lafitte was sailing into history.

No one knows what happened to Lafitte after Galveston. Stories persist that much of his treasure is hidden at various points of the New Orleans Gulf area. But on one point all are agreed: Lafitte was one of the most fascinating rogues ever to strut across the stage of history.

VALOR AT GALVESTON

It was 5:30 on the morning of November 10, 1883, and the men on the morning watch at the San Luis Lifesaving Station at the west end of Galveston Island, Texas, were having their first cup of coffee. In the chilly morning air, the coffee tasted especially good. Routinely, one of them trained his binoculars on the Gulf. In the distance he could make out a barkentine standing in before a strong southerly wind, heading toward the south breaker at the San Luis Pass. Obviously, her skipper wasn't aware that he was dangerously close to land.

Quickly, the lifesaver relayed the news to the station. The international code signal then in use, M.F.G., meaning "Do not stand in so close," was hoisted immediately. But in the early morning mist the oncoming vessel couldn't see it. A few minutes later, the *Laura R. Burnham* of Boston, Mass., stranded on a shoal about three and a half miles southwest of the station. She was carrying a cargo of coal.

By the time the unlucky vessel ran ashoal, the lifesaving crew was already on its way down the beach with a boat. Reaching the Pass, they managed to launch the lifeboat in a vicious surf.

Half an hour later, after battling an extraordinarily rough sea, they reached the vessel. They were drenched, and the boat was partly filled with water.

Then began some difficult maneuvering to get the stranded *Burnham* off the shoal. At first an effort was made to heave her off by running an anchor from the starboard quarter, but it failed. After spending several hours vainly trying to free the vessel, the rescuers decided to head back for shore. On their arrival, they sent a message requesting a tug and lighters.

The weather grew steadily worse. When the lifesavers boarded the *Burnham* at noon, the surf was much heavier than in the morning. To make matters worse, she had begun to leak badly. To keep her afloat, the lifesavers joined the crew at the pumps. But there was no let up in the storm. By nightfall, the seas had risen so high they were washing over the freighter's rail, and the surf boat narrowly missed being smashed to pieces.

Meanwhile, the *Burnham* was working farther up on the shoal, and the water was flooding in faster than the tired men at the pumps could handle it. The sea had gone berserk. A heavy rain storm set in to further harass the exhausted men at the pumps. Spray from towering waves flew as high as the main top. Jagged shafts of lightning ripped the inky sky, throwing a lurid light on the haggard men. They made the blackness seem all the more intense. All the devils of the sea seemed to be assaulting her.

Only one thing mattered now, and that was to save all hands. As soon as the lifeboat could be manned, the captain of the *Burnham* and four of his men tumbled in. The remaining five crew members stayed on the ship to await rescue. So violent was the sea that it was necessary for the lifeboat to pull a mile or two to the east. After several narrow escapes from swamping, the boat was beached at about 4:00 o'clock. The party headed for the station, and at five o'clock arrived exhausted but safe.

After a short rest, the lifesaving crew again set out to rescue the five men still on the *Burnham*. Returning to that hell was even worse than the original attempt, especially after the warmth and security of the station. They had no choice, however. But this time, the tug *Estelle* and the lighter *Buckthorn* had arrived and anchored during the night.

For the men on the *Burnham*, the situation had become desperate. At dawn, their nerves all but shattered by the nightmare of the storm, they hoisted their colors Union down, the classic signal of distress. They had good reason for anxiety. The sea was still breaking in huge cataracts over the ship and a violent squall was approaching from the northeast. Just as the lifeboat succeeded in getting alongside, the squall struck with all its fury. In that savage sea, no thought could be given to saving baggage. The five men were transferred to the lifeboat, and half an hour later were safely ashore. It was now two o'clock in the afternoon of November 11.

The story doesn't end there, however. The tenacious lifesavers were determined to reach the abandoned *Burnham* and recover the crew's possessions. On the morning of November 12, after an early breakfast, they tried to board the bark. It was no use. After a thorough soaking and half swamping the boat, they were forced to give it up. On the following day, the wind and sea calmed down a bit. This time they reached the almost wrecked ship. The sea was still breaking over her, the cabin was full of water, and the forward house was demolished. Nevertheless, the rescuers secured most of the crew's personal possessions as well as cabin stores and other articles.

The last act of the drama took place on November 14 when a party of wreckers arrived from Galveston to strip the vessel. Dangerous seas, however, made it impossible to remove everything of value. The remains of the *Burnham* still lie at the spot where she was abandoned. Her exact location, along with other pertinent data, is given in the table in this chapter.

CHAPTER 4 — TABLES. The following listing gives the position (latitude and longitude); type, name of vessel, and tonnage; the Coast and Geodetic Survey charts covering the area; and general information concerning dates, cargo and estimated value.

Lat/Long	Type, Name, Tonnage	Charts	Remarks

COAST OF FLORIDA

Lat/Long	Type, Name, Tonnage	Charts	Remarks
24-57.1 81-54.0	Ftr. EDWARD LUCKENBACK (7934)	1113	Sunk by mine July 2, 1942, with cargo of ore. 48 feet over wreck.
24-56.9 81-46.6	Ftr. GUNBOR (1121)	1113	Torpedoed June 14, 1942. 39 feet over wreck.
24-57.0 87-57.5	Ftr. BOSILJKA (3009)	1113	Sank June 19, 1942, in 60 feet.
25-14.0 82-27.0	Ftr. BAJA CALIFORNIA (1648)	1113	Torpedoed July 18, 1942, in 115 feet.
——	GASPARILLA	1113 1255	Sank in 1821 off south end of Gasparilla Island. Loss reported at $1,000,000, including gold and silver.
27-21.0 82-38.0	ZALOPHUS	1113 1256	Sank before World War II.
27-35.0 83-06.0	Bge. BLUE STACK (669)	1114	Foundered March 1, 1954, in 75 feet.
27-40.5 82-55.8	BELMONT (1521)	1114 1257	Sank in 1939 in 33 feet.
27-46.5 82-32.7	Tug, 125 feet long	1114 1257	10 feet over wreck.
27-52.1 83-07.4	Clearwater wreck	1114	In 45 feet.
27-57.0 84-00.0	NORLINDO	1114	Sank in 1942.

Lat/Long	Type, Name, Tonnage	Charts	Remarks
28-29.5 84-01.0	Ftr. HOLLISWOOD (1141)	1114	Sank June 30, 1920, in 114 feet.
29-00.0 84-23.0	Ftr. S. C. LOVELAND (1288)	1114	Sank Nov. 17, 1948, in 100 feet.
29-19.0 84-55.0	Dge. GELMER	1114 1262	Sank before World War II, in 85 feet.
——	Unidentified	1114 1262	Sank in mouth of lagoon off Apalachicola in 1819. Gold reported on board. Loss estimated at $200,000.
29-18.9 85-21.2	Tkr. EMPIRE MICA (8032)	1114 1262	Torpedoed June 29, 1942. 50 feet over wreck.
29-54.0 85-27.8	Ftr. VAMAR (598)	1115 1263	Sank March 21, 1942 in 18 feet.
30-03.2 85-37.3	Tug E. E. SIMPSON	1115 1263	Sank in 1936 in 12 feet.
29-38.0 85-57.0	Sch. THELMA (525)	1115	Sank May 5, 1925, in 150 feet.
30-23.0 86-48.4	Sch. JAMES BAIRD (391)	1115 1265	Wrecked Feb. 1, 1899.
30-12.0 87-13.5	Ftr. SAN PABLO	1115 1265	Torpedoed in 1944 in 80 feet.
30-17.5 87-18.7	Shp. BRIDE OF LORNE (1324)	1115 1265	Wrecked April 8, 1887.
30-17.8 87-18.7	Ftr. MASSACHUSETTS	1115 1265	Stranded in 1921. Partly above water.
30-19.1 87-18.8	Bk. ANNA PEPPINA (620)	1115 1265	Wrecked July 19, 1896.
30-19.3 87-10.7	Bk. HATTIE G. McFARLAND (546)	1115 1265	Wrecked Feb. 6, 1891.
30-18.9 87-19.5	Shp. EASTERN LIGHT	1115 1265	Wrecked Dec. 23, 1890, on Caucus Shoal.

COAST OF ALABAMA

Lat/Long	Type, Name, Tonnage	Charts	Remarks
30-12.8 88-02.2	CGC MAGNOLIA (916)	1115 1266	Sank Aug. 1945.
——	Str. WADDON (5500)	1115 1266	Wrecked Aug. 5, 1917, on Diamond Point, Mobile.
30-00.0 88-05.0	Ftr. TULSA (607)	1115	Sank March 11, 1943.

Lat/Long	Type, Name, Tonnage	Charts	Remarks
30-12.4 88-20.1	Ftr. MANHORTON	1115 1267	Sank in 1938.

COAST OF MISSISSIPPI

30-09.5 88-29.3	Sch. LEWIS BROTHERS	1115 1267	Sank Sept. 19, 1925.
——	Bk. MAGDALA (800)	1115 1270	Wrecked March 18, 1876, off Chandeleur Island.

COAST OF LOUISIANA

29-19.0 88-50.0	Pass. BAYARD (2160)	1115 1272	Torpedoed July 6, 1942, in 150 feet, with 2200 tons of general cargo on board.
28-59.2 89-08.1	Ftr. LOUISIANA	1115 1272	Sank Oct. 28, 1926.
28-53.0 89-15.0	Tkr. RAWLEIGH WARNER (3663)	1115 1272	Torpedoed June 1942, in 266 feet, with 38,909 barrels of gasoline on board.
28-56.6 89-26.6	Ftr. YUMA	1116 1272	Sank March 17, 1926. Wreck is visible.
28-52.6 89-27.5	Tkr. VIRGINIA (10731)	1116 1272	Torpedoed May 12, 1942, with 152,393 barrels of gasoline on board. Wreck completed silted over.
29-16.0 89-49.4	Twr. PEARL HARBOR	1116 1273	Sank in 1955. 22 feet over wreck.
29-10.0 90-00.0	Ftr. EL VIVO (199)	1116 1273	Sank April 25, 1945.
28-42.0 90-08.0	Tkr. HALO (6986)	1116	Torpedoed May 20, 1942, in 140 feet.
29-03.0 90-09.0	Tkr. BENJAMIN BREWSTER	1116 1273	Torpedoed July 9, 1942, with cargo of aviation gasoline and lube oil. 36 feet over wreck.
28-55.2 90-35.0	Tkr. DAVID McKELVY (6820)	1116 1274	Torpedoed May 14, 1942, with 80,000 barrels of light crude oil on board.
28-47.0 90-45.0	U-166 German Submarine (740)	1116 1274	Sank Aug. 1, 1942, in 60 feet.
28-47.0 90-45.0	Tkr. R. M. PARKER (6779)	1116 1274	Torpedoed Aug. 13, 1942.
28-32.0 90-59.3	Tkr. R. W. GALLAGHER (7989)	1116	Torpedoed July 13, 1942, in 90 feet with 83,000 barrels of bunker "c" oil on board.
28-30.4 90-59.5	Ftr. HEREDIA (4732)	1116	Torpedoed May 19, 1942, in 100 feet with 1500 tons of general cargo on board.

Lat/Long	Type, Name, Tonnage	Charts	Remarks
28-42.3 91-23.0	Tkr. SHEHEROZADA (13,467)	1116 1275	Torpedoed March 10, 1945, in 70 feet.
28-32.0 91-30.0	Tkr. HAMLET (6578)	1116	Torpedoed July 10, 1945, in 126 feet.
29-08.0 91-41.9	Bge. PIONEER	1116 1276	Sank in 1954.
29-04.0 91-43.0	Tkr. CITY OF TOLEDO (8192)	1116 1276	Torpedoed June 12, 1942, in 12 feet with part of wreck protruding four feet above water.
29-06.9 91-43.3	Bge. CARIBE	1116 1276	Sank Dec. 19, 1954.
29-21.4 91-55.0	Twr. POLARIS	1116 1277	Sank Feb. 14, 1956.
29-24.3 92-01.0	Twr. RAMOS III	1116 1277	Sank Nov. 21, 1955, in 12 feet.
——	M/V CORAL FAYE (111)	1116 1277	Burned and sank Nov. 27, 1959, on Tiger Shoals.
29-20.0 92-23.8	ATLANTIC	1116 1277	Sank in 1954.
29-27.0 92-37.0	Twr. SHOAL HARBOR	1116 1278	Sank Oct. 23, 1955. 36 feet over wreck.
29-08.0 92-35.0	Twr. DR. H. E. WHITE	1116	Sank July 25, 1954.
29-22.0 93-00.0	Ftr. E. F. CONEY (153)	1116 1278	Sank Jan. 28, 1930.
29-45.2 93-07.0	Twr. BELLE	1116 1278	Wrecked in 1953.
29-35.0 93-14.0	LEO HUFF (157)	1116 1278	
29-43.9 93-14.3	Twr. WEST BEUFORT	1116 1278	Sank Nov. 28, 1953.

COAST OF TEXAS

Lat/Long	Type, Name, Tonnage	Charts	Remarks
29-45.8 93-26.2	Twr. DEWEY	1116 1279	
29-44.9 93-36.0	Twr. LINDA	1116 1279	Shows above water, 850 yards from shore.
29-15.8 93-39.5	Dge. GULF TIDE	1116 1279	Sank Sept. 30, 1947. 40 feet over wreck.

Lat/Long	Type, Name, Tonnage	Charts	Remarks
29-44.0 93-42.0	Twr. WAWA	1116 1279	
29-40.0 93-59.9	Str. SAN SABA (703)	1116 1280	Burned Oct. 15, 1948. 2 feet over wreck.
29-17.9 94-40.3	LCT BESCO	1117 1282	
29-12.7 94-40.8	Tug PROTECTOR (116)	1117 1282	Sank Nov. 28, 1954.
29-20.4 94-40.8	Dge. GALVESTON (3375)	1117 1282	Sank July 29, 1943.
29.09.4 94-58.4	Sch JOHN S. AMES (963)	1117 1282	Sank in 1899 with cargo of coal.
——	Str. HIGH FLYER (6214)	1117 1282	Destroyed April 17, 1947 in Texas City explosion.
29-00.0 95-00.0	Ftr. MARGATE (199)	1117 1283	
29-04.6 95-07.0	Bk. LAURA R. BURNHAM (673)	1117 1283	Wrecked Nov. 10, 1883, with cargo of coal.
29-03.2 95-07.1	Sch. JENNIE S. BUTLER (943)	1117 1283	Wrecked March 22, 1900, with cargo of coal.
29-02.0 95-10.0	GLORIA COLITAUS	1117 1283	
29-55.4 95-17.6	Str. HONDURAS (2350)	1117 1283	Wrecked Oct. 29, 1911, with general cargo. Loss estimated at $285,000.
28-41.0 95-27.7	Twr. V. TILEMAN	1117 1283	Sank in 1956. 36 feet over wreck.
28-23.0 96-11.0	Pass. OAXACA (4351)	1117 1284	Torpedoed July 26, 1942, with general cargo and caustic soda in 60 feet.
28-21.0 96-23.0	LCT SALTDOME No. 1	1117 1284	Sank in 1955. Partly above water.
27-52.5 96-58.5	Twr. LIBORIA C.	1117 1286	Sank June 27, 1954. 23 feet over wreck.
27-40.0 97-05.0	Twr. EMPRESS	1117 1286	Sank Oct. 30, 1955 in 50 feet.
27-30 97-20	Ftr. ORION	1117 1286	Sank March 1, 1945.

Lat/Long	Type, Name, Tonnage	Charts	Remarks
——	SAN PEDRO	1117 1288	Wrecked in 1811 on west end of Padre Island. Gold and silver reported on board. Loss estimated at $500,000.
——	MARIA THERESA	1117 1288	Sank in 1880 in Brazos Pass, off Padre Island. Gold reported on board. Loss estimated at $210,000.
26-03.8 97-08.7	L.S.T. PALMETTO	1117 1288	Sank in 1954.
——	JESSIE	1117 1288	Foundered on sand bar off mouth of Rio Grande River in 1875. Gold and silver reported on board. Loss estimated at $100,000.

U.S. Coast and Geodetic Survey Charts Covering Southern States Gulf Coastal Waters — Chapter 4

Florida, Alabama, Mississippi, Louisiana, Texas

Chart	Price	Title	Scale	Size
1113	$1.00	Habana to Tampa Bay	1:470,940	31x45
1114	.75	Tampa Bay to Cape San Blas	1:456,394	30x34
1115	1.00	Cape St. George to Mississippi Passes	1:456,394	35x41
1116	1.00	Mississippi River to Galveston	1:458,596	36x49
1117	1.00	Galveston to Rio Grande	1:460,732	36x44
1255	1.00	Estero Bay to Lemon Bay, including Charlotte Harbor	1:80,000	34x44
1256	1.00	Lemon Bay to Passage Key Inlet	1:80,000	34x46
1257	1.00	Tampa Bay to St. Josephs Sound	1:80,000	34x43
1262	1.00	Apalachicola Bay to Cape San Blas	1:80,000	34x44
1263	1.00	St. Joseph and St. Andrew Bays	1:80,000	34x45
1265	1.00	Pensacola Bay and approaches	1:80,000	33x44
1266	1.00	Mobile Bay	1:80,000	34x46
1267	1.00	Mississippi Sound and approaches — Dauphen I. to Cat. I.	1:80,000	31x43
1270	1.00	Chandeleur and Breton Sounds	1:80,000	36x44
1272	1.00	Mississippi River Delta	1:80,000	35x43
1273	1.00	Barataria Bay and approaches	1:80,000	35x40
1274	1.00	Timbalier and Terrebonne Bays	1:80,000	35x40
1275	1.00	Isles Dernieres to Point au Fer	1:80,000	35x44
1276	1.00	Point au Fer to Marsh Island	1:80,000	34x46
1277	1.00	Vermilion Bay and approaches	1:80,000	35x46
1278	1.00	Rollover Bayou to Calcasieu Pass	1:80,000	35x45
1279	1.00	Calcasieu Pass to Sabine Pass	1:80,000	34x44
1280	1.00	Sabine Bank to East Bay, including Heald Bank	1:80,000	33x44
1282	1.00	Galveston Bay and approaches	1:80,000	33x45
1283	1.00	San Luis Pass to East Matagorda Bay	1:80,000	34x46
1284	1.00	Matagorda Bay and approaches	1:80,000	34x44
1286	1.00	Aransas Pass to Baffin Bay	1:80,000	34x41
1288	1.00	Southern part of Laguna Madre	1:80,000	34x43

Crew abandoning the sinking SS MALDEN *in North Atlantic in 1926.*
(Official U.S. Coast Guard Photograph)

CHAPTER 5

Great Lakes

Lake Ontario, Lake Erie,

Detroit River, Lake Huron,

Lake Superior, Lake Michigan

ON THE MAP, the five Great Lakes look like the ventricles of a giant heart pumping the lifeblood of commerce to all parts of the United States. Around their shores has developed a huge agricultural-industrial complex which provides billions of dollars worth of manufactured goods and farm commodities annually. If that great heart should falter, our country would be mortally ill.

In all the world there is nothing like these great inland seas, which constitute the largest bodies of fresh water on earth. Their combined shore lines total 8,300 miles, enclosing about 94,710 square miles of water. Four of the Lakes are shared by the United States and Canada. Only Lake Michigan lies wholly within our boundaries.

Anyone who has travelled the Great Lakes knows that some of the most vicious storms in the world arise in Lake Erie. Coming up suddenly, they can unleash stunning blows on vessels unlucky enough to be in their path. Under their brutal assaults, many passenger and cargo ships have gone down.

How did the Lakes come into being? Geologists think that they were scooped out of the earth by the gigantic glacier which once covered much of the Midwest. As the ice receded, water filled the great basins made by the glacier.

The epic of the Great Lakes begins in the New France established in Canada during the reign of Louis XIV. French interest in this vast area was limited mainly to the valuable furs so much in demand in the luxury markets of Europe. One of the first to engage in this trade was Samuel de Champlain, who in 1608 set up a trading post at Quebec, near the "narrows" of the St. Lawrence. Thus, from the very start, the St. Lawrence, a turbulent river with rapids and dangerous falls, was destined to play a key part in the development of the Lake region. Together with the Great Lakes, it provided a magnificent inland waterway which extended nearly 2000 miles into the heart of North America.

As France's New World empire grew, her enterprising *voyageurs* and *coureurs de bois* began to take increasing advantage of the Lakes. Evidence of French martime activity is to be found in the wreck of the frigate *La Jean Florin* which sank in Lake Erie in July, 1721, with gold and silver on board at a combined loss of $500,000. Some years later, in 1764, the French vessel *Le Blanc Henri* was wrecked on Wolf Island Spit, near Kingston, Ontario, carrying gold and silver bullion. The loss is estimated at $100,000.

It was not until the early 1800's that the United States turned its attention to the development of the lands adjacent to the Lakes. The new settlers were mostly immigrants from the overcrowded countries of Europe, seeking a new life. Unlike the early French, who were interested in quick exploitation of the natural wealth of the region, they were anxious to establish themselves permanently in the free New World. On their arrival in the United States they found that most of the land along the eastern seaboard was already being farmed. Where it was available in the East, land had become expensive, but in the underdeveloped territory to the Northwest there was virgin country waiting to be developed. Not only was land cheaper, but the Government was making attractive offers to homesteaders to speed its development.

The first to feel the impact of this northwesterly movement was Lake Erie. In 1818, the Genesee route became the route of the Erie Canal. Three thousand Irish workmen began clearing the forest and shoveling out the Big Ditch, as it was called. The canal was completed in 1825 with great pomp. A procession of packet boats passed from Buffalo to New York harbor, with cannon booming, bands playing, and church bells ringing in every town along the way. As the crowning ceremony, a cask of fresh Lake Erie water was poured into the sea, uniting the inland waters with the ocean. With the Erie Canal, the United States had made a major breakthrough to the development of the entire region.

By the 1840's, a thriving commerce had grown up on Lake Erie, if we judge by the vessels lost there during this period. In 1841, the steamer *Erie* sank four miles off Silver Creek, New York, with specie and whiskey on board at a total loss of $100,000. In 1845, the steamer *Kent* went down with gold and specie for an overall loss of $65,000. A few years later, in 1850, the *Anthony Wayne* sank six and one-half miles northwest of Buffalo, N.Y., with specie and whiskey. The estimated loss is $96,500. Evidently, our ancestors had a great thirst.

Along the Erie Canal, which is imbedded deep in American folklore, business was brisk. Barges left at every hour of the day, carrying plows, axes, anvils, and immigrants to the West. They brought back pork, wheat, wool, apples, cheese, and whiskey from what was, at that time, the frontier.   ,

The wharves of Buffalo resembled a Tower of Babel as people speaking many tongues booked passage on immigrant ships for Cleveland, Toledo, Detroit, Milwaukee, and Chicago. The line of steamers running up the Lakes was well known in the market and embarkation towns of Europe, and nearly all of the immigrants were buoyantly optimistic about the future. It may have been the confidence of ignorance, but apparently it worked. A newspaperman of the time who visited one of the ships tells of Swiss, German, Scotch, Scandinavian, Irish, and English migrants stretching out among their baggage and their household possessions. A painted German wagon was loaded with ploughs, shovels, and other implements. Its owner had no idea of what might lie ahead, but he was supremely confident that he was equal to the task. And, in the great majority of cases, he was.

Migration to the Midwest kept pace with the changing rhythms of national expansion. The first big wave came shortly after the passage of the Harrison Land Act of 1800, opening the public domain to the small farmer. For a short time, migration was slowed by the War of 1812. With the end of the war, a tidal wave of migration began which continued for about five years. There were occasional setbacks, either as a result of economic crises or war, but the march pushed inexorably forward.

After the country had begun to bind up the wounds inflicted by the Civil War, a new surge of settlement started. There were prairies to plow, forests to fell, and minerals to mine. The need for settlers was so great that the States sent immigration agents abroad to recruit new citizens. Germans came in large numbers to Chicago, to Milwaukee, and to lake towns all the way to Green Bay. Dutch immigrants thronged to Lake Michigan, settling communities they called Holland, Vreeland, and Vriesland. By the 1870's, Poles were arriving in large numbers. One group was hired by a lumber company near Lake Huron to cut timber. They bought the cleared land with their wages and developed some of the best farms in Michigan.

Thousands of additional Polish settlers arrived between 1910 and 1920, many of them settling in the industrial centers of Michigan and Wisconsin. During the first World War, the first Negroes came to the Lake cities. They had come as the result of intensive recruitment in the southern states. Trainloads of Negro workmen and their families arrived to take their places in the industrial centers along the Lakes.

Behind the surge of migration to the Midwest were many factors. And they were not exclusively economic ones. Essentially, the pioneers were inspired by the same dream that had motivated earlier generations of Americans to accept the challenge of the wilderness. The mid-18th century was a period of great unrest in Europe. Among the masses there were stirrings of revolt against the doctrine of hereditary privilege. Also, the Old World was weary from its many wars and set in its ways. Increasingly its philosophy was one of resignation and despair. America, especially the Midwest, offered a chance to start afresh. The American Dream was moving from the Atlantic seaboard to the new frontier which was pushing steadily westward.

What made the Lake region especially attractive to settlers was its highly varied population and its diversity of natural resources, including forest and prairie, lakes and wide rivers, coal, oil, gas, copper, iron, and a good, rich soil. In a letter to his brother, a Welsh settler wrote: "We have done very well in this country.

Have a fine farm which would sell for about 6,000 dollars, and every other thing in proportion . . . Thank God no orthodoxy, no tithes, no high church, no king, but good and wholesome laws."

Their buoyant optimism was reflected in the great cities which were springing up on the shores of the Lakes.

At the time of Moses Cleaveland's death in 1806, there were less than 40 people in the little hamlet he had begun on the shore of Lake Erie. By 1840, Cleveland had acquired a population of 40,000 (dropping the 'a' en route). Its harbor was filled with canal boats, lumber scows, and grain schooners. At its wharves lay high-masted sailing vessels loaded with wool, lard, lime, fish, and grindstones. But Cleveland's hour of destiny didn't arrive until 1852, when six barrels of iron ore were shipped from Lake Superior, after being hauled around the falls at Sault Ste. Marie, Mich., and reloaded into a second vessel. With that cargo, Cleveland was on the way towards becoming a giant among American cities. Three years later, in 1855, the St. Mary's Falls Canal was opened, linking Lake Superior to the lower lakes. That year 1,447 tons of iron ore passed through the Soo Locks.

Within half a century, Cleveland became a great commercial center. Although many other cities were involved, the growing commerce on the Lakes centered around Cleveland. Its iron merchants, as well as the nearby coal fields of Pennsylvania, made Cleveland the pivotal point for the Great Lakes trade. All this came about in an incredibly short time. It was as though a young and vigorous America was demonstrating its unique ability to achieve miracles out of a wilderness.

Detroit, today the auto capital of the world, was a straggling settlement six miles long and one street wide in 1800. Its first commerce consisted of canoe caravans which brought the furs of the north to the French fur traders. Picturesque French cottages looked across the river to a Wyandot Indian village, where life was going on just as it had for centuries before the white man's arrival. Three decades later, as the Erie Canal poured commerce into the western waters, Detroit became the busy gateway to new settlements in Michigan and northern Indiana. Its waterfront was filled with merchants, speculators, army men, assorted adventurers, cattle traders, and westward-moving Yankees, as well as a mixed tide of immigrants. The event that started Detroit's change from a frontier outpost to the automobile center of the world took place in Indiana in 1894 when Elwood Haynes cranked up an odd-looking contrivance and drove three miles down Pumpkin Vine Pike. From that modest beginning grew the industrial giant which is today's Detroit. If Elwood were to return to his home town, he would see long freighters loaded with shiny new autos steaming along the river, past the glass and steel buildings of the Civic Center. The River Rouge, which he probably knew as a hunting ground for waterfowl, is filled with blast furnaces and vast spreads of motor factories. The town has changed a lot since Elwood's time.

Chicago, that "tall, bold slugger among cities" as Sandburg describes it, started with little more than its strategic location at the juncture of Lake Michigan and the prairies. In 1803, the city that was to become the greatest metropolis of the Midwest and one of the great cities of the world was a lonely outpost called Fort Dearborn. Hostile Indians, in 1812, burned the settlement and massacred the garrison, putting an end to the little town. After four years, it was rebuilt and a few log houses were constructed on the river bank. The era of development, however, began in 1830 when surveyors began running lines for the Illinois and Michigan Canal. By 1837, it was a city with 4,117 inhabitants. The streets of that early Chicago were soft and were paved with heavy planks. It wasn't until the 1850's that Chicago raised its streets above their natural level and put new foundations under thousands of buildings.

After that, there was no stopping Chicago's headlong rush to eminence. With the dredging of sand bars and the deepening of the Chicago River channel, the city became accessible to lumber schooners, grain schooners, and passenger vessels. Later, when wheat fields were spreading over the prairies, two grain merchants built Chicago's first elevator, and the brig *Osceola* loaded the first cargo of grain for Buffalo. Railroads came into Chicago from six directions in the middle of the 19th century, linking it with the East and with the Mississippi River. Chicago was on its way to becoming the greatest railroad center in the world. Into its growing stockyards, trains of cattle cars brought western cattle. Almost limitless cargoes of lumber came down the Lakes to speed the building of the new frontier.

The terrible fire of 1871 temporarily checked Chicago's phenomenal growth. But such was its vitality that within a few years, the damage had been repaired and a newer, more attractive Chicago was rising out of the ashes of the old. Today, Chicago, perhaps more than any other American city, typifies the drive, dynamics, and soaring aspiration which are so much a part of our heritage. With the opening of the St. Lawrence Seaway, making the Great Lakes accessible to foreign commerce, Chicago has entered upon a new era as one of the great seaports of the world.

As the most important system of inland water transportation in the world, the Great Lakes are an economic asset of incalculable value. Their future is limited only by the economic growth of the nation. Over an intricate network of interconnecting waterways flow hundreds of millions of tons of bulk materials. Cargoes carried on the Lakes today include iron ore from Minnesota, Wisconsin, and Michigan; coal from the Appalachian fields; and wheat from the vast farms of the United States and Canada. Stone moves down the Lakes from Michigan, and pulp wood and petroleum move up the St. Lawrence. America's inland heart is strong and healthy. It will continue to serve us well for years to come.

During the critical days of World War II, shipping and industry in the Great Lakes area moved into high gear. Mines and factories which had formerly produced for the peacetime market, directed all their energies toward meeting war requirements. In a steady stream, their products poured into the war effort. The hard won experience of the past paid off in huge dividends. The people of the Lakes proved to the world what could be accomplished by a free people determined to preserve what they had won by toil and sacrifice.

Heavily increased traffic on the Lakes resulted in higher ship losses. On September 3, 1942, the *Steelvender* sank in Lake Superior with a cargo of steel billets. The steamer *James H. Reed* went down in Lake Erie in April, 1944. It was part of the price of victory.

Many other ship losses could be cited in recounting the long history of the Great Lakes. Mention should be made of the sloop *Ontario* which in 1783 vanished in Lake Ontario, near Oswego, N.Y., with 190 persons, and a cargo of gold and silver valued at

$500,000. Seventy-three years later, in 1856, the *J. S. Brooks* was wrecked while approaching Sackets Harbor, Lake Ontario, with a stupendous $4,000,000 in her safe. The steamer *Young Zion* sank two miles off Walnut Creek, Lake Erie, in 1881, with a cargo of gold specie and railroad iron valued at $225,000.

Those with a taste for well-aged whiskey, as well as for gold and silver specie, might investigate the remains of the steamer *Lexington* which met her end four miles off Point Moullie, Lake Erie. She carried a cargo of gold specie and whiskey with a combined valuation of $100,000. There is also the *Smith Mare*, wrecked in Lake Superior in 1889 while carrying 150 barrels of high grade silver ore and 350 kegs of whiskey. In addition, the *Chicora* has been lying in Lake Michigan since 1895 with specie and 120 barrels of fine whiskey.

Somewhat more exotic are the cargoes which went down with the brig *Black Hawk* and the yacht *Gunilda*. The *Black Hawk*, which foundered in Lake Michigan in 1862, carried stained glass and specie. The *Gunilda* lies in Lake Superior, still encasing a reported $500,000 in jewels.

THE UNLIKELIEST THANKSGIVING

THE SKY was gray, the water was gray, and the coffee tasted more bitter than usual to Captain Green of the *Calumet* as he surveyed the dismal scene around him. Why the devil couldn't the cook prepare a decent cup of coffee?

His broodings were suddenly interrupted by the voice tube from the engine room, "The fluke of an old anchor is sticking right up through the bottom plates, Cap'n."

Green remembered with a shock that they were passing through the shallowest part of the Detroit River. Here on the cold river, just a few days before Thanksgiving, 1889, his spanking new 1500-ton ship had struck her bottom. Remorselessly, the voice continued, "The water is flooding in faster than we can pump it out." Green's coffee tasted bitter as gall. It sure looked like a terrible Thanksgiving. "Set her course for Detroit," he ordered.

At Detroit, workmen repaired the *Calumet* by placing vertical timbers against the overhead. Using wedges they forced iron plates down over the holes. They then filled the bilge with cement. "That ought to hold her," one of them remarked.

Green wasn't so sure. For a really thorough repair job, the *Calumet* should have been dry docked and patched from the outside. But that couldn't be done without unloading the thousands of tons of coal she had in the holds, and her owners were already grousing about the lost time. They wanted Green in Milwaukee by Thanksgiving. As a precaution, Green purchased an emergency steam pump.

The *Calumet* had barely entered Lake Michigan through the Straits of Mackinac, when, without warning, one of the worst blizzards in years shrieked out of the northeast. Snow-laden blasts piled the water into mountains which pummelled the ship. She creaked and groaned as she wallowed deeply. The thermometer plummeted. Ice coated the wave-swept decks. Under constant twisting of the hull, the temporary patches gave way. Soon the rush of water into the hull was beyond control of the ship's pumps. All that stood between the crew and the icy water was the emergency pump.

Finding the lights of Milwaukee in the sleet-filled darkness was like looking for a toothpick in a London fog. The only alternative was to head for Chicago and wait out the storm. Green gave the order and the *Calumet* continued southward with the wind on her tail.

But the *Calumet's* troubles weren't over. Just when it seemed that they might reach the haven of Chicago, Green heard the grim news from the engine room, "Cap'n, the emergency pump just gave out. Don't know what's wrong. Can't fix it."

This was far worse than anything Green had anticipated. Within minutes he would have to make one of the most agonizing decisions to face a skipper: whether to sacrifice his ship or risk the lives of those on board. His face was tense as he gave the order, "Starboard your helm. Steer due west." He was condemning his ship to death.

The *Calumet* lumbered westward in the troughs of the walls of water which beat on the starboard side. The foundering vessel sank deeper as the water poured into the holds. The water-lubricated coal shifted easily now, causing the *Calumet* to roll farther to port and hang there longer after each terrible battering. At 10:30 p.m., an ear-rending screech came up out of the bowels of the ship as rocks laid open her hull.

The *Calumet* had grounded on a bar 1,000 yards from the beach off Fort Sheridan. To keep her from breaking apart immediately, Green ordered the engineer to open the seacocks. The ship settled to the bottom with only a few feet of freeboard left. The wind had become a vengeful demon, blowing the tops off the waves, and filling the air with spray. A thick coating of ice entombed all exposed surfaces. The captain and 17 crew members huddled in the pilot house forward, certain that death awaited them in the swirling water sweeping across the decks.

As the *Calumet* lay helpless in the pounding surf, she was sighted by A. W. Fletcher of Highland Park. He quickly sent a telegram to the U. S. Lifesaving Service Station at Northwestern Academy in Evanston, about 12 miles to the south. At 12:30 a.m. Thanksgiving Day, an Evanston police officer wakened Keeper Lawson, "Here's a message that says there's a large ship aground off Fort Sheridan."

Lawson dressed quickly and hurried to the railroad station. "When's the next train north?" he asked the operator.

"Not until 7:30 in the morning," was the reply. "There's a freight train due to come through here about 2:00 a.m.," the operator continued. "We can flag her down." He telegraphed Chicago. The train had already started for Evanston.

It was too late to couple on an extra car to carry the boat and breeches buoy gear to Highland Park. The train would arrive in 35 minutes.

Lawson ran through the heavy snow to the livery stable, hired a team of horses and dashed back to the campus where he rounded up his crew of students. Keeper Lawson was the only full-time member of the station. Students from Northwestern filled in as surfmen on a part-time basis. Lawson directed one of them to stay behind and wait for the surfman walking the beat along the bluffs to the north of the station. When he came in, the two were to drive the team of horses with the boat and the beach gear along the snow-clotted roads to the site of the wreck. Lawson, four surfmen, and the police officer boarded the train which had just come in. A hot train-wheel journal caused delay. They jumped off at Highland Park at 4:00 a.m.

There they were met by Fletcher, who had found a guide to take them the remaining two miles. The shore opposite the *Calumet* was an almost vertical bluff, 70 to 80 feet high. The bluff was sliced through by deep gullies filled with trees and dense underbrush extending to the water's edge. In the darkness and the blinding flurries, the guide became confused. After struggling in and out of several gullies in the hip-deep snow, the group reached the bottom of the ravine opposite the *Calumet*. The temperature had fallen to 10° above zero. With brush, the student-surfmen built an immense fire to light the area and keep themselves and the now-gathering crowd warm until the beach gear arrived at daylight.

By 7:00 in the morning, it was light enough to make out the steamer. She was rocking under the deluge flooding her main deck. With several inches of ice encasing her rigging and topsides, she looked like a ship out of a legend. It was obvious that she would soon break up, and the crew would be lost unless they got help quickly. From the bluff, the *Calumet* appeared to be in range of the Lyle gun. Lawson ordered it hauled to the top. The gun boomed and a projectile with a line attached hurtled toward the ship. It fell several hundred yards short. Hoping to avoid the near-suicidal boat trip through the surf furiously lashing at the foot of the bluffs, Lawson fired two more shots. They, too, fell short. They would have to go out in the boat!

Captain G. C. Penny, Sixth U. S. Infantry, Fort Sheridan, volunteered his contingent of 50 soldiers. Civilian onlookers, headed by Fletcher, also volunteered to help. With axes they cleared a path through the trees and brush. Others shoveled snow and hacked steps in the stiff blue clay. Together they slid the boat down the ravine to the water's edge.

They had to haul the boat some 500 yards along the foot of the bluff to a position upwind of the *Calumet* to avoid rowing into the teeth of the gale. The men pushed as hard as they could along the narrow shelf of the beach. As wave after wave thundered toward the bluff, each man braced himself against the onslaught. In spite of the bitter cold, they soon found themselves sweating. As water engulfed the boat, the men next to the bluff were in danger of being crushed against the hard clay walls. As the cataract roared lakeward again, the men on the outboard side were nearly swept off their feet. The boat swamped three times. Each time progress stopped while it was bailed out. Eventually they managed to get upwind.

The surfboat was pointed lakeward. Lawson timed the breakers. When the boat lifted as the next wave dashed itself against the bluff, Lawson shouted, "Man your oars, Lads." The young surfmen sprang to their thwarts, shoving their oars out ready to row on the command, "Give way together."

With a mighty shove from the soldiers, the little boat shot lakeward in the torrent of backwash. Crossing the first bar, an immense breaker nearly threw the boat end over end. Lawson was torn from the sweep oar and knocked down, nearly going overboard. Before he could recover, a massive cascade swamped the boat to the thwarts. The boat was nearly unmanageable. Five oarsmen could barely keep steerage way while the stroke oarsman bailed with a bucket. Getting through the lines of white water, they found that they had been swept southward well to the leeward of the *Calumet*. In steady cadence keyed by the count from Lawson, they started the long strength-sapping pull into the raging snowstorm. Flying spray from every white-streaked crest added to the glaze of ice covering them. The oars, encased with ice, constantly slipped out of the rowlocks.

Lawson's boat finally reached the *Calumet's* stern. None of the frightened crew in the forward deckhouse would risk crossing the ice-shrouded decks to toss them a line. After endless rowing, the boat pulled abreast of the bow. Green threw them a line. It was hastily secured to a thwart. On shore, and on the steamer, all breathed easier as the surfboat swung alongside. "You did the impossible," Captain Green shouted.

One at a time, the shipwrecked sailors jumped into the surfboat, wildly tossing in the slamming surf curling around the bow.

George M. Cox stranded on Rock of Ages in Lake Superior.
(Official U.S. Coast Guard Photograph)

One slip and a man would be crushed between the ship and the boat. Once in the rescue boat, each donned a cork-filled life jacket. When six were aboard, they started for shore. The current carried them a quarter of a mile down the beach from the blazing fire. The boat stranded high on the beach after almost broaching on the way in. Volunteers rushed the survivors and the surfmen to the fire where they beat the ice out of their clothing and filled them with hot coffee. Others began the tedious and dangerous job of pushing the boat upwind from the wreck again.

There were still twelve men on the *Calumet*. After a brief rest, Lawson and his crew headed lakeward again into the towering curlers. This time he steered more into the current. They made it to the ship with little wasted motion. The last of the 18 crew members were brought ashore on the third trip.

After the final rescue trip, the lifesavers were in worse condition than the men they had saved. They were so completely exhausted they could scarcely walk or talk. They were warmed, given more coffee, and put on the first train to Evanston, where they arrived early in the afternoon. The survivors were taken to Fort Sheridan for attention.

Within a few hours of the rescue, the *Calumet* was torn apart by the awesome seas. The following morning, nothing was left of the once proud ship except the sternpost and the stem, sticking up out of the water like grim specters.

For their bravery, Keeper Lawson and his student crew were awarded Gold Lifesaving Medals. What had looked like certain disaster had been turned by the courage of Captain Lawson and his crew into an occasion of thanksgiving. As Captain Green reflected some time later, November 28, 1889, was probably the finest Thanksgiving he had ever known. It was certainly the unlikeliest one.

CHAPTER 5 — TABLES. The following listing gives
the position (latitude and longitude); type, name of
vessel, and tonnage; the Coast and Geodetic Survey charts covering the area; and general information concerning dates, cargo and estimated value.

Lat/Long	Type, Name, Tonnage	Charts	Remarks
		LAKE ONTARIO	
——	Sch. GLENDORA	2, 21	Sank Nov. 19, 1887, 2½ miles SW of Amherst Island, Ont., with gold and silver specie on board. Loss estimated at $60,000.
——	LE BLANC HENRI	18, 21	Wrecked June 17, 1764, on Wolf Island Spit near Kingston, Ont. Gold & silver bullion reported on board. Loss estimated at $100,000.
43-57.1 77-07.3	J. S. BROOKS	2, 211	Sank Nov. 4, 1856, in approach to Sackets Harbor with cargo of steel billets. $4,000,000 reported in safe.
43-31.5 76-27.5	Sloop ONTARIO	2, 22	Vanished Nov. 23, 1783, within 3 miles of Oswego. 190 lives lost. Gold and silver reported on board. Loss estimated at $500,000.
48-32.5 76-34.9	Sch. ATLAS	2, 22	Foundered in 1839 with cargo of pig iron.
43-26.5 76-37.3	Sloop LADY WASHINGTON	2, 22	Vanished Nov. 11, 1803, with a mixed cargo and chinaware.
43-13.3 79-15.9	Sch. DELAWARE	2, 25	Sank in Nov. 1887 with cargo of pig iron.
		LAKE ERIE	
——	Str. ANTHONY WAYNE	3, 31	Reported sank April 28, 1850 6½ miles NW of Buffalo, N.Y. Specie and liquor reported on board. Loss estimated at $96,500.
43-34.6 79-12.0	Str. YOUNG ZION	3, 31	Sank June 13, 1881, 2 miles off Walnut Creek with gold specie and RR iron, reported on board. Loss estimated at $225,000.

Lat/Long	Type, Name, Tonnage	Charts	Remarks
——	Str. ERIE	3, 32	Sank Aug. 9, 1841, 4 miles off Silver Creek, N.Y. Specie and whiskey reported on board. Loss estimated at $100,000.
——	Str. DEAN RICHMOND (1432)	3, 32	Sank Oct. 10, 1893, in positions variously reported from 1 mile off Van Buren Point to a few miles NE of Dunkirk, N.Y. $141,000 in bullion reported in safe. Cargo reported to include 200 tons of lead, 100 tons of spelter, and 40 tons of copper ore. Loss reported at $300,000.
42-24.0 79-36.0	Str. CITY OF DETROIT	3, 32	Sank Sept. 3, 1873. Gold Specie and copper reported on board. Loss estimated at $100,000.
42-17.5 79-42.0	Str. CITY OF ROME	3, 32	Burned then beached. Awash 1,000 feet offshore.
42-18.0 79-54.1	Frigate LA JEAN FLORIN	3, 33	Sank July 2, 1721, 10 to 15 miles offshore. Gold and silver bullion reported on board. Loss estimated at $500,000.
42-33.0 79-57.0	Str. ATLANTIC	3	Sank Aug. 19, 1852. Gold and silver specie & whiskey reported on board. Loss estimated at $60,000.
42-30.0 80-07.0	Str. IDAHO (1111)	3	Foundered Nov. 6, 1897, near Long Point with general cargo. 19 lives lost.
42-02.3 80-24.0	Car Ferry MARQUETTE & BESSEMER (3818)	3, 33	Foundered Dec. 7, 1909, with specie, iron, and railroad cars reported on board. Loss estimated at $65,000. 31 lives lost.
42-01.5 80-34.0	Str. CHESAPEAKE	3, 33	Sank June 9, 1847. $8,000 in specie reported on board.
42-16.8 80-47.5	Str. JAMES H. REED (5265)	3	Sank April 27, 1944. Demolition crews leveled wreck to a depth of 35 feet.
41-50.5 81-04.0	Str. CHARLES B. HILL (1731)	3, 34	Beached Nov. 22, 1906, with cargo of coal.
41-37.6 81-32.2	CLEVECO Bge.	3, 35	Sank Dec. 2, 1942. Specie, fuel oil (1,000,000 gals.). Loss estimated at $80,000.
——	Sch. ALGERIA (2038)	3, 35	Sank May 9, 1906, in vicinity of Cleveland, Ohio, with cargo of iron ore.
——	Sch. MABLE WILSON (1225)	3, 35	Sank May 28, 1906, in vicinity of Cleveland, with cargo of iron ore.
41-31.0 81-43.0	Sch. WAHNAPITAE (1432)	3, 35	Sank Oct. 26, 1890.
41-50.5 82-23.5	Str. KENT	3	Sank Aug. 12, 1845. Gold & silver specie reported on board. Loss estimated at $65,000.

Lat/Long	Type, Name, Tonnage	Charts	Remarks
41-29.2 82-12.7	Str. JOHN M. McKERCHEY (506)	35 357	Foundered Oct. 16, 1950, 6,680 feet, 298 degrees from Lorain, Ohio West Breakwater Light.
41-54.0 82-31.0	Str. GEORGE STONE (1841)	3, 36	Sank Oct. 13, 1909, with cargo of coal.
41-39.0 82-36.0	Str. F. H. PRINCE (2047)	3, 36	Sank Aug. 8, 1911.
41-47.8 82-49.0	Str. CASE (2278)	3, 364	Sank May 1, 1917, near Quarry Rocks with cargo of coal.
——	Str. CLARION	3, 364	Reported sunk Dec. 8, 1909, 7 miles SE of Point Moullie in 1918. Gold, silver and 12 locomotives reported on board. Loss estimated at $120,000.
——	Str. LEXINGTON	37, 41	Reported sank 4 miles off Point Moullie. Gold specie & whiskey reported on board. Loss estimated at $100,000.

DETROIT RIVER

Lat/Long	Type, Name, Tonnage	Charts	Remarks
——	Sch. FONTANA (1163)	3, 41	Sank Aug. 3, 1900, in Detroit River with cargo of iron ore.
——	Str. BRITANNIE (1122)	3, 41	Sank Aug. 9, 1895, in Detroit River with cargo of iron ore.
——	Str. KASTOA (1661)	3, 41	Sank July 17, 1890, in Detroit River with cargo of iron ore.
42-05.5 83-08.8	Str. TASHMOO (1344)	41	Struck obstruction June 18, 1936, in Sugar Island Channel.

LAKE HURON

Lat/Long	Type, Name, Tonnage	Charts	Remarks
43-05 82-25	Str. WILLIAM R. LINN (4328)	5, 51	Collided and sank Nov. 4, 1918.
43-05 82-25	Str. NORTHERNER	5, 51	Collided and sank April 18, 1856, with $25,000 in specie and 60 barrels of whiskey reported on board.
44-06.3 82-41.0	Str. PHILADELPHIA (1464)	5, 51	Collided and sank Nov. 7, 1893, in 126 feet, with cargo of coal and merchandise. 16 lives lost.
44-07.0 82-40.0	Str. ALBANY (1918)	5, 51	Collided and sank Nov. 7, 1893, in 210 feet. 8 lives lost.
44-04 83-00	Str. KEYSTONE STATE	5, 52	Sank in 1861 with hardware, crockery and $3000 in gold reported on board.
44-05 83-00	Str. SACRAMENTO (2380)	5, 52	Sank May 5, 1917.

A GUIDE TO SUNKEN SHIPS IN AMERICAN WATERS

Lat/Long	Type, Name, Tonnage	Charts	Remarks
44-05 83-03	Str. HOWARD M. HANNA JR. (5905)	5, 52	Sank Nov. 9, 1913, with cargo of coal.
43-57 83-28	Str. NEW YORK (704)	5, 52	Sank Oct. 14, 1876.
44-25 83-19	Str. WATER WITCH	5, 52	Sank Nov. 1863.
44-25 83-20	Str. BALTIMORE (1160)	5, 52	Sank April 24, 1901, with cargo of coal.
45-02 83-11	Str. JAMES DAVIDSON (1456)	5, 53	Sank Oct. 4, 1883, with cargo of coal.
45-06 83-13	Str. PEWABIC	5, 53	Sank Aug. 12, 1865. Gold & silver specie, 300 tons of copper reported on board. Loss estimated at $250,000.
45-52 83-25	Str. BRUNO	5	Sank Nov. 13, 1890. 100 kegs of whiskey reported on board.
45-30 83-55	Str. JOSEPH S. FAY (1220)	5, 53	Sank Oct. 19, 1905, with cargo of iron ore. Specie & copper reported on board.
46-13 83-42	GRIFFON	5	Sank Sept. 1679. Gold specie reported on board. Loss estimated at $12,000.

LAKE SUPERIOR

Lat/Long	Type, Name, Tonnage	Charts	Remarks
46-48.5 85-04.4	Str. JOHN M. OSBORN (891)	9, 92	Sank after collision July 27, 1884, with cargo of iron ore.
46-46 85-16	SS ALEX NIMICK (1968)	9, 92	Stranded Sept. 21, 1907, 1/3 mile off beach with cargo of iron ore.
46-47.0 85-18.0	Str. NESHOTA (2255)	9, 92	Sank Sept. 27, 1908, with cargo of iron ore. Loss estimated at $65,000.
46-41.0 85-40.0	Str. WESTON RESERVE (2392)	9, 92	Sank Aug. 30, 1892.
46-41.0 85-40.0	Str. STORUCCA (1313)	9, 92	Sank Nov. 15, 1888, with a general cargo. Loss estimated at $80,000.
46-46 85-58	Str. A. A. PARKER (1660)	9, 92	Sank Sept. 19, 1903, with cargo of iron ore.
46-40.9 85-58.7	Str. H. E. RUNNELS (889)	9, 93	Wrecked Nov. 14, 1919, 1/4 mile off Grand Marais with cargo of coal.
46-41.0 86-08.5	Str. GALES STAPLES (2197)	9, 93	Sank Oct. 1, 1919, with cargo of coal.

Lat/Long	Type, Name, Tonnage	Charts	Remarks
46-34.0 86-35.0	Str. SMITH MARE	9, 93	Sank June 13, 1889, with 150 barrels of high-grade silver ore and 350 kegs of whiskey reported on board.
——	Str. SUPERIOR	9, 93	Sank Oct. 29, 1856, off Grand Island, Mich., with specie and 216 barrels of whiskey reported on board. Loss estimated at $30,000.
47-24.5 87-16.0	M/V STEELVENDER (1695)	9	Sank Sept. 3, 1942, loaded with steel billets.
46-30.0 87-21.0	Str. CHARLES J. KERSHAW (1324)	9, 93	Sank Sept. 29, 1895.
——	Str. E. W. OGLEBAY	9, 935	Wrecked Dec. 9, 1927, on Shot Point.
47-25.0 87-40.0	Str. L. C. WALDO (4466)	9, 94	Sank Nov. 8, 1913, with cargo of iron ore.
47-24.0 87-42.0	Str. ALTADOC	9, 94	Sank Dec. 8, 1927.
47-29.0 87-47.8	Pass. Str. SUNBEAM	9, 94	Sank Sept. 28, 1863, with 112 barrels of whiskey and $10,000 in safe reported on board.
47-28.5 87-48.0	Str. R. G. COBURN	9, 94	Sank Oct. 15, 1871. Gold reported on board. Loss estimated at $105,000.
47-28.0 88-16.0	Pass. Str. MANISTEE	9, 94	Sank Nov. 16, 1863, with 100 tons of copper ingots and passengers' valuables.
47-26 88-17	Str. WILLIAM C. MORELAND (7514)	9, 94	Stranded Oct. 18, 1910, with cargo of iron ore.
47-26 88-17	Str. JAMES PICKANDS (1546)	9, 94	Sank Sept. 22, 1894, with cargo of iron ore.
47-28 88-09	Str. HUDSON (2294)	9, 94	Sank Sept. 16, 1901.
47-28 88-09	Str. S. R. KIRBY (2338)	9, 94	Sank May 8, 1916.
47-28 88-09	Str. BANGOR	9, 94	Sank Nov. 1926.
47-14 88-40	Sch. PASADENA (2076)	9, 94	Sank Oct. 8, 1906, with cargo of coal.
47-00.0 90-54.0	Str. SEVONA (3166)	9, 96	Sank Sept. 2, 1905, with cargo of iron ore.
47-11.2 91-22.0	Sch. MADEIRA (5039)	9, 96	Sank Nov. 28, 1865.

Lat/Long	Type, Name, Tonnage	Charts	Remarks
47-05.0 91-33.0	Str. LAFAYETTE (5113)	9, 96	Sank Nov. 28, 1905.
46-56.0 91-46.0	Str. BENJAMIN NOBLE	9, 96	Sank in 1914. $250,000 cargo reported on board.
46-46.9 92-04.0	Str. THOMAS WILSON (1713)	9, 96	Sank June 7, 1902, with cargo of iron ore.
47-44.0 88-45.5	Str. HENRY STEINBRENNER (4345)	9 98	Foundered May 11. 1953 15 miles due south of Isle Royale Light.
48-12.4 88-30.0	Str. EMPORER	9, 98	Struck Canoe Rocks and sank June 1947. Search failed to locate wreck.
48-16.0 88-56.0	Sch. MAGGIE McRAE	9, 98	Sank June 4, 1888, with 300 tons copper ore and liquor on board.
47-52.0 89-19.0	Str. GEORGE M. COX	9, 98	Wrecked May 27, 1933, on reef near Rock of Ages Light.
——	Str. ALGOMA (1173)	9, 98	Sank Nov. 7, 1885, off South Shore Isle Royale, with 200 tons of steel and 100 tons of copper reported on board. 48 lives lost.
——	M/V Q. E. PARKS	9, 98	Sank in 1929, 2 to 3 miles west side of Thunderbay Island.
——	Yct. GUNILDA	9	Sank off Rossport, Sept. 30, 1911, in 200 feet of water. Jewels valued at $500,000 reported on board.
——	Str. KAMLOOPS	9, 98	Sank ¾ mile off Isle Royale with cargo valued at $500,000.
——	Str. MONARCH	9, 98	Sank Dec. 6, 1906, off Isle Royale.

LAKE MICHIGAN

Lat/Long	Type, Name, Tonnage	Charts	Remarks
45-48 86-19	Str. MATOA (2311)	7, 701	Sank Nov. 10, 1913, with cargo of coal.
45-34 85-34	Str. PANTHER (1634)	7, 704	Sank Nov. 21, 1910, with cargo of coal.
44-42 86-16	Brig BLACK HAWK	7, 705	Foundered Nov. 1862 with $4,000 in specie and stained glass reported on board.
45-00 86-09	Str. WALTER L. FROST (1322)	7, 705	Sank Nov. 4, 1903, with general cargo on board. Loss estimated at $65,000.
45-06 86-04	Str. WILLIAM T. GRAVES (1075)	7, 705	Sank Nov. 31, 1885.

Lat/Long	Type, Name, Tonnage	Charts	Remarks
45-55.0 85-12.5	Str. J. OSWALD BOYD (1806)	70, 704	Stranded Nov. 11, 1936 on Simmons Reef, Straits of Mackinaw.
43-58 86-35	Str. WILLIAM B. DAVOCK (4220)	7, 77	Foundered Nov. 11, 1940 between Ludington and Pentwater, Michigan.
44-40 86-16	Str. ST. LAWRENCE (1437)	7, 77	Stranded Nov. 25, 1898, 350 yards from shore
43-58 86-28	Sch. J. H. RUTTER (1224)	7, 77	Sank Nov. 1, 1878.
43-45 86-28	Str. ANNA C. MINCH	7, 77	Sank Nov. 1940.
43-13 86-15	Str. AMAZON OF DETROIT (1406)	7, 76	Sank Nov. 28, 1879.
43-04 86-15	Sch. MONTPELIER (1290)	7, 76	Sank Nov. 1, 1878.
42-47 86-13	Str. ARGO (1089)	7, 76	Sank Nov. 24, 1905, with miscellaneous cargo. Loss estimated at $102,000.
42-46.3 86-13.0	Str. BURLINGTON (2029)	76, 763	Stranded Dec. 6, 1936, 200 feet off North Breakwall, Holland.
42-41 86-42	Str. H. C. AKELEY (1187)	7, 76	Sank Nov. 13, 1883.
42-07 85-30	Str. CITY OF DULUTH (1310)	7, 75	Sank Jan. 26, 1898 with general cargo. Loss estimated at $47,000.
42-04.3 87-04.0	Str. GEORGE W. MORLEY (1046)	7, 75	Wrecked Dec. 5, 1897, just north of Northwestern University.
42-00 86-37	Str. CHICORA	7, 75	Sank Jan. 1, 1895, with specie and 120 barrels of whiskey. Loss estimated at $50,000.
41-45 86-52	Str. F. W. WHEELER (1688)	7, 75	Sank Dec. 3, 1893, with cargo of coal.
41-44 86-55	Str. HORACE A. TUTTLE (1585)	7, 75	Sank Oct. 26, 1898.
42-12 87-43	Str. CALUMET (1526)	7, 74	Sank Jan. 28, 1889, with cargo of coal, 1,000 yards from shore.
42-22 87-40	Str. SEABIRD	7, 74	Reported sank April 9, 1886, with gold and silver specie, banknotes, 66 barrels of whiskey. Loss estimated at $40,000.
——	Str. WISCONSIN	7, 74	Foundered Oct. 29, 1929 off Kenosha, Wisc.

Lat/Long	Type, Name, Tonnage	Charts		Remarks
43-05 87-52	Str. APPOMATTOX (2643)	7,	74	Sank Nov. 2, 1905, with cargo of coal.
43-23 87-52	Str. TOLEDO	7,	74	Sank Oct. 22, 1956.
43-45 87-39	Str. SELAH CHAMBERLIN (1207)	7,	73	Sank Oct. 13, 1886.
44-09 87-30	Str. VERNON	7,	73	Sank Oct. 29, 1887. Specie valued at $30,000 reported on board.
44-56 86-06	Str. WESTMORELAND	7,	70	Sank March 2, 1865, with specie, whiskey, copper on board. Loss estimated at $95,000.
45-37 86-03	M/V CARL D. BRADLEY (10,028)	7,	70	Foundered Nov. 18, 1958.

U.S. Army Corps of Engineers Charts Covering
Great Lakes — Chapter 5

Lake Ontario, Lake Erie, Detroit River,
Lake Huron, Lake Superior, Lake Michigan

Chart	Locality	Scale	Size	Price
0	Great Lakes, General Chart, including Lake Champlain and New York Canals	1:1,200,000	36x52	$1.00
2	Lake Ontario	1:400,000	24x38	1.00
3	Lake Erie	1:400,000	30x44	1.00
5	Lake Huron, including Georgian Bay and North Channel	1:500,000	36x42	1.00
7	Lake Michigan, including Green Bay	1:500,000	30x48	1.00
9	Lake Superior	1:500,000	31x52	1.00
18	St. Lawrence River — Cape Vincent, N.Y., to Allan Otty Shoal, N.Y., and Kingston, Ont.	1:30,000	30x38	1.00
21	Coast chart — Clayton, N.Y., and Kingston, Ont. to Stony Point, N.Y., and False Duck Island, Ont.	1:80,000	30x38	1.00
22	Coast chart — 6 miles south of Stony Point, N.Y., to 8 miles west of Little Sodus Bay, N.Y.	1:80,000	30x38	1.00
25	Coast chart—Thirty Mile Point, N.Y., to Port Dalhousie, Ont., including lower Welland Canal	1:80,000	30x38	1.00
211	East End of Lake Ontario, including Chaumont, Henderson, Black River Bays, and Sackets Harbor	1:30,000	30x38	1.00
3	Lake Erie	1:400,000	30x44	1.00
31	Coast chart — East end of Lake Erie, Morgans Point, Ont., to Sturgeon Point, N.Y., including Niagara River and Welland Canal	1:80,000	30x40	1.00
32	Coast chart — Sturgeon Point, N.Y., to 20 Mile Creek, Pa.	1:80,000	30x40	1.00
33	Coast chart — 16 Mile Creek, Pa. to 7 miles west of Conneaut, Ohio	1:80,000	30x40	1.00
34	Coast chart—8 miles east of Astabula, Ohio to 15 miles west of Fairport, Ohio	1:10,000	30x40	1.00
35	Coast chart — Moss Point to Vermilion, Ohio	1:80,000	30x40	1.00
36	Coast chart — Vermilion, Ohio to Port Clinton, Ohio and Point Pelee, Ont., to Colchester, Ont.	1:80,000	30x40	1.00

Chart	Locality	Scale	Size	Price
37	Coast chart — Port Clinton, Ohio and Colchester, Ont., to mouth of Detroit River.	1:80,000	30x40	1.00
364	Islands in Lake Erie, including Sandusky Bay, Ohio	1:40,000	34x48	1.00
41	Detroit River — 3 miles south of Detroit River Light to Windmill Point, Mich.	1:30,000	34x40	1.00
51	Coast chart — Head of St. Clair River to Pte. aux Barques, Mich., and to Port Albert, Ont.	1:120,000	36x48	1.00
52	Coast chart — Pte. aux Barques, Mich. to 11 miles north of Oscoda, Mich., and Saginaw Bay	1:120,000	36x48	1.00
53	Cast chart — 6 miles north of Oscoda, Mich. to Forty Mile Point Light, Mich., including Great Duck Island	1:12,000	3 x48	1.00
70	North end of Lake Michigan, including Green Bay	1:240,000	36x48	1.00
73	Coast chart — Algoma, Wis. to 18 miles south of Sheboygan, Wis. Insets: Kewaunee, Wisc. and Two Rivers, Wis.	1:120,000	36x48	1.00
74	Coast Chart — 10 miles north of Port Washington, Wis. to Waukegan, Ill.	1:120,000	36x48	1.00
75	Coast chart — South end of Lake Michigan from Waukegan, Ill. to South Haven, Mich.	1:120,000	36x48	1.00
76	Coast chart — South Haven, Mich. to Benona, Mich.	1:120,000	36x48	1.00
77	Coast chart — Benona, Mich. to Point Betsie	1:120,000	36x48	1.00
701	Coast chart — Farnsworth Point, Mich. to 15 miles southwest of Escanaba, Mich. including Big Bay de Noc and Little Bay de Noc	1:80,000	36x48	1.00
704	Coast chart — Beaver Island Group, Waugoshance Point, Mich. to Bou'der Reef and north shore from Brevort, Mich. to Seul Choix Point, Mich.	1:80,000	36x48	1.00
705	Coast chart — Platte Bay, Mich. to Lake Leelanau, Mich. including the Manitou and Fox Islands	1:80,000	36x48	1.00
92	Coast chart — St. Marys River to Au Sable Point, Mich. and to Montreal Shoal, Ont.	1:120,000	36x48	1.00
93	Coast chart — Grand Marais, Mich. to Big Bay Point, Mich.	1:120,000	36x48	1.00
94	Coast chart — Big Bay Point, Mich. to Redridge, Mich., including Keweenaw Peninsula and Keweenaw Waterway.	1:120,000	36x48	1.00
96	Coast chart — Little Girls Point, Mich. to Silver Bay, Minn.	1:120,000	36x48	1.00
97	Coast chart — Beaver Bay, Minn., to Pigeon Point, Minn.	1:120,000	36x48	1.00
98	Coast chart — Isle Royale, Mich. including Thunder Bay, Ont., and coast from Grand Portage Bay, Minn. to Shesheeb Point, Ont.	1:120,000	36x48	1.00
935	Marquette and Presque Isle Harbors, Mich.	1:15,000	26x38	1.00

CHAPTER 6

Great Rivers

Illinois River, Kanawha River,
Mississippi River, Cumberland River,
Tennessee River, Allegheny River,
Missouri River, Monongahela River,
Ohio River

ROLL THE NAMES over on your tongue: Mississippi, Missouri, Kanawha, Tennessee, Monongahela. There's music in them. They make up an important part of the history of America. To the men who first took up the challenge of the wilderness they provided pathways to the otherwise inaccessible heart of the continent. Along their shores grew the first settlements, which later developed into great cities. As the nation prospered, the rivers became broad highways of commerce bringing the goods and produce of one section of the country to another.

Many are the legends which have flourished around our rivers. They have become celebrated in song and story. But by far the most famous is "Old Man River," the mighty Mississippi, which rolls its sinuous length down the middle of North America. Frequently muddy and slow moving, this fantastic river has wound its way through all the eras of American history. The Indians with their aptitude for poetic expression, called it, "The Father of Waters." The name is eminently appropriate. Beginning as a tiny rivulet in Minnesota, it widens and gains increasing strength to become a majestic stream.

For the Mississippi, the greatest days came in the years preceding the Civil War. Cotton had brought a new prosperity to the

South and all along the winding river, levees were piled high with goods from the huge plantations which lined its banks. These were days described by Mark Twain in his "Life on the Mississippi", and later by Edna Ferber in her novel, "Showboat." The Mississippi was more than a river. It was a way of life.

As commerce grew on the river, the steamboats entered into their most fabulous era. Lady Emmeline Stuart Wortley, a visitor to the United States in the early 1850's, describes a procession of riverboats this way: "By night the scene is one of startling interest and magical splendor. Hundreds of lights are glancing in different directions on shore and from the magnificent "floating palaces" of steamers, that frequently look like living moving mountains of light and flame, so brilliantly are these enormous leviathans illuminated outside and inside . . . steamer after steamer coming, sweeping, sounding, thundering on . . ."

In ornately furnished lounges, with rich rugs, oil paintings, and lines of chandeliers, frock-coated dandies flirted elegantly with ladies in crinoline skirts. Menus on these floating hotels were rich and varied, the chefs in many cases having been taken from famous restaurants. Surviving menus show scores of dishes with as many as seven soups and 15 desserts from which to choose. For the men there were mirrored bars, which always did a capacity trade.

The captain of a river steamer had a power second to none. He enjoyed almost unlimited authority over passengers and crew. His style of living both on land and water was regal and his merest whims were treated with the greatest respect.

Enjoying an authority almost as absolute as the captain's was the pilot. He was deferred to by all on board, including the captain. He received the highest pay and there is no question that he earned it. The safety of the ship, passengers and crew hinged on his ability to spot a danger before it could cause disaster. His knowledge didn't lie in books alone, but came from long experience during which he learned to know every changing mood of the river, as well as its many treacherous points. Like the aviators of a generation ago, the river pilot often had to navigate "by the seat of his pants."

For the towns along the Mississippi, the steamboat whistle was one of the most exciting sounds in the world. Much of the social life centered around the comings and goings of the steamboats. Townspeople would flock to the river to see who was arriving or leaving, hear bits of news the crew might have picked up along the way, and find out how much cotton was being shipped.

To feed the engines which swallowed fuel hungrily, men cut vast quantities of cordwood and stacked them for quick pickups when needed. At isolated spots, people would stand on the banks for hours waiting for a vessel. Eager for business, the steamboats would stop nearly anywhere to pick up an extra passenger.

Even more exiciting were the showboats. They brought the glamorous world of the theater to the towns along the river. Their repertoire consisted of vaudeville and the tear-jerking melodramas of which our ancestors were so fond. It was on the showboats that the dashing riverboat gamblers would engage prospective victims in conversations which led to marathon card games, some of them lasting for 36 hours or more. At the end of these grueling sessions, a gambler might leave with a year's plantation profits.

Most of the boats were worked so hard that they seldom lasted more than four or five years. Poor construction and inadequate maintenance contributed to frequent mishaps. Always, there was intense competition among the boats to provide faster schedules. The price of all this was the death of about 4,000 persons in riverboat accidents between 1810 and 1850.

The Civil War virtually halted steamboat traffic on the river. Gunboats replaced river boats in the great struggle to gain control of the strategic Mississippi. But the era of the steamboat was not yet over. Shortly after the war's end, steamboating started to revive. In 1865, the famous old steamboat *Sultana* was destroyed in a disastrous explosion on the Mississippi, which claimed the lives of more than 1,500 men. The full story of this tragedy is given later in this chapter.

CHEATING THE OHIO

Sunday, March 5, 1882, was a drizzly day in Louisville, Ky., but the rain didn't dampen the spirits of the large crowd which had gathered on the wharf to bid goodby to the 505-ton stern-wheeler, *James D. Parker*. Enroute from Cincinnati to Memphis, the *Parker* had made her regular stop at Louisville to pick up additional cargo. She was carrying 50 crewmen, 55 passengers, including women and children, and a cargo estimated at $25,000. The wind had whipped the Ohio into a heavy chop, and old timers could see that it was running unusually deep.

To avoid going through the canal, her captain had decided to take the *Parker* through the Indiana Chute of the Ohio Falls. To do this, he had engaged a veteran river pilot with the improbable name of Pink Varble. Varble foresaw no danger. For some unknown reason he overlooked the haphazard stowage of the *Parker's* cargo in the forward part of the vessel. Since the *Parker* drew only six feet of water forward and three aft, it was a surprisingly serious oversight, especially for a vessel about to navigate the fast-running Chute.

Ashore, it was a gala occasion. People were dressed in their Sunday best. The men were imposing in their high white collars and luxuriant mustaches. The women were resplendent in ruffled shirtwaist blouses, elaborate coiffures and long, sweeping skirts. Parasols and umbrellas were very much in evidence as the spectators waved handerchiefs and shouted the usual farewells.

At 12:30 p.m., the bell on the hurricane deck clanged the signal for the deckhands to let go the lines. Majestically, the *Parker* crunched and clanked her way into the swift-running Ohio. Plumes of smoke and steam hovered over her as she steamed up the river, stopped, turned, and straightened herself for the descent into the Chute. A sharp, signal stroke of the ship's bell meant that she was going ahead slow. Then she swept past the crowd and over the full waters of the dam into the rapids.

For a few moments, the *Parker* superbly held her course in the foaming waters. Suddenly she began to veer to the left. Varble, first by himself, then with the help of the captain and others, spun the wheel hard to full right. But the ship continued to swerve off course. Since she drew only three feet aft, the rudders were too high to get a good grip. Varble, whose face was now ashen, saw a huge rock looming ahead. He rang up "Back Full," but it was too late. The shuddering ship bounced off the rock on her left side. A desperate effort at the wheel straightened her out for a moment. But again she swerved and continued smashing against the rocks, her bow gradually submerging.

To the horrified spectators on the wharf, it looked hopeless. For a while, the *Parker* seemed to undertake a course of her own, sheering to the left and wobbling sideways until her bow disappeared. Then she careened to starboard, knocking her stern completely off as the after end swung into the channel towards the Indiana shore. Her tall smoke stacks toppled over, and a volcano of steam shot into the air as the water flooded her furnaces. Finally she sank in 18 feet of water 200 feet below the railroad bridge, listing as she settled. Her upper works fell in a crashing shower.

Aboard the *Parker* there was utter panic. The ship became a mass of frightened humanity. Women, crying in terror, clutched their children to their bosoms. Many of them were scrambling for the cabin door when the boat careened, throwing them to the deck. Tables, glass, and dinnerware scattered across the deck. As the supports of the hurricane deck gave way, a shower of barrels, boxes, and merchandise thundered down on the frantic people.

The rush and gurgle of water into the hull added to the hellish cacophony of shrieking, sobbing women and children, shouting men, and the creaking and splitting of ship's timbers. In her agony, the *Parker* shivered violently, careened once more, and broke apart from stem to waist.

The shock of the *Parker's* death spasm momentarily stilled the clamor. As order returned, women and children, one by one, slowly climbed out of the steeply slanting cabin. To help them, chairs had been piled one on the other so that they could climb to the doorway. But the water was now flooding so fast that it was waist-deep by the time the last woman had been pulled out through the overhead hatch by the captain.

A new threat appeared. Sometime during the *Parker's* final moments, the stove in the saloon had overturned. Snake-like tongues of flame darted through the dense clouds of smoke curling up from below. The male passengers, regaining their self-possession, assisted the crew as they doused the fire with buckets of water. It was a stubborn blaze, but they finally subdued it.

The entire nightmarish episode had taken less than ten minutes, but already boats from the U. S. Lifesaving Service, Louisville, were racing to the scene. The stricken *Parker* was about 400 yards from shore when they pulled alongside. Wrenching a door off a cabin to serve as a gangway, the rescuers began helping the shaken passengers into the boats.

It required 12 trips to transfer 80 passengers to the Indiana bank. Twenty-five more, clinging to boxes and casks, were picked up by a bizarre flotilla of craft which had been hastily assembled and rushed to the scene. All on board were rescued, some having drifted as far as two miles downstream. All that was lost was the ship and her cargo. The courage and skill of the rescuers had cheated the Ohio.

SOLDIER REST! THY WARFARE O'ER

The war was over, but peace had not yet come. Wounds were still too fresh, past bitterness too recent to be forgotten, as straggly columns of men in shabby Union blue and equally shabby Confederate grey began the long homeward trek.

One of these groups had gathered at the old Mississippi port town of Vicksburg. Their tattered blue uniforms said they were the victors. But they didn't look much like victors. Their gaunt faces bore the marks of recent suffering. Some seemed dazed by their surroundings, detached, emotionless.

These men in Union blue had been freshly liberated from a Confederate prison camp at Chaba, Ala., after two years confinement. Short days ago they had lived in constant fear of death. Now they were free, but the sensation was so new that it took some time getting used to.

They had been in the inhospitable southern city for two days waiting for the steamboat *Sultana* to take them to St. Louis, the first leg of the journey home. With two years back pay in their pockets, bored and restless, they were only too willing quarry for the gamblers, moonshiners, and campfollowers who had streamed into Vicksburg like ants to sugar. All had the same objective: to lighten the purses of the sad-faced men waiting to go home.

Now the waiting was finally over. It was time to board the old riverboat and leave the war behind them forever. All was shouting and confusion on that mild spring day of April, 1865. One of the men produced a mouth organ and started to play a Negro spiritual born out of the bondage they had set out to destroy so long ago. The notes rose softly and sweetly above the clamor:

"*Swing low, sweet chariot*
Comin' for to carry me home."

Two Negro stevedores on the dock began to sing the verses. Soon the men on board the *Sultana* were singing with them. Tense faces relaxed and softened. There were tears on the faces of some that weren't brushed away. They were good tears, cleansing and washing away the stain and ugliness of war. The warm tears dissolved the hard outer shell of indifference and they were men once more, capable of feeling. They wept for the lost years that would never come again.

Had the men on the *Sultana* known the condition of the boat on which they counted so heavily, their rejoicing might not have been so unrestrained. She carried no safety equipment of any kind and her boiler plant was an invitation to disaster. Built to carry about 400 persons and cargo, the 1720-ton riverboat was carrying an incredible load. Besides two companies of fully armed infantry, she carried about 2,000 former prisoners of war, horses, mules, and 100 hogsheads of sugar. There was scarcely room to stand, let alone lie down. Privacy was out of the question, but nobody complained. They would gladly have stood all the way to St. Louis to put the past behind them.

Late in the afternoon, the *Sultana* started backing out of the harbor. Suddenly her whistle stuck and, for what seemed an eternity, the ear splitting blast assailed the exhausted men's nerves. Someone shouted, "Shut that thing off or I'll go crazy." Then nearly everyone else joined in the cry until the boat seemed a bedlam. At last the engineers shut the valve leading to the whistle and peace once more reigned on the *Sultana*.

Darkness had settled on the river, and many of the men stretched out on deck to enjoy the beauty of the spring night. It was a time for private thinking, each man wrapped in thoughts of his own future. The slapping of the water against the sides of the boat made an agreeable accompaniment. For the first time, they felt really at peace. They had survived. They were going home. Life had never seemed so good.

Two hours upstream from Memphis, the *Sultana* was passing through a group of islands known to natives as "Hens and Chickens," just opposite Tagleman's Landing. Abruptly, the ship was rocked by a violent explosion. The men could feel the vessel shudder as if smashed by a giant fist. Hatches leading to the engineroom were blown off their hinges and propelled across the deck, narrowly missing some of the sleeping men.

Black smoke laced with hissing steam billowed from the openings. Shrieks of scalded men and horses added to the horror. Some of the horses broke loose and shots rang out as the men tried to protect themselves from being trampled to death.

Blind panic had taken possession of the ship. Men threw themselves into the inky water — their bodies lit up briefly in the orange glow of the *Sultana* until they disappeared in the water. Those who couldn't swim crowded ever closer to the edge.

The *Sultana* had become a flaming torch, lighting up the water for miles around. The water was filled with men desperately trying to stay alive. All about were flailing arms and bobbing heads. Cries for help came from everywhere. Gradually the cries ceased and the silence of death hung over the grisly scene. The *Sultana* had gone down. She had taken with her the lives of more than 1,500 men. They never got home after all. And yet, perhaps they did.

U. S. Coast Guard river cutter KANKAKEE *built in 1919 by Dubuque Boat and Boiler Works in Dubuque, Iowa. The vessel was commissioned in 1919 and decommissioned on May 31, 1936 at Evansville, Indiana, her home port. This paddle wheeler was powered by steam and displaced 383 tons.*

(Official U.S. Coast Guard Photograph)

CHAPTER 6 — TABLES. The following listing gives the location (mile); name of vessel, and tonnage; and general information concerning dates, cargo and estimated value. All mile locations are from the mouth of the river, except the Mississippi, which is divided into Lower and Upper Sections. Locations on Lower Mississippi River are from the mouth at the Gulf. Locations on Middle and Upper Mississippi River are from Cairo, Ill., where the Ohio joins the Mississippi.

Mile	Name, Tonnage	Remarks
	ILLINOIS RIVER	
60.0	Barge	Sank June 26, 1947.
166.2	Barge	Sank March 16, 1949.
173.3	Barge	Sank May 8, 1950.
188.4	Barge	Date Unknown.
302.2	H. S. HENNEN	Sank Sept. 12, 1950.
	MIDDLE AND UPPER MISSISSIPPI RIVER	
1.9	Barge	Sank Feb. 19, 1947.
50.0	Steamboat hull	Sank Nov. 2, 1948.
51 0	MOP-4	Sank April 10, 1949.
78.0	GOLDEN EAGLE	Sank May 18, 1947.
86.2	TESSLER	Sank June 26, 1949.
127.5	R.J.V.	Sank June 1941.
176.5	Barge #108	Sank May 20, 1947.
179.6	Barge	Sank Oct. 27, 1949.
179.9	CT-425	Sank Oct. 4, 1949.
187.6	Barge	Sank Nov. 2, 1948.
189.0	**GEORGE BULZ**	Sank in 1949.

Mile	Name, Tonnage	Remarks
217.9	Barge	Sank Feb. 28, 1947.
272.5	Barge #BL316	Sank June 26, 1947.
374.8	CITY OF NAUVOO	Sank in 1945.
415.8	BARNETT	Sank in 1942.
480.1	LONE DEER	Sank in 1947.
481.2	PEARL	Sank in 1945.
481.2	W. J. QUINLAND	Sank in 1946.
481.2	J. P.	Sank in 1943.
486.2	MARQUETTE	Sank in May 1939.
849.8	HARRY R. HARRIS	Sank in Oct. 1948.

LOWER MISSISSIPPI RIVER

Mile	Name, Tonnage	Remarks
170.0	Barge MV656 (911)	Collided with SS TRIMBLE'S FORD and sank on Sept. 23, 1960, near Burnside, La.
344.4	Barge	Sank May 26, 1950.
344.4	OBL-378	Sank May 20, 1950.
352.5	WYCHEM 112, Bge. (765)	Foundered March 23, 1961, 7 miles below Natchez, Miss.
373.3	Barge	Sank Dec. 19, 1948.
449.0	OLIVER BEIRNE, Str. (1018)	Destroyed by fire at Millikens Bend, Oct. 29, 1891.
491.7	Str. NATCHEZ (757)	Collided March 4, 1948, with pier of Greenville Hiway Bridge.
507.0	U.S.E.D. Quarterboat	Sank Sept. 15, 1947.
519.8	Barge	Sank Dec. 7, 1948.
540.6	Barges (three)	Sank Nov. 13, 1947.
540.6	Barge	Sank Sept. 15, 1947.
589.9	Barge	Sank May 16, 1950.
659.9	WACOUTA	Sank March 27, 1950.
700.0	SULTANA, Str. (1720)	Exploded and burned April 27, 1865, in Hens and Chickens Islands, opposite Tagleman's Landing, Tenn. 1500 lives lost. (Mileage approximate).

Mile	Name, Tonnage	Remarks
732.7	Barge	Sank Dec. 15, 1948.
732.7	IWC-#212	Sank Jan. 28, 1950.
885.0	Bge. BL 203 (612)	Foundered Nov. 26, 1958
911.7	Barge #208	Sank Feb. 11, 1949.
939.0	ABL-#201	Sank Oct. 1, 1949.
940.0	Barge	Sank March 27, 1950.

KANAWHA RIVER

54.7	HENRY C. YEISER	Sank Aug. 15, 1940.

CUMBERLAND RIVER

19.6	CTC-431	Sank Feb. 22, 1949.
38.5	YOCONA	Sank July 10, 1939.
191.0	SUSIE A.	Sank Oct. 9, 1942.
237.0	PATTY T.	Sank Jan. 1, 1940.

TENNESSEE RIVER

0.1	MARGARET HALL	Date Unknown.
19.6	Barge	Sank Feb. 14. 1946.
22.0	PHILLIP RITCHIE	Sank Aug. 12, 1944.
47.2	Barge	Sank Aug. 14, 1946.
205.0	JAY HAWKER	Sank Jan. 25, 1939.
241.7	Barge	Sank Feb. 6, 1947.
251.1	Barge	Sank April 7, 1948.
275.0	Barge	Sank March 25, 1945.
300.7	ELIZABETH SMITH	Sank April 14, 1944.
304.5	ZENALE	Sank Feb. 19, 1946.

MISSOURI RIVER

299.6	RED WING	Sank Oct. 31, 1948.
311.5	MARGUERITE B.	Sank Sept. 17, 1949.

Mile	Name, Tonnage	Remarks
336.3	Str. MINNESOTA (1332)	Foundered June 21, 1951, near mouth of Fishing River, Mo.
504.0	Ferry Boat #20	Sank April 24, 1939.

ALLEGHENY RIVER

Mile	Name, Tonnage	Remarks
19.0	E. K. DAVIDSON	Sank in 1950.
60.2	WIRLER #1	Sank in 1949.

MONONGAHELA RIVER

Mile	Name, Tonnage	Remarks
1.0	Str. ISLAND QUEEN (1213)	Burned Sept. 7, 1947, at Pittsburgh.
1.0	STEEL CITY	Sank in 1941.
37.0	ALRISA	Sank in 1946.
42.0	LEONA	Sank in 1942.
42.0	RICHARD	Sank in 1940.
57.0	JOE CARTER	Sank in 1948.
70.0	RECRUCIBLE	Sank in 1948.
70.0	MIDLAND	Sank in 1940.

OHIO RIVER

Mile	Name, Tonnage	Remarks
47.6	Barge #126	Sank March 22, 1948.
68.2	Barge	Sank April 15, 1949.
86.0	U.S.E.D. Boat	Sank May 2, 1939.
94.5	KATIE L. LYONS	Sank in 1942.
128.2	Barge	Sank Feb. 3, 1949.
137.7	KIWANIS	Sank April 27, 1948.
219.9	CALVIN B. BEACH	Sank Feb. 19, 1939.
265.5	VALLEY BELLE	Sank Feb. 24, 1943.
269.7	JOHN W. LANE	Sank Jan. 22, 1947.
305.8	PAUL F. THOMAS	Sank Jan. 30, 1948.
305.8	SAM D. SUIT	Sank March 22, 1948.
318.0	JULIUS FLEISCHMAN	Sank March 21, 1945.

Mile	Name, Tonnage	Remarks
329.3	CTC #402	Sank Sept. 26, 1942.
356.0	ECLIPSE	Sank April 27, 1947.
357.4	Barge #81	Sank Oct. 17, 1946.
357.4	Barge #263	Sank Dec. 1, 1944.
389.1	Barges (two)	Sank July 6, 1939.
391.4	W. C. MITCHELL	Sank Feb. 18, 1945.
397.3	Barge OR #2	Sank March 13, 1947.
412.3	JANE NELSON	Sank March 3, 1939.
417.7	CHIEF BLACK HAWK	Sank Aug. 24, 1948.
430.1	A. C. INGERSOLL	Sank Aug. 23, 1940.
461.4	O & K #2	Sank June 8, 1947.
465.7	ONK #107	Sank April 18, 1944.
469.4	Derrick Boat	Sank May 19, 1945.
470.0	G. W. McBRIDE	Sank Feb. 22, 1942.
470.1	KASKASKIA	Sank Jan. 9, 1942.
471.1	Barge	Sank Aug. 15, 1949.
472.3	CT-420	Sank June 30, 1949.
473.2	OR-218	Sank Sept. 6, 1947.
474.6	OFS #45	Sank May 1, 1943.
482.0	Barge #3	Sank March 26, 1947.
487.4	Barge	Sank April 1, 1948.
493.0	Barge IC-25	Sank Feb. 14, 1946.
493.0	Barge IC-18	Sank Feb. 14, 1946.
496.3	R. W. TURNER	Sank July 11, 1947.
504.0	CAPTAIN BEATTY	Sank Nov. 26, 1947.
514.1	LITTLE EDDIE	Sank Dec. 17, 1947.
523.8	Coal Digger	Sank Jan. 7, 1950.
602.8	PLYMOUTH	Sank Jan. 9, 1945.

Mile	Name, Tonnage	Remarks
700.0	JAMES PARKER, Str. (505)	Sank in Falls of Ohio Chute. 105 passengers saved. $25,000 cargo lost. (mileage approximate)
757.3	OWENSBORO	Sank Feb. 15, 1945.
766.0	Pontoon	Sank May 28, 1947.
794.9	OBL-362	Sank Feb. 28, 1950.
809.6	BOB GRESHAM	Sank Feb. 17, 1945.
836.7	CT-429	Sank Feb. 24, 1950.
844.0	ABL-208	Sank Sept. 26, 1950.
976.5	HARTFORD	Sank Sept. 15, 1949.
979.3	CGR #2347	Sank Sept. 23, 1943.

Refer to Appendix B for details on available maps covering Great Rivers of the United States.

CHAPTER 7

Pacific Coast

California, Oregon,

and Washington

BETWEEN the northern boundary of Washington and California's southern border lie about 1,800 miles of the most spectacularly beautiful coastline in the world. It offers a panorama of unparalleled magnificence, ranging from the craggy coves and inlets of Washington and Oregon, on through the High Sierras and lush valleys of central California, to the golden beaches of California's southern coast, all framed by the vastness and splendor of the Pacific Ocean.

On this western coast our ancestors finally realized their dream of a mighty nation whose borders would reach from "sea to shining sea." After terrible hardships and much sacrifice they had broken through to a land whose scenic grandeur was more than matched by its natural resources. "I hear America singing" wrote Walt Whitman. On the Pacific coast, the song becomes a mighty symphony of foam-flecked surf breaking against rock, of gleaming cities reaching far into the sky and of virgin forests already old when Columbus first stepped upon the shore of the New World. It is in fact, a symphony of human aspiration. In many ways, the West Coast is still young in spirit. It is a place where most things are possible if one has the will to achieve.

The first to touch the shores of this fabulous land were the roving Spanish conquistadors. Driven by an all-consuming lust for gold, these hardy soldiers of fortune reached the wilderness which was to become California during the 1520's. They must have had incredible stamina to have undertaken so great a voyage in their small galleons. One cannot help but admire their courage.

To Hernando Cortes falls the honor of having first ventured into the country of which he had read in the absurd but imaginative travel books of his time. One of these was written by Ordonez de Montalvo whose language is so quaint that it is worth repeating: "There is an island California, very close to that part of the Terrestrial Paradise which was inhabited by black women . . . In this island, named California, there are many griffins. In no other part of the world may they be found. And there ruled over that island of California a queen of majestic proportions, more beautiful than all the others . . . their arms were of gold and so was the harness of the wild beasts they tamed to ride for in the island was no metal but gold." Senor de Montalvo may have been an indifferent geographer, but he certainly had a way with words.

This obsession with gold spurred most of the many Spanish expeditions of the 16th century. Also, nearly all of them were looking for that magic Northwest Passage that would lead them to the wealth of the East. If they had not been so blinded with gold lust, they might have seen that they had come close to finding the *El Dorado*, the Golden Country, for which they hungered. But perhaps these early Spaniards were not very different from the men of other ages who fell into the same tragic error, hunting for treasure which was before their very eyes.

One of the earliest expeditions to reach northern Mexico was headed by Niño de Guzman, whose atrocities eventually sickened even the Spanish and led to his arrest. Unable to find the rich Aztec-like civilization they were sure was there for the plunder, de Guzman and his men vented their frustrations on the Indians. Their incredible brutality created a hatred for the white man that would plague settlers for more than three centuries. To rid themselves of their torturers, the Indians fed them tales of wealth to be found — further on, always further on.

Following in de Guzman's wake, Cortes sent expeditions by foot and by ship as far into the interior as the Colorado River. The results were disappointing, but Cortes, convinced that treasure lay within his grasp, refused to give up. He sailed up the Pacific Coast and went ashore on what he thought was the legendary island of California. He had no way of knowing it, but the treasure he hunted lay far beyond the tip of lower California, about 1,500 miles to the northwest. It was locked up in the granite vaults of the Sierra Nevada Mountains. It would be another three centuries before the vault would be unlocked.

Cortes finally left California, a disappointed man. He was succeeded by Antonio de Mendoza, first Viceroy of New Spain. It was Mendoza who ordered another conquistador to go into the Southwest at the head of an army with banners to search for the Seven Cities of Cibola whose houses were supposedly made of emeralds, turquoise, and gold. Mendoza also dispatched Hernando Alarcon into the unknown waters of the Sea of Cortes, now called the Gulf of California, to hunt for them by sea and river. Alarcon was under orders to effect a juncture with Coronado's army. Alarcon succeeded in reaching the Colorado, but instead of waiting for Coronado, he pushed his way up the Colorado. In 1540 at a point near the Gila River, he erected a cross with the inscription: *Alarcon reached this place, there are letters under the tree.* That made the haughty Alarcon the first white man to stand on the soil of California.

Many Spanish adventurers took up the search for treasure in succeeding generations. They learned a good deal about the California coastline and something about the interior. Bartolome Ferrer sailed as far as the southern coast of Oregon. He missed the bay of San Francisco, as did Sir Francis Drake in 1602 on his famous voyage.

Yet the early history of California was not exclusively Spanish. For a long time, Russia's Czar, Peter the Great, had nursed the ambition of establishing an eastward passage between the Pacific and Atlantic oceans. Soon after his death, Russia started to explore the coast of Alaska, build ships on Kodiak Island, and encouraged her fur traders to hunt in the Aleutians.

To bar Russian expansion and to stimulate the local economy, Spain sent out teams of soldiers and priests to set up a chain of missions. This would be visible evidence of Spanish claims to the territory. This turned out to be one of the most productive measures undertaken by Spain in the New World. It is a tribute to the power of the spirit that the influence of the missions survives so long after their building. Many of them remain intact, dotting the California landscape from San Diego to San Francisco. Against a dark blue California sky, they suggest gentleness and peace. One of the most famous missions was established in 1776, the year of United States independence, in San Francisco. A presidio which still stands was also built at that time.

A memento of early Spanish exploration is the galleon *San Agustin*, wrecked in 1599 off Point Reyes with a reported $500,000 in treasure on board. More than a century later, 1717, the *Santa Rosa* sank off Bishop's Rock with gold and silver on board. The loss was estimated at $700,000.

By the late 17th century, Spanish power in the North America had begun to fade. Already, the first vanguards of American settlers were arriving. Some came by overland trek and others by the equally dangerous journey around Cape Horn. By the time of the war with Mexico in 1847-48, a number of American communities had been set up in the Golden State.

Like the Spaniards before them, they had been spurred by the hope of finding treasure. Their appetites had been whetted by news that Sam Brannan in 1848 had found gold in the American River. Nearly everyone capable of carrying a pick and shovel raced out to get his share of the precious metal. Working a full day, anyone could pan about $15.00 of gold dust. Many a man made his fortune in those incredible days. A miner named Hudson, dug $20,000 in gold in six weeks near Coloma. A Frenchman discovered $5,000 while cutting down a tree stump.

Brannan's shout of "gold" didn't reach the East until the following year, starting a migration which has never been equalled. By the tens of thousands the "49'ers" came by wagon and by horseback. About 16,000 sailed around the Horn. Others came via the Panama route, risking serious illness and death. From all over the United States they came.

Within a year, 100,000 persons, exclusive of Indians, were in California. America's newest frontier was growing. But it was still largely uninhabited and the possibilities were limitless. Ships moved in and out of San Francisco Bay in a never-ending stream.

Often cargoes failed to reach their destinations because the demand for them was so great that they were sold at the wharves. Prices were astronomic. Flour cost $400 a barrel, cabbages went for $2.00 a piece, and pills sold for $20.00 each. Doctors tended the sick at $32.00 a visit — a rather odd fee — and ordinary tents rented for $20.00 a week. Ladies of pleasure, imported from Paris, charged $16.00 just to sit on a bar stool with a patron. A night's entertainment cost $250.00. Gold was not being mined exclusively in the mines and rivers.

For the City of the Angels, times were not so booming. The city had some of the romantic quality of a Spanish town with guitars very much in evidence. Lola Montez, notorious ex-mistress of Ludwig, the half-mad King of Bavaria, performed her "Spider Dance" at $65.00 a ticket. But most of the younger and more vigorous men headed for San Francisco as part of the gold rush.

Los Angeles might have remained a somnolent Spanish town were it not for the vision and stubborn courage of a Franciscan priest, first administrator of the missions, Father Junipero Serra. Long before the days of the gold rush, Father Serra saw clearly that the spiritual and economic salvation of the area depended on agriculture. He recognized that unless something could be done to stimulate the sagging economy, many of the Indian converts would leave the Church in disillusionment. Working tirelessly, he founded nine missions before his death in 1784. His work was continued by another outstanding personality, Father Lasuen. Ultimately, 21 of these missions were established, extending for about 600 miles along the Royal Highway (*El Camino Real*). Each mission controlled about 100,000 acres.

Under the direction of the priests, the Indians set out orchards and vineyards, raised livestock, built irrigation dams and ditches, and mills for grinding wheat and corn. Women were taught to spin and weave. It was a great achievement, and it helped to prevent a complete economic breakdown in a crucial period of development.

Eventually, the missions were taken over by the Spanish crown and later by the Mexican government. By 1848, they had been broken up into hundreds of ranchos. The mission buildings themselves were abandoned and the fine old churches sold for a pittance. San Juan Capistrano sold for $710, and San Luis Obispo for $500.

The country was changing rapidly now. San Francisco was the unquestioned cultural and commercial center of the new territory. Despite frequent violence caused by outlaws and other reprehensible characters, it continued to move ahead.

Los Angeles, hitherto overshadowed by its bigger and more glamorous neighbor to the north, began to grow. What gave Los Angeles a firm lease on life was the completion of the Southern Pacific Railway. Anticipating Madison Avenue by several generations, the city put on an intensive advertising campaign to lure visitors to Southern California. Today, Los Angeles outranks San Francisco as a seaport and is one of our great harbors.

By the turn of the century, California was well on the way towards a brilliant future. To meet rising demands of the new western market, many ships, often heavily laden with valuable cargo, came to California harbors. Not all of them arrived, however. In July, 1896, the 3616-ton *City of Columbia* was wrecked for a loss of $680,000.

One of the worst disasters in this history of the West Coast took place in 1901 when the *City of Rio de Janeiro* struck an obstruction while entering the Golden Gate at San Francisco and went down with a reported $2,000,000 in silver on board. A few years later, in 1907, the steamer *Corona* sank with a total loss of about $200,000.

California, too, was deeply involved in World War II. Its ports were important embarkation centers for Pacific operations. On July 17, 1944, the steamships *Quinalt Victory* and *E. A. Bryan* were loading ammunition at Port Chicago. Suddenly, the *Bryan's* cargo of about 5,000 tons of ammunition exploded. This terrific explosion destroyed both vessels and was felt for 200 miles. Damage extended for ten miles, and there were isolated cases of broken windows 50 miles away. The pier and buildings of Port Chicago were badly damaged and all aids to navigation in the area were ruined. During this disaster, Coast Guard fireboat CG-60041F was destroyed and its crew of five killed. Thousands of persons, mostly naval personnel, were injured, and about 325 lives lost.

In this aerial photo taken from a U.S. Coast Guard heli-
copter, a barely visible cross marks the hull of the USS
BENEVOLENCE, where she sank on August 25, 1950, after colliding with the SS MARY LUCKENBACH four miles outside the
Golden Gate Bridge. The naval hospital ship, returning to
San Francisco after a shakedown run, was hit by the LUCKEN-
BACH in a dense fog and sank in 20 minutes. Of the over 500
people on board the BENEVOLENCE, 400-odd were rescued, 18
were killed, and an undetermined number are still missing.

Unlike California, the Pacific Northwest didn't begin to develop until relatively late in our history. It was next to the last piece to be fitted into the continental United States, the last being Alaska.

As far back as 1782, the intrepid Captain Robert Gray had explored the Columbia River. This was the same Captain Gray who was to take the American flag around the world for the first time. Before then the Spaniards had had a glimpse of the Oregon coast early in the 16th century, and about a century later they were followed by Sir Francis Drake. But these visits were brief and without lasting result. For a long time, the Northwest was a disputed territory. Great Britain claimed it as part of Canada, while the United States insisted that it was part of the Louisiana Purchase. Happily, the issue was settled by treaty rather than gunfire in 1846.

Only a handful of people were aware of the immense wealth and variety of this region, which extends approximately 500 miles north and south and 350 miles east and west. This fertile corner of the continent runs the gamut from almost total desolation to lush green forests of nearly tropical density.

Not long after Gray made his epochal voyage up the Columbia, Lieutenant George Vancouver of His Majesty's Royal Navy entered the Columbia. He traveled far upstream as far as "a remarkable mountain covered with snow" which he named Mount Hood. He also explored Puget Sound and named such other geographic features as the Hood Canal and Mount Rainier.

American claims to the Northwest were greatly strengthened by the famous expedition carried out in 1804 by Captain William Clark and Lieutenant Merriwether Lewis. After a long voyage up the Missouri, they reached the Columbia the following year in mid-October. On November 7 of that year they were rewarded by their first sight of the Pacific. "Ocian in view, O! the joy!" Clark exclaimed rhapsodically in his journal.

In spite of the Lewis and Clark achievement, the Northwest remained for the most part unknown and undeveloped territory. However, the expedition had dispelled the myth of the "Northwest Passage" and had given Americans a more realistic view of the territory's potential.

The United States did not move into the Northwest Territory in force until the climatic year of 1843. An expansion-minded United States was demanding all of the Northwest up to the Russian territory of Alaska. British men-of-war anchored in the Columbia River. This was met by the dispatch of an American warship. Tension rose and James K. Polk was elected President of the United States on the slogan "Fifty-four-forty or fight." Eventually, a compromise solution was found which favored the United States. Britain's Hudson's Bay Company moved out of Oregon to set up new headquarters in British Columbia.

Intensive development of the Northwest began with the coming of the railroads. Until then, the territory could be reached only by a long and hazardous transcontinental journey or by an equally arduous voyage around Cape Horn. Soon timber cruisers came by railroad from the Midwest. A chain of sawmills sprang up between Spokane and Portland, Tacoma and Seattle. All over the great region, towns began to flourish. The frontier was beginning to fade. With that unflagging vigor that marked America's other pioneers, the people of the Northwest showed an amazing capacity to build cities and industries where only wilderness had been before.

The great port of Seattle, chief commercial, industrial and financial center of the Pacific Northwest, was founded in 1852 by 21 white settlers. Gradually the little trading post grew into one of the world's great harbors. Today, Seattle is one of the principal gateways to the Orient, a natural meeting place between East and West. Its trade arteries crisscross the seven seas via the more than 90 steamship lines which offer service to every port of the free world. In Seattle's harbor lie vessels flying the flags of many countries. By all standards, Seattle is a cosmopolitan city whose influence is felt around the world.

Second only to Seattle is Portland, Oregon, a deep-sea port more than a hundred miles from the ocean. Portland is one of the world's largest exporters of grain and of forest products, and it has close shipping ties with Hawaii and Japan. Few cities can boast a more dramatic setting. Two great rivers flow through and around it and three major peaks of the strikingly beautiful Cascade Mountains dwarf the steel and concrete evidences of its growth.

THE MYSTERY OF THE CHINESE SILVER

On the bottom of the Pacific, just outside San Francisco Harbor, lies more than $2,000,000 in Chinese silver. It has been there since February 22, 1901, when the 3548-ton American steamer *City of Rio De Janeiro* went to the bottom, carrying with her the valuables of 95 passengers and 114 crewmen, as well as holds crammed with general cargo.

The *Rio* was en route from Hong Kong via Honolulu. Entering the Golden Gate in a heavy fog just before dawn, she struck a reef of rocks, and sank almost immediately. It happened so quickly no one knew of the disaster until 7:20 a.m., when surfman Ellingsen of the Fort Point Lifesaving Station sighted a lifeboat jammed with 81 persons coming around the Point. He informed the keeper of the station who ordered the immediate launching of a lifeboat. The ebb tide current was then running very strongly.

After taking the badly shaken survivors to the station, the Fort Point crew, along with two tugs, undertook a search of the area. Although they combed the area thoroughly, they found no other survivors.

To this day, no one has come up with an adequate explanation of the shipwreck. From the evidence available, the *Rio* carried 11 lifeboats, three of which were swung by davits from the sides of the ship. The remaining eight were on skids on the roofs of the deck houses. Her equipment and launching apparatus were good. Ordinarily, the boats could have been lowered within five minutes. At the time the *Rio* struck the rocks, the water was calm. Passengers and crew behaved well and there was no panic. Immediately on contact with the rocks, the captain sounded the alarm and called the crew to the boats.

What happened to upset what should have been a routine operation? The closest thing to an answer is to be found in the make-up of the *Rio's* crew, which consisted of 84 Chinese commanded by Americans. None of the officers and only two of the crew spoke English and Chinese. Orders had to be communicated either through the boatswain or fireman or by signs and signals.

Apparently this system worked well during the voyage, but it broke down completely under the stress of sudden emergency. The sailors could not understand the officers' commands and it was too dark to use hand signals. Only one of the two Chinese who spoke English knew anything about lowering a boat, and there had been no drill.

It wasn't surprising, therefore, that of the three boats lowered, only one was launched successfully. The other two were swamped as a result of inexpert handling. A tragic inability to communicate lay at the bottom of this tragedy. Many persons have looked for the *Rio* since, but this is one secret the sea will not give up easily.

THE SHOESTRING RESCUE

Sweat mingled with rain as Captain Nikolai Majolin struggled to control his ship, the Soviet freighter *Lamut*, caught in a vicious storm off the coast of Washington. Rampaging seas had edged the *Lamut* onto dangerous shoals off Teakwhit Head, where a jagged rock ripped a gaping hole in her hull. With tons of water rushing into her, she was already listing dangerously. It was only a matter of time before she capsized into the foaming water.

Majolin ordered the radio operator to broadcast a continuous SOS. Suddenly, dead ahead, Majolin saw an enormous rock reaching to shore, flanked on the right by a smaller one. If he could maneuver his ship into the sheltered area between the rocks, there was a fighting chance of survival. It would be difficult to navigate, but there was little choice. Majolin ordered full speed ahead. Slowly, the *Lamut* labored forward and, as by a miracle, she reached the refuge. She was now listing so badly that her deck nearly touched the raging sea.

In the shelter, things were a little calmer, and there was time to survey the situation. Looking about him, Majolin could see that he was in a pool of shallow water almost surrounded by knife-edge ridges.

But, while the *Lamut* was in a better position than before, she was by no means out of danger. At best Majolin's maneuver had gained him only a few minutes respite. Unless he could get his crew off the ship quickly there was not much hope for them.

Majolin ordered the lowering of the ten-ton motorboat with ten men and 19-year-old Alexamira Kovshova, a stewardess, on board. The attempt ended in disaster as the boat falls gave way and the boat went sliding down the freighter's side. The men managed to hold on, but the woman was not so lucky. She was struck by a falling barrel and flung to her death in the angry sea, as the crew, helpless, watched in horror.

Fifty-four people were now trapped on the *Lamut*. The only other lifeboat had been smashed to bits on the starboard side. Also, the chief stewardess, Antonia Shmelova, had fractured a hip when she was caught in a rope fall.

On April 1, 1943, the *Lamut* sailed from Astoria, Ore., for Seattle. She was travelling in ballast, having unloaded her cargo at Astoria. It was a routine voyage which the 24-year-old freighter had made many times before. After navigating the tricky Columbia River bar, Majolin had lowered the pilot over the side and ordered his helmsman to remain "steady on course 324 degrees." Ordinarily this should have taken the *Lamut* to within 14 miles of the Washington coast, heading north.

But almost immediately after turning north, misfortune struck. Vicious rain squalls cut visibility, and winds began picking up gale force. Worse than that, the *Lamut* was off course. This was caused in part by a strong northeasterly current off the Washington coast, running at two and one-half knots. Strong winds made the situation even more dangerous.

To make matters worse, the *Lamut* was almost totally without navigational equipment. She carried no fathometer, no radio direction finder or gyro-compass. All she had was a magnetic compass and a lead line good for 36 fathoms.

By 9:50 p.m. Majolin decided that it would be safer to remain well out to sea until morning. There was no point in tempting fate by trying to enter the treacherous Straits of Juan DeFuca at night.

A few moments later, the lookout came to the bridge and reported land dead ahead. Majolin ordered all engines astern. He was too late. At precisely 9:58 p.m. the ship ripped her hull on a rock in the Quillayute Needles.

This was the situation as Majolin waited anxiously for help to reach him. But while his signals were being received clearly enough, they gave no indication of his longitude. All the rescuers had to go by was an approximate latitude which put the *Lamut* on the "Kost." Direction finder stations at Eureka, Calif., and Tatoosh Island, Wash., were working frantically to plot her position. Their work was made more difficult by distress calls which were being received at about the same time from another Russian freighter, the *Uzrekistan*. This unfortunate vessel was in much the same situation, just off the Canadian coast to the north.

While waiting for help, Captain Majolin assembled his crew on the port board deck near the radio shack. His broad, Slavic face was haggard with anxiety which was reflected on the faces of the men and women before him. Just as Majolin began to speak, the radio shack was washed ashore. With it seemed to go all hope of rescue. Fortunately, the ship had reached its final position on the rocks. Hiding his own fears, Majolin tried to calm his shattered crew, assuring them of eventual rescue.

As if in answer to his unspoken prayer, the first rescue vessels appeared. They were lifeboats from the former Point Badah Lifeboat Station at Neah Bay. They had braved 75-mile-an-hour winds to reach the *Lamut*. But so rough were the seas, that they couldn't get close enough to help. They stood by until the first grey light of morning disclosed the wretched survivors huddled high on the steeply sloping deck.

Soon a land party was hacking its way through a mile of swampy thickets. Two miles south of the *Lamut*, they broke through, and began their perilous climb across wet and slippery boulders to the summit of the cliff overlooking the ship. From their narrow perch they looked down on one side at the freighter and on the other at a sandy beach and calm sea.

But how could help be gotten to the Russian seamen? The ledge on which they were standing was so narrow that it could only be traversed one man at a time. Primarily a searching party, they were not equipped with the rope and other equipment needed for this difficult rescue. Behind them was a second group on its way to the dying *Lamut*, but they would be some time in coming. Meanwhile, time was running out for the vessel and her crew.

With help only a few hundred yards away, the Russians now felt sure of rescue. From the expressions on their faces, it was plain that they regarded the small group as their salvation. Their rescuers, however, were not nearly so sanguine. The relatively short distance separating them from the Russians might just as well have been a couple of miles. Even if they had a surfboat, launching it would have been out of the question in that furious surf. The only possible means of rescue was to get a line out to the *Lamut*. But they had no rope to send out. To be so close to rescue and to be unable to accomplish it was frustrating, but there it was.

Just when the situation seemed hopeless, the Chief Petty Officer hit upon an idea. He had suddenly noticed the long shoelaces worn by his crew on their heavy all-duty shoes. There was his answer. To his surprised crew he ordered, "Okay, you guys, take the laces out of your shoes. We're going to try to tie them into some kind of a line to send out to the ship." The laces were tied together and with the aid of some gauze bandage, they managed to put together a makeshift line. A rock was tied to one end, and the line was lowered to the anxious Russians.

The Russians tied a heavier line to the shoestring and passed it to the rescuers. Now there was a bridge of rope connecting the *Lamut* with the shore. But it was a perilous bridge and had to be negotiated hand over hand. One by one, the woman first, the Russians climbed from the deck of the broken *Lamut* to an under-cut ledge, halfway up the cliff. Never had shoelaces been put to a more unlikely or more laudable use.

The Soviet freighter LAMUT *lying capsized in the cove the day after she was wrecked. On cliff above right, rescuers are still bringing the crew to safety.*

But there was still much work to be done before the rescue could be completed. As the Russians huddled together on the cliff ledge, chilled by driving wind and rain, the stage was set for the second step, the ascent to the upper cliff.

When the Soviet seamen reached the top of the ridge, they were lowered down the landward side to the beach and safety. The journey down was an agonizing one. To check their descent, the seamen had to cling to roots and crevices in the rock face. Especially trying was the rescue of the injured girl, who had been placed on a stretcher.

Safety was now assured, but there was still hardship ahead. This was one of the wildest spots on the Pacific Coast. Nevertheless, the Russians tackled the problem cheerfully as they trudged through swamp, sometimes sinking to their knees in slime and water. As darkness fell, the last of the mud-covered crew staggered from the trail to waiting Coast Guard trucks and ambulances.

Nearly two decades have passed since that fateful day. The *Lamut* still lies in her shallow grave at the Quillayute Needles. Her rusty iron plates are the only monuments to a day of great valor. No one knows what has happened to Captain Majolin or the members of his crew. But it's a cinch that if any of them are still around, they will always think of shoelaces with affection.

CHAPTER 7 — TABLES. The following
listing gives the position (latitude and longitude); type, name of vessel, and tonnage;
the Coast and Geodetic Survey charts covering the area; and general information concerning dates, cargo and estimated value.

Lat/Long	Type, Name, Tonnage	Charts	Remarks

COAST OF CALIFORNIA

Lat/Long	Type, Name, Tonnage	Charts	Remarks
——	SANTA ROSA	5101	Sank off Bishops Rock, Cortes Bank, in 1717 in 120 feet. Gold and silver reported on board. Loss estimated at $700,000.
——	SANTA CECILIA	5101 5112	Sank three miles off Ship's Rock, Santa Catalina Island, in 1852. Gold and silver reported on board. Loss estimated at $200,000.
——	Bk. GEORGE U. HIND (1389)	5101	Foundered Sept. 1936, off Carlsbad.
33-23.9 118-22.0	Twr. DIXIE	5101 5112	Sank in 1954 in 10 feet.
33-39.4 118-13.8	Twr. OLYMPIC (1766)	5101	Sank Sept. 4, 1940. 48 feet over wreck.
33-43.6 118-11.7	PIERPONT	5101 5148	Sank Oct. 17, 1951.
——	Sch. PHILIPPINE (523)	5101 5147	Stranded Jan. 1, 1934, on Terminal Island.
33-59.8 118-31.2	STAR OF HOLLYWOOD	5101 5144	Sank Feb. 14, 1942, in 42 feet.
——	M/V SOUTHLAND (119)	5202	Foundered Sept. 24, 1960, approximately 15 miles from Anacapa Island.
——	Str. CHICKASAW (6131)	5202 5116	Stranded Feb. 7, 1962, between Cluster Point and South Point, southwesterly portion of Santa Rosa Island.

Lat/Long	Type, Name, Tonnage	Charts	Remarks
——	Bge. MINNIE A. CAINE (880)	5101	Stranded Sept. 24, 1939, 6 miles west of Santa Monica.
34-23.0 119-41.0	JANE STANFORD (970)	5202 5261	Sank before World War II.
34-26.1 120-01.1	BRANT M/V (149)	5202	Burned May 8, 1960.
34-27.0 120-36.3	BERKLEY Ftr. (571)	5202	Sank Nov. 14, 1907.
34-29.3 120-29.5	CGC McCULLOCH	5202	Sank June 13, 1917, after colliding with SS GOVERNOR.
34-37.0 120-37.5	Six U.S. Navy Destroyers	5302	Squadron ran aground Sept. 8, 1923, at Honda while proceeding to port in thick fog. 73 lives lost.
34-39.3 120-37.3	I. G. KULUKUNDIS Ftr. (4380)	5202	Grounded and broke up July 11, 1949.
35-36.0 121-17.0	MONTEBELLO Tkr. (8272)	5302	Torpedoed Dec. 23, 1941, with 75,346 barrels of crude oil.
——	Str. HOWARD OLSON (2477)	5402 5476	Collided with MARINE LEOPARD off Point Sur, May 14, 1956.
——	Sch. AURORA (1211)	5402 5403	Stranded Jan. 18, 1935, at Monterey.
37-10.6 122-22.9	CITY OF COLUMBIA Str. (3616)	5402	Wrecked on rocks July 14, 1896, with cargo of merchandise. Loss valued at $680,000.
37-11.0 122-25.0	Str. SAN JUAN	5402	Sank before World War II after colliding with Str. DODD.
37-25.0 122-40.0	OCEANIA	5402	Sank before World War II in 250 feet.
37-28.5 122-29.0	Sch. JAMES ROLF (586)	5402 5520	Sank Aug. 2, 1910, with cargo of merchandise.
——	Shp. RYDAL HALL	5402 5520	Wrecked Oct. 17, 1876, on Pillar Point with cargo of coal.
37-34.0 123-00.0	Sch. LOUIS (831)	5402	Sank June 19, 1907.
37-38.9 122-29.9	Bk. GIFFORD (2245)	5402	Wrecked Sept. 25, 1904, on Muscle Rock with cargo of coal.
37-40.5 122-47.5	Ftr. J. LUCKENBACK (7869)	5402	Collided July 1953 with HAWAIIAN PILOT in 165 feet.

Lat/Long	Type, Name, Tonnage	Charts	Remarks
——	Pass. CITY OF RIO de JANEIRO (3548)	5402 5532	Struck rock or other obstruction Feb. 22, 1901, and sank while entering the Golden Gate. $2,000,000 in silver reported on board.
——	SS CITY OF CHESTER (1106)	5402 5532	Sank Aug. 22, 1888 off Fort Point, in the Golden Gate with cargo of merchandise.
37-45.0 123-00.0	Ftr. HENRY BERGH (7176)	5402	Wrecked May 31, 1944, on Farallon Islands.
37-46.9 122-30.9	Str. OHIAN (5153)	5402 5532	Stranded Oct. 7, 1936.
——	Str. KATHERINE DONOVAN (993)	5402 5532	Stranded Jan. 22, 1941, in the vicinity of Seal Rocks.
——	Str. FRANK H. BUCK (6076)	5402 5532	Collided with PRESIDENT COOLIDGE in the Golden Gate Channel, Mar. 6, 1937.
37-46.9 122-33.0	USS BENEVOLENCE (11,000)	5402 5532	Collided and sank Aug. 25, 1950. 51 feet over wreck. (See page 145.)
37-48.0 122-31.0	COOS BAY	5402 5532	Sank Oct. 22, 1927.
——	Str. CITY OF NEW YORK (3010)	5402 5532	Wrecked Oct. 26, 1893, on rocks off Point Bonita with general cargo. Loss valued at $454,000.
37-49.0 122-30.0	CITY OF ROEDE	5402 5532	
37-49.2 122-27.5	FERNSTREAM (4980)	5402 5532	Sank Dec. 25, 1952. 60 feet over wreck.
——	Shp. ELIZABETH (1866)	5402 5532	Lost Feb. 21, 1891, near Tennessee Cove, with general cargo.
——	Ftr. E. A. BRYAN (7212)	5575	Lost July 17, 1944, in explosion at Port Chicago.
——	Ftr. QUINALT VICTORY (7608)	5575	Lost July 17, 1944, in explosion at Port Chicago.
37-54.6 122-43.8	Str. HANALEI (666)	5402 5599	Wrecked Nov. 23, 1914, on reefs off Bolinas Point, with cargo of merchandise. 23 lives lost.
37-56.0 122-59.7	Sch. ANNIE E. SMALE (845)	5502 5599	Sank July 9, 1910 with cargo of coal.
37-56.0 122-55.0	ITUNA (201)	5502 5599	Sank before World War II in 180 feet.
37-59.0 122-58.0	SAMOA	5502 5599	Sank Jan. 28, 1913, in 60 feet.

Lat/Long	Type, Name, Tonnage	Charts	Remarks
37-59.3 122-57.7	Sch. GASPAR	5502 5599	Wrecked in 1937.
38-00.0 123-03.0	Ftr. MUNLEON	5502	Wrecked before World War II. 50 feet from shore.
——	SAN AGUSTIN (300)	5502	Wrecked 1599 off Point Reyes. $500,000 treasure reported on board.
——	Sch. GOLDEN SHORE (699)	5576	Foundered in 1928 at Pittsburgh.
38-02.5 122-59.7	Bk. HADDINGTONSHIRE (1119)	5502 5599	Sank Aug. 20, 1885.
——	Bk. FRANCOIS COPPEE (2289)	5502 5603	Sank Nov. 20, 1903, off Tomales Point, with cargo of coal.
38-21.0 123-05.0	NEWBERG	5502	Sank Oct. 8, 1918.
38-38.2 123-35.5	Ftr. WINTERMORE (2010)	5502	Sank Sept. 17, 1938.
38-42.0 123-32.0	Str. DOROTHY WINTEMOTE (2010)	5502	Foundered Sept. 17, 1948, near Fish Rock.
38-47.0 123-36.0	Ftr. ARCTIC	5502	Sank July 6, 1922, in 180 feet.
——	Str. SAN BENITO (3789)	5602	Sank Nov. 22, 1896, near Point Arena.
38-58.0 123-45.7	PACIFIC ENTERPRISE M/V (11,000)	5602	Stranded Sept. 9, 1949.
39-04.0 123-44.0	ALLIANCE	5602	Sank Oct. 18, 1915, in 180 feet.
——	SS COLUMBIA (2722)	5602 5773	Lost July 21, 1907, off Point Delgada, with general cargo.
——	Str. ST. PAUL (2440)	5602	Wrecked Oct. 5, 1905, near Point Gorda, with general cargo valued at $165,000.
40-27.0 124-28.5	ALASKA	5602 5795	Wrecked on Blunts Reef.
40-28.0 124-24.5	Str. TRICOLOR (2498)	5602 5795	Sank July 25, 1905, with cargo of coal.
40-44.6 124-13.7	Str. WEEOTT (557)	5602 5832	Wrecked Dec. 1, 1899, with general cargo.
40-46.0 124-18.5	USS MILWAUKEE (9700) Cruiser	5602	Sank Jan. 13, 1917.

Lat/Long	Type, Name, Tonnage	Charts	Remarks
40-46.5 124-14.9	Str. CORONA (1492)	5602 5832	Wrecked March 1, 1907, with general cargo on board. Loss estimated at $200,000.
40-48.8 124-11.9	SOTOYOME M/V	5602 5832	Sank Dec. 7, 1907.
40-54.0 124-10.0	WILMINGTON (990)	5602	Sank before World War II in 60 feet.
41-13.7 124-09.0	SS DAISEY MATTHEWS (933)	5702	Foundered May 4, 1940.
——	Str. BROTHER JONATHAN (1360)	5702 5895	Hit NW Seal Rocks, Trinidad Head, and sank in 1865. Gold and paper money worth $250,000 reported on board.
41-44.6 124-11.2	Tkr. EMIDIO REMOVEA (6912)	5702 5895	Sank Dec. 20, 1941.
——	CELILO M/V (177)	5702 5895	Burned at Cresent City.
41-52.0 124-25.0	Ftr. SUSAN OLSEN (953)	5702 5895	Sank Nov. 15, 1942.

COAST OF OREGON

Lat/Long	Type, Name, Tonnage	Charts	Remarks
42-36.5 124-29.5	SS WILLAPA (1185)	5702	Foundered Dec. 3, 1941.
——	Str. PHYLLIS (1266)	5702	Stranded Mar. 9, 1936, 1 mile north of Humbug Mountain.
——	Str. COTTONEVA (1113)	5702 5952	Stranded Feb. 10, 1937, at Port Orford.
42-46.0 124-36.0	Str. SINALOA (1648)	5802 5952	Sank June 15, 1917.
——	ELIZABETH OLSEN M/V (275)	5802 5971	Sank Nov. 30, 1960, at entrance to Bandon Harbor.
——	Str. OLIVER OLSON (2235)	5802 5971	Stranded Nov. 3, 1953, off the south jetty of Coquille River, Brandon.
——	Bge. NORTH BEND (976)	5802 5984	Foundered Oct. 23, 1940, at entrance to Coos Bay.
43-10.3 124-24.5	Sch. SANTA CLARA (6309)	5802	Sank Nov. 2, 1915.
43-17.0 124-26.0	Str. ARAGO (947)	5802	Sank Oct. 20, 1896. 13 lives lost.

Lat/Long	Type, Name, Tonnage	Charts	Remarks
43-19.0 124-30.0	Ftr. BRUSH	5802	Sank April 26, 1923, in 300 feet.
43-20.5 124-22.0	Sch. CHINOOK (785)	5802 5984	Sank April 12, 1907, with cargo of merchandise.
43-22.0 124-21.0	COLUMBIA	5802 5984	Sank Feb. 17, 1924.
43-22.0 124-21.0	Ftr. C. A. SMITH	5802 5984	Sank Dec. 16, 1923.
——	Ftr. GEORGE OLSON (1428)	5802 5984	Stranded June 23, 1944, on Coos Bay Bar.
——	Str. CHARLES W. WETMORE (1340)	5802 5984	Wrecked Sept. 8, 1892, on North Spit of Coos Bay Bar, with cargo of coal.
43-31.3 124-15.0	Ftr. ALVARADO (1994)	5802	Wrecked March 17, 1945. Forward part on beach. After part 100 yards offshore.
43-38.0 124-19.0	Sch. NOVELTY (592)	5802	Sank Oct. 23, 1907.
43-40.0 124-14.0	C. C. LINDAUER	5802	Sank before World War II.
43-44.0 124-11.5	Str. TACOMA (2119)	5802 6004	Sank Jan. 29, 1883, with cargo of coal.
44-21.5 124-06.0	Shp. ATALANTA (1753)	5802	Stranded Nov. 17, 1898.
44-36.0 124-06.0	MELBA	5802 6056	Sank before World War II.
44-37.0 124-06.0	BUTCHER	5802 6056	Sank before World War II.
44-37.3 124-04.8	SS JOSEPH ASPDIN (5000)	5802 6055	Wrecked in 1948.
45-05.0 124-24.0	Tug MOBILE POINT (1117)	5902	Sank Dec. 23, 1944, after colliding with SILVER STATE PARK.
——	Shp. EMILY REED (1564)	5902 6122	Stranded Fed. 14, 1908, on Nehalem River Bar, with cargo of coal.
45-47.2 124-03.3	Shp. GLENESSLIN (1818)	5902	Sank Oct. 1, 1913.
45-56.2 124-01.1	Bk. LUPATA	5902	Wrecked Jan. 1881 on Tillamook Rock.
46-12.0 124-07.1	Sch. ADMIRAL (683)	5902 6151	Sank Jan. 13, 1912.

Heroic Coast Guardsmen battle gale to rescue the captain and entire crew of 25 from the 1113-ton SS COTTONEVA which foundered on reefs off Port Orford, Oregon, on February 10, 1937. Breeches buoy aided rescue workers as they saved every life aboard the doomed vessel. Raging sea broke the ill-fated ship in two shortly after the last man was on shore.

Lat/Long	Type, Name, Tonnage	Charts	Remarks
46-14.6 124-01.8	Str. SEA THRUSH (5807)	5902 6151	Stranded in 1932 on Clatsop Spit.

COAST OF WASHINGTON

Lat/Long	Type, Name, Tonnage	Charts	Remarks
46-15.1 124-01.3	Bk. DILHAREE (1293)	6002 6151	Sank March 10, 1880, 1 mile SW of lower end of Sand Island.
46-15.5 124-06.0	Bk. WILLIAM H. BESSE (1027)	6002 6151	Sank July 23, 1887, with cargo of railroad iron.
——	Str. LAUREL	6002 6151	Wrecked in 1929 on Peacock Spit, Cape Disappointment.
——	Bk. CAVOUR (1429)	6002 6151	Wrecked Dec. 8, 1903, on Peacock Spit, Cape Disappointment.
——	SS VAZIAV VOROSVSKY	6002 6151	Stranded April 3, 1941, on Peacock Spit, Cape Disappointment.
46-16.5 124-07.3	IOWA	6002 6151	Sank before World War II.
46-17.0 124-08.0	SS GREAT REPUBLIC (3882)	6002 6151	Sank April 19, 1879, 600 yards offshore with general cargo. Loss estimated at $356,000.
46-18.0 124-05.0	Sch. FRANK W. HOWE (573)	6002 6151	Wrecked Feb. 22, 1903.
46-18.7 124-09.5	Ftr. DREXEL VICTORUS (6654)	6002 6151	Foundered Oct. 10, 1942.
46-18.1 124-05.5	Str. ROSECRANS (2976)	6002 6151	Stranded Jan. 7, 1913.
46-20.8 124-04.6	Bk. POTRIMPOS (1246)	6002	Sank Dec. 19, 1896.
46-25.8 124-03.7	Str. STRATHBLANE (1364)	6002 6185	Sank Nov. 3, 1891.
46-31.3 124-03.6	Shp. ALICE (2509)	6002 6185	Sank Jan. 15, 1909, with cargo of cement.
——	Str. TRINIDAD (974)	6002 6185	Stranded May 7, 1937, at Willapa Harbor on North Spit.
46-46.6 124-31.2	Ftr. CAMDEN (6653)	6002	Sank Oct. 10, 1942, in 330 feet.
46-53.0 124-20.0	Ftr. MULTNOMAH (969)	6002	Sank before World War II in 180 feet.

Lat/Long	Type, Name, Tonnage	Charts	Remarks
46-53.0 124-20.0	Str. SKAGIT CHIEF (502)	6002	Foundered Oct. 29, 1956, approximately 12 miles west of Grays Harbor.
——	Bk. TORRISDALE (2184)	6002 6195	Stranded Dec. 28, 1912, on South Spit near rocks of jetty on lower side of entrance to Grays Harbor.
——	SS TEXMAR (7146)	6002 6195	Stranded Dec. 30, 1960, at Range #4 in Grays Harbor.
46-59.7 124-10.4	SS TELLUS (2522)	6002 6195	Sank Sept. 21, 1907, with cargo of coal.
——	Bk. ABERCORN (1262)	6002	Wrecked Jan. 30, 1888, on Damon's Point north of Grays Harbor, with cargo of railroad iron.
47-09.0 124-12.0	Bk. FERNDALE (1350)	6002	Sank Jan. 29, 1892, with cargo of coal.
47-15.0 124-50.0	Ftr. J. C. KIRKPATRIUS (1430)	6002	Sank before World War II in 500 feet.
47-36.1 122-22.5	Bge. M.T. #6 (1315)	6401 6446	Collided with FAIRLAND, Dec. 31, 1949. In 347 feet.
47-40.5 124-29.1	Shp. EMILY FARNHAM (1193)	6002	Wrecked Nov. 18, 1875, on Destruction Island with cargo of railroad iron.
47-52.0 124-36.0	SS LAMUT (2694)	6102	Wrecked March 31, 1943, in Quillayute Needles. (See page 153).
——	Shp. PRINCE ARTHUR (1666)	6102	Wrecked Jan. 2, 1903, at Cape Johnston.
48-00.0 125-00.0	NIHA	6102	Sank before World War II in 370 feet.
48-10.2 123-42.2	DIAMOND KNOT M/V	6102	Sank Aug. 13, 1947, after collision with SS FENN VICTORY. 21 lives lost.
48-15.0 125-40.0	Ftr. COAST TRADER (3286)	6102	Torpedoed June 7, 1942, in 550 feet with 1200 tons of newsprint on board.
48-20.8 124-30.0	SS ANDALUSIA	6102	Stranded Nov. 4, 1949. ¼ mile from shore.
——	Bge. W. J. PIRRIE (4000)	6102	Broke up Nov. 26, 1920, on rocks opposite south end of Waada Island, in Neah Bay.
48-22.2 124-44.0	SS SKAGWAY (1838)	6102 6265	Burned in 1930.
48-23.0 124-37.0	ALICE B.	6102 6266	Sank before World War II.

Lat/Long	Type, Name, Tonnage	Charts	Remarks
——	PACIFIC	6102	Collided and sank Nov. 4, 1875, off Cape Flattery. $79,220 in cash and gold reported on board.
48-42.9 125-03.0	UZBEKISTAN		Sank April 1, 1943, in Canadian waters. ¼ mile from shore in 18 feet.
48-45.0 125-15.0	Ftr. MALAHAT (1544)	6102	Sank March 23, 1944.
48-25.4 122-44.7	Tkr. BUNKER HILL (10,000)	6300	Exploded, broke in two, and sank March 6, 1964, in 250 feet.

U.S. Coast and Geodetic Survey Charts Covering
Pacific States Coastal Waters — Chapter 7
California, Oregon, Washington

Chart	Price	Title	Scale	Size
5101	$1.00	San Diego to Santa Rosa Island	1:234,270	35x50
5202	1.00	Point Dume to Purisima Point	1:232,188	33x48
5302	1.00	Point Conception to Point Sur	1:216,116	33x46
5402	1.00	Point Sur to San Francisco	1:210,668	33x42
5502	1.00	San Francisco to Point Arena	1:207,840	34x42
5602	1.00	Point Arena to Trinidad Head	1:200,000	33x48
5702	1.00	Trinidad Head to Cape Blanco	1:196,948	33x43
5802	1.00	Cape Blanco to Yaquina Head	1:191,730	33x48
5902	1.00	Yaquina Head to Columbia River	1:185,238	33x44
6002	1.00	Columbia River to Destruction Island	1:180,789	33x41
6102	1.00	Approaches to Strait of Juan de Fuca — Destruction Island to Amphitrite Point	1:176,253	35x44
5112	.75	Santa Catalina Island	1:40,000	29x40
5144	.50	Santa Monica Bay	1:40,000	24x36
5148	1.00	San Pedro Bay	1:18,000	32x47
5261	.25	Santa Barbara	1:20,000	22x28
5520	.25	Halfmoon Bay	1:20,000	21x22
5532	1.00	San Francisco Entrance	1:40,000	36x45
5575	1.00	Suisun Bay — Port Chicago and vicinity	1:40,000	36x44
5599	.50	Drakes Bay	1:40,000	25x32
5603	1.00	Bodega and Tomales Bays	1:30,000	35x44
5773	.25	Shelter Cove	1:15,000	15x19
5795	.75	Cape Mendocino and vicinity	1:40,000	28x40
5832	.75	Humboldt Bay	1:25,000	33x39
5895	.50	St. George Reef and Crescent City	1:40,000	29x29
5952	.50	Port Orford to Cape Blanco	1:40,000	24x29
5971	.50	Coquille River Entrance	1:10,000	24x29
5984	.75	Coos Bay	1:20,000	32x43
6004	.50	Umpqua River Pacific Ocean to Reedsport	1:20,000	26x33
6055	1.00	Yaquina Bay and River	1:10,000	36x42
6056	1.00	Approaches to Yaquina Bay	1:50,000	36x41
6122	.50	Nehalem River	1:20,000	22x35
6151	.75	Columbia River — Pacific Ocean to Harrington Point	1:40,000	27x43
6185	1.00	Willapa Bay	1:40,000	33x45
6195	.75	Grays Harbor	1:40,000	27x40
6265	.75	Cape Flattery	1:40,000	31x41
6266	.50	Neah Bay	1:10,000	24x30

Steamship COOS BAY *stranded on the rocks about one and three-quarter miles south by west from Fort Point Coast Guard Station, Calif., October 22, 1927. Her crew of 35 was rescued by means of the breeches buoy and lifeboats from the Fort Point, Golden Gate, and Point Bonita Coast Guard Stations. The operation of the breeches buoy apparatus from the side of the hill proved a hazardous and difficult task.*

CHAPTER 8

Northern Pacific

Alaska

WHEN WILLIAM SEWARD, Secretary of State under Presidents Lincoln and Johnson, purchased Alaska from Russia's Czar, Alexander II, for $7,200,000, he was roundly criticized. "Seward's Folly," "Icebergia," and "Walrussia" were among the unflattering names given his purchase. Editors and others, who should have known better, pictured it as an icy waste suitable only for polar bears and Eskimos. They denounced it as a reckless squandering of taxpayers' dollars.

Time has shown how wrong they were. Yet, for generations, most Americans were only dimly aware of this vast and sprawling land which covers an area of about 586,000 square miles. Superimpose a map of Alaska on one of the continental United States. Its total spread is as deep and wide, running 2,700 miles from Ketchikan to Attu, and 1,400 miles from south to north at Point Barrow. Point Barrow, Alaska's northern tip, lies well within the Arctic Circle. Within Alaska itself there are at least three principal climate zones: coastal, interior and northern.

Most Alaskans live along the Pacific or southern coast where most of its principal cities are located. In this zone, according to the U.S. Weather Bureau, "warm winters and cool summers are the rule . . . To those whose conception of Alaska is that of a desolate waste of perennial ice and snow it will come as a surprise to know that the mean temperature of January at Sitka is nearly a degree higher than the mean for that month in St. Louis. And Juneau, 1000 miles north of the United States-Canada border, experiences on the average only about one day a year with minimum readings below zero." That's a far cry from the land of perpetual winter so often associated with Alaska.

Even though Alaska has become our 49th state, there is still amazing ignorance of its great natural wealth. It took the gold strike in the Yukon in the late 1890's to make the great mass of Americans conscious of Alaska. All at once, Alaska was in the headlines. Stories by Jack London and poems by Robert W. Service further popularized the territory. In Alaska, Americans found a new frontier to replace the vanishing frontier of the west. And it was true that at the turn of the century, Alaska resembled the California of an earlier era. Adventurers and "fast buck" operators from all over the United States came there to reap a golden harvest. Most of them stayed a while and returned to the States when the pickings turned out to be leaner than they had expected. In 1901 at the height of this hectic period, one of the most valuable cargoes ever lost at sea went down with the *Islander* in Stevens Passage. On board was $3,000,000 in gold dust and $400,000 in currency.

The gold rush has been over a long time. Since then we have learned there is much more to be found in Alaska than gold. There is, for example, the important salmon industry which started in 1878. Headquarters for this pioneer industry were originally in San Francisco and later in Puget Sound. Today, the Alaskan fishing industry includes crab, halibut, clams and shrimp, and constitutes a major part of the Alaskan economy.

The total value of Alaska's mineral output since its purchase may be estimated conservatively in billions of dollars. In addition to gold, Alaska has deposits of silver, coal, lead, tin, platinum, palladium, antimony, tungsten, natural gas, petroleum, marble, gypsum, graphite, barite, and sulphur. Two great natural forests, the Tongass in southeastern Alaska, and the Chugach on Prince William sound are important sources of lumber. Seward's modest investment has paid for itself many times since his widely criticized purchase in 1867.

As in the case of California, the first important migration to Alaska was stimulated by reports of gold. The first discoveries were made in United States territory in 1887 at Forty Mile Creek. But it was the reports of big strikes along the upper Yukon in Canada, in 1897, that attracted prospectors in large numbers. To reach this area, the prospectors had to travel through Alaska. Many of them remained there.

Seward's purchase of Alaska was dictated by military and political, rather than economic factors. With a foresight not shared by many of his contemporaries, he saw that the Russian presence on the North American continent could eventually be dangerous to the United States. Essentially, he was extending the Monroe Doctrine to cover this northern American outpost.

The United States knew little about its territory, and, soon after the purchase, dispatched the Revenue Cutter *Lincoln* to make the first exploration of Alaskan waters and to carry out such investigations as might be feasible. That was the first Federal action in Alaska. It was also the start of a historic relationship between Alaska and the Revenue Cutter Service, later succeeded by the U. S. Coast Guard.

In the early brawling days of the territory, the captains of cutters were virtually the only law in that part of the world. Their powers were vast, including both administrative and judicial functions. It was not unusual in that far off time for a captain to try a case, and make appropriate disposition.

One of the first crises confronting the United States was the butchery of seal herds on their breeding grounds of the Pribiloff Islands by Russian, Japanese, and other hunters. Entire herds, including nursing mothers and their pups, were being destroyed in the hunters' greed for profit.

Because of these and other raids on Alaska's natural resources, the United States entered into treaties with the countries primarily involved to conserve fish and wildlife. Enforcement of the treaties was placed in the hands of the Revenue Cutter Service and subsequently, the U.S. Coast Guard. That halted the brutalities, but serious damage had already been done.

Alaska's early history is dominated by the Russia of the Czars. In 1728, Vitus Bering, a Danish sea captain, sailing for the Czars, passed through the strait named after him and sighted the American coast. Bering made a second expedition in 1741 during which he located the mainland of America and numerous islands. Many of these still carry their Russian names. Bering's ship was wrecked in November, 1741, and he and his crew faced the bleak prospect of an Alaskan winter. Nevertheless, they managed to survive. For the next three decades, the Russians continued to be active in exploring the coast and islands, and in developing a trade with the natives.

Private exploitation of the territory turned out to be a pretty sordid affair. Traders and companies robbed, massacred and otherwise abused the native Indians. The situation became so intolerable that in 1799 the Russian Government moved to restrict Alaskan trade to the Russian-American company. Its most famous director, Alexander Baranof, proved to be a first-rate administrator. He ended the abuses of the Russian traders and founded Sitka, which became the headquarters of the company.

By the 1850's the United States was actively interested in the Russian possession. But the country was on the verge of Civil War, and its attention was focused almost entirely on domestic issues. With the end of the war, American interest revived, culminating in the Seward purchase of 1867.

Alaska's dramatic rise to statehood was one more proof of the existence of the pioneer spirit so frequently demonstrated in the past. In what had been largely a wasteland, new cities sprang up: Ketchikan, Sitka, Juneau, Anchorage, Skagway, Cordova, Wrangell, Petersburg, Douglas, Haines, Fairbanks, and others.

For a long time, Alaskan development was handicapped by lack of communication with the mainstream of American life. Gradually, this isolation was overcome by the building of new roads under the Federal Aid Highway Act. The Alcan Highway, begun after the United States entered World War II, has been an important factor in Alaskan development.

The Second World War intensified shipping activity off the Alaskan coast. This activity was especially heavy during 1942 and 1943 as is evidenced by the numerous ship losses occurring during that period. The *SS Rescuer* was stranded on December 31, 1942, at Scotch Cap, off Unimak Island, and the *SS Crown City* met a similar fate on September 2, 1942, at the Sledge Island Light, off Sledge Island. The year 1943 had its share of sinkings, including the freighter *Mapele, SS Slocum,* and *Dellwood,* to name just a few.

ALASKAN TREASURE TROVE

A fortune in gold dust lies in the cold waters of Stevens Passage, between Douglas and Admiralty Islands, off the southern coast of Alaska. It has lain there since August 15, 1901, when the good ship *Islander* went down with heavy loss of life.

The story began on August 14, 1901, when the *Islander,* out of Victoria, B.C., departed Skagway with 109 passengers and 69 crewmen. She was bound for Vancouver as part of her regularly scheduled run between that city and various southern Alaska ports. She was considered a stout vessel by the standards of the time. Her commander, Captain Hamilton Roberts Foote, was a seasoned mariner.

Times were booming in the Klondike where gold had been reported several years before. A motley throng of adventurers had been pouring into the Yukon hoping to strike it rich in a hurry. Some of them were lucky enough to find substantial deposits of gold. News of their good fortune, filtering back into the States, spurred thousands of other men to undertake the hazardous journey.

By 1901, the gold fever was at its peak. The general sense of prosperity was reflected by the gay crowd on board the *Islander.* On that clear summer day, the future seemed entirely serene. Many of the passengers were women and children, returning to the mainland to renew family ties and enjoy some of the comforts of more civilized living.

Unknown to all but the crew, the *Islander* was carrying a cargo of gold dust and currency valued at about $3,400,000 for the Alaska Pacific Express Co. It was indicative of the new prosperity that the vessel had carried similar amounts on previous trips.

About seven hours after the *Islander's* departure, the lookout noticed a large object off the port bow. Before he could sound an alarm, a heavy tremor shook the vessel. Razor sharp, floating ice cut deeply into her port side, tearing open the water-tight bulkheads into the coal bunkers.

Water pouring in, the vessel started to go down almost immediately. Within about 20 minutes, she had disappeared in the cold waters of Stevens Passage, about midway between Douglas and Admiralty Island. So sudden was the disaster that about 40 lives were lost. Locked in those icy waters is a fortune in gold dust still waiting there to be claimed.

TRAGEDY IN THE ALEUTIANS

As Captain R. O. Crisp, commanding officer of the Revenue Cutter *Tahoma* mounted the bridge of his ship, the sun was just coming up. The cool morning air felt good on his face and the day ahead promised to be a good one.

So far the *Tahoma's* patrol of Alaskan waters had been routine, except for a rescue of the master and crew of the small schooner *Trilby* two days before on September 18, 1914. Now he was returning to Alaid Island, most westerly of the Semechi group, to strip the unfortunate *Trilby*. It didn't seem to be a very difficult assignment.

But northern waters are deceptive, and by the time Captain Crisp arrived south of Alaid Island, the weather and sea in his words, "looked none too good for wrecking operations." A prudent navigator, the captain decided to make for the open water since the passage from Attu could be made only in daylight. At about 9:30 in the morning, he passed through the strait, sometimes referred to as the Semechi-Agattu Pass.

Passengers being taken off the sinking SS PRINCESS KATHLEEN. *The 365-foot, 5980-ton passenger ship grounded on the tip of Point Lena, 17 miles north of Juneau, Alaska, September 7, 1952. All the 146 passengers and crew were rescued.*

Four hours later, Crisp was congratulating himself on having successfully negotiated a difficult passage. He was reassured by the absence of broken water, seaweed, or other signs of shallow water. Besides, there was a line of deep soundings on the chart just a little outside the usual track of the *Tahoma*.

The afternoon wore away and darkness began to settle down on the far northern sea. The sea was calm with a moderate swell. The wind was southeast and light. Convinced that everything was in good order, Crisp retired to his cabin where he settled down comfortably with a pipe and a book.

His peaceful reverie was suddenly shattered by a grating noise as the *Tahoma's* hull scraped the bottom. This was followed by frantic signals to back full speed given by the officer of the deck. Adding to the confusion was the crashing and pounding of the ship as she pitched forward over the reef, accompanied by a ringing of the general alarm.

As the color drained from the captain's face, he raced to the deck and made his way to the bridge. By now all hands had come on deck and were clearing away the boats. Crisp ordered the boats lowered to the rail only, outfitted there, and griped in. The crew was then to await further orders.

The *Tahoma* had come to a full stop. Crisp ordered one of the crew to man the searchlight, but the pounding of the vessel had broken the supports of the projector and the light was unusable. Soundings showed that the ship was reef-locked. At no point was the depth of water alongside sufficiently deep to permit an exit.

The captain maneuvered to back off the reef, first going slow and then increasing to full speed. The wounded *Tahoma* would move forward and backward a little, but each attempt was damaging her more. The wheel and rudder were striking against the rocks and the rudder extension stock was forcing its way up through the spar deck. The situation became more complicated when the main steam pipe in the engine room pulled loose from the bulkhead flange, creating a bad leak. Any further attempts to dislodge the *Tahoma* might pull it out altogether and scald the working force.

It was now 10:30 p.m. and nothing more could be done before daylight. Nothing remained but to spend a wakeful night, hoping for better luck on the morrow.

Daylight on the morning of September 21 showed that the *Tahoma* was entirely surrounded by kelp for about a mile. Crisp sent out reconnoitering parties to find the nearest deep water and to see if there were any exits from the reef in which the *Tahoma* was imprisoned. Their search was fruitless. In the meantime things had worsened on the ship. The feed pump and the fire pump had been knocked out of commission by the heavy lunging of the vessel. Only the circulator pump remained intact to keep water down in the engine room. But the broken fire pump made it impossible to free the fore and main holds which were filling up rapidly.

Captain Crisp was a veteran sailor and a realist. He knew that the moment was rapidly approaching when he would have to make the decision to abandon ship. However before making this terrible decision he exhausted every possible means of saving his ship. Distress calls were sent out continually. The lifeboats were provisioned and readied for lowering.

Nevertheless, Crisp decided to stand by the *Tahoma* in the hope that she would remain upright with her main deck slightly above water, if she did sink. This would provide a safe place to await help.

The sea was now punishing the stricken ship brutally as she continued to smash against the reef. Already the afternoon shadows were lengthening. Soon it would be too dark to leave the ship. The time had come. Crisp ordered the circulator pump stopped, and the sea inlets and berth deck air ports opened.

The *Tahoma* now began to settle rapidly. When she started to list starboard instead of going down straight, Crisp gave orders to abandon ship.

The crew managed to carry out the operation without mishap. As darkness fell, the wind increased and heavy breakers rolled across the reef. Fearing that the tide might turn, the captain gave orders to make for Agattu Island. A plan had been agreed upon with the station on the island that the *Tahoma's* boats would make for the east end of the island, if this course of action became necessary.

In that rough sea, it was impossible for all of the lifeboats to remain together. It took Captain Crisp two hours to work off the reef in his boat, handicapped by the rough sea. At eight o'clock of September 21, he looked for the last time at the lights that had been hoisted on the *Tahoma*.

The *Tahoma* is still at the spot where she was abandoned so many years ago; her exact position is given on page 179.

———————

CHAPTER 8—TABLES. *The following listing gives the position (latitude and longitude); type, name of vessel, and tonnage; the Coast and Geodetic Survey charts covering the area; and general information concerning dates, cargo, and estimated value.*

Lat/Long	Type, Name, Tonnage	Charts	Remarks
		COAST OF ALASKA	
54-49.5 130-37.1	MT. BAKER	8102 8141	Burned and beached Feb. 22, 1944.
——	M/V NORCO (615)	8075 8074	Sank March 8, 1944, in Tomgas Harbor, off Annette Island.
——	Str. DENALI	8102	Wrecked April 19, 1935, on rock off Zayas Island.
——	Bge. P. T. & B. (1651)	8102 8094	Stranded Feb. 26, 1947, on Louis Reef, in Tongass Narrows. 3½ miles north of Ketchikan.
——	SS TONDELEYO	8102 8124	Foundered Oct. 23, 1941, near Meyers Chuck and Ship Island Light, off Three Islands.
——	Bk. STAR OF BENGAL (1877)	8152 8173	Stranded Sept. 20, 1908, on Coronation Island.
——	Str. ISLANDER	8202	Sank Aug. 15, 1901, in Stevens Passage, in 365 feet. $3,000,000 in gold and $400,000 in currency reported on board. 70 lives lost.
——	Bge. ARR 738 (2297)	8202 8304	Stranded Nov. 8, 1948, in vicinity of Taylor Island.
58-23.5 134-46.7	Pass. PRINCESS KATHLEEN (5980)	8202	Grounded and sank Sept. 7, 1952, off Point Lena, 17 miles north of Juneau. (See page 173).
——	M/V CORAL SEA (148)	8252	Burned July 19, 1960, in Frederick Sound.
——	Ftr. PORT ORFORD (1293)	8252	Stranded Dec. 22, 1942, on Yasha Island, in Chatham Strait.

Lat/Long	Type, Name, Tonnage	Charts	Remarks
——	Bge. PACIFIC (3238)	8457	Stranded Dec. 28, 1960, at Icy Bay.
——	Pass. CLEVEDON (7314)	8402 8455	Sank Jan. 11, 1942, off Yakutat Pass.
——	Ftr. COLDBROOK (5104)	8551	Stranded June 3, 1942, at Middleton Island.
——	Lighthouse Ship USLHS ARMERIA (1052)	8520 8551	Wrecked May 20, 1912, on Cape Hinchinbrook, Prince William Sound.
——	USN YR-43	8551 8520	Wrecked March 28, 1945, at entrance to Hinchinbrook.
59-55.5 148-50.9	Str. YUKON (5746)	8552 8528	Stranded Feb. 4, 1956, at Cape Fairfield. Wreck partially above water.
——	USRC WOLCOTT	8556 8542	Wrecked approximately 1900, at Uyak Bay, Kodiak Island.
——	Bk. MEROM (1204)	8556 8541	Lost Oct. 6, 1900, at Karluk, Kodiak Island.
——	Bk. SERVIA (1886)	8556	Lost Nov. 6, 1907, off Kodiak Island.
——	M/V FEARLESS (145)	8556	Foundered Jan. 31, 1960, off Cape Chiniak, Kodiak Island.
——	Str. USAT ELNA (5746)	8556	Stranded Dec. 27, 1943, in Shelikof Straits, Wide Bay.
55-15.0 159-00.0	Ftr. JOSEPH P. GAINES (7176)	8859	Broke in two and foundered Nov. 24, 1943.
54-52.0 159-10.0	SS NORTH WIND (2448)	8859	Stranded Dec. 15, 1944, on Simianof Island.
55-23.0 160-08.0	Ftr. MAPELE (3297)	8859 8700	Stranded June 15, 1943, on Cape Devine.
——	SS SLOCUM	8859 8703	Stranded Feb. 19, 1943, on Bold Cape.
——	Dge. EVERETT	8860 8701	Stranded Sept. 24, 1942, on Cape Pankof.
——	Shp. ONEIDA (1131)	8860 8841	Wrecked Apr. 26, 1890, on Henning Rock, Sanak Island, with general cargo.
——	Str. YUKON	8860	Wrecked June 11, 1913, on reefs west of Sanak Island.
54-15.0 163-30.0	Ftr. JOHN STRAUB (7176)	8860	Sank April 19, 1944, with 7,176 tons of general cargo.

Lat/Long	Type, Name, Tonnage	Charts	Remarks
54-23.0 164-44.0	Pass. MOUNT McKINLEY (4861)	8860	Stranded March 11, 1942, at Scotch Cap.
——	Str. ALLOWAY	8860 8720	Wrecked Feb. 8, 1929, on Ugamak Island.
——	St. FRANCIS (1898)	8860	Wrecked May 14, 1917, on Unimak Island, with cargo of canning supplies.
——	SS RESCUER	8860	Stranded Dec. 31, 1942, at Scotch Cap, Unimak Island.
——	SS TURKSIB	8860	Stranded Nov. 21, 1942, at Scotch Cap, Unimak Island.
——	Shp. PARAMITA (1582)	8860 8720	Stranded May 16, 1914, at Lost Harbor, Akun Island, with cargo of cannery supplies.
——	LST A.T.T.	8861 8862	Went aground Nov. 10, 1946, on NE shore of Amutka Island.
51-53.0 175-53.0	CGC TAHOMA (1215)	8863 9140	Struck reef and broke up Sept. 20, 1914. (See page 172).
——	M/V CROWN REEFER	8864 9123	Stranded Jan. 27, 1946, at Kirlof Point, Amchitka Island.
——	M/V DULCINEA (622)	8864	Stranded Oct. 9, 1956, on Buldir Island.
——	Ftr. SCOTIA (2649)	9198 9125	Stranded Dec. 23, 1943, at Shemya Island.
——	Ftr. DELLWOOD (3923)	9198 9128	Stranded July 19, 1943, in entrance to Massacre Bay off Alexai Point, Attu Island.
——	GREAT BEAR (367)	9380 9383	Wrecked Aug. 25, 1916, on Pinnacle Rock, Nome, with cargo of general merchandise.
——	SS CROWN CITY (5433)	9380	Stranded Sept. 2, 1942, at Sledge Island Light.
——	Str. CLEVELAND (1160)	9380	Lost Oct. 23, 1900, at Cape Rodney, with cargo of coal.

U.S. Coast and Geodetic Survey Charts Covering
Alaskan Coastal Waters — Chapter 8

Chart	Price	Title	Scale	Size
8074	.75	Harbors in Clarence Strait (4 plans)	———	25x40
8075	1.00	Revillagigedo Channel,	1:80,000	35x44
		Ryus Bay, Duke Island	1:20,000	
8094	.75	Tongass Narrows	1:30,000	34x38
8102	$1.00	Hecate Strait to Etolin Island, including Behm and	1:229,376	34x43
		Portland Canals		
8124	.50	Harbor Charts — Clarence Strait and Behm Canal		30x30
		(5 plans)		
8141	.75	Portland Inlet to Nakat Bay	1:40,000	34x40
8152	1.00	Dixon Entrance to Chatham Strait	1:229,376	33x45
8173	1.00	Southern Entrances to Sumner Strait	1:40,000	33x47
8202	1.00	Stephens Passage to Cross Sound, including Lynn Canal	1:209,978	34x45
8252	1.00	Coronation Island to Lisianski Strait	1:217,828	35x45
8402	.75	Cross Sound to Yakutat Bay	1:300,000	33x42
8455	.75	Yakutat Bay	1:80,000	30x34
8457	.75	Icy Bay	1:40,000	31x33
8520	1.00	Prince William Sound — eastern entrance	1:80,000	34x45
8541	.75	Cape Ikolik to Cape Kulluk, Kodiak Island	1:80,000	34x37
8542	1.00	Uganik and Uyak Bays, Kodiak Island	1:80,000	33x44
8551	1.00	Prince William Sound	1:200,000	36x46
8556	1.00	Kodiak Island	1:350,000	35x46
8700	.75	Shumagin Islands — Nagai Island to Unga Island	1:100,000	35x41
8701	.75	Morzhovoi Bay and Isanotski Strait	1:80,660	35x41
8703	1.00	Cold Bay and approaches, Alaska Peninsula	1:80,000	35x48
8720	1.00	Krenitzin Islands	1:80,000	35x48
8841	.25	Harbors and Anchorages, Sanak Island (3 Plans)		22x23
8859	1.00	Shumagin Islands to Sanak Islands	1:300,000	35x42
8860	1.00	Unimak and Akutan Passes and approaches	1:300,000	35x44
8861	1.00	Unalaska I. to Amukta I.	1:300,000	36x48
8862	1.00	Amukta Island to Igitkin I.	1:300,000	36x47
8863	1.00	Igitkin I. to Semisopochnoi I.	1:300,000	36x48
8864	1.00	Rat Islands — Semisopochnoi I. to Buldir I.	1:300,000	36x42
9123	.50	Constantine Harbor, Amchitka Island	1:10,000	23x30
9125	1.00	Shemya Island, Semichi Islands	1:20,000	36x43
9128	1.00	Massacre Bay, Attu Island	1:25,000	36x48
9140	1.00	Tagalak Island to Little Tanaga Island, Andreanof Islands	1:30,000	35x48
9198	1.00	Near Islands — Ingenstrem Rocks to Attu Island	1:160,000	33x45
9380	1.00	Norton Sound	1:400,000	35x42
9383	.75	Nome Harbor and approaches, Norton Sound	1:20,000	35x41

The SS H. F. DeBARDELEBEN, *caught in a storm, became unmanageable and was abandoned on March 10, 1932. Carrying ballast, the merchant-ship sprang a leak after three days of buffeting by the heavy seas. Her crew was transferred to the steamship* LAGANBANK *before the* DeBARDELEBEN *sank in Lat. 39°32′N — Long. 58°30′W.*

APPENDIX A

QUESTIONS AND ANSWERS ON YOUR RIGHTS

It's one thing to find a sunken vessel, but another to know your legal rights to it. This section is intended to give you a few of the highlights of the subject. Reading it won't make you a sea lawyer, but it may give you some idea of where you stand. If the going gets too rough, your best bet is to consult an attorney. Nevertheless, here are some questions and answers on claiming your find. They should clarify some of the major points:

Q. *What are your rights to your find?*
A. Generally speaking, the find is yours under the law of "finders keepers." However, where salvage law applies, the find belongs to you subject to certain legal requirements.

Q. *What are these requirements?*
A. There are three major requirements:
    (1) The property must be found or rescued from navigable waters of the United States.
    (2) The property must be saved from impending marine peril.
    (3) The service rendered to the vessel or cargo must be entirely voluntary on the part of the "salvor" as the rescuer is known.

Q. *What are "navigable waters"?*
A. That is a very tricky term upon which even lawyers are not agreed. In general, it applies to all waters under Federal jurisdiction.

Q. *Who determines the amount of the salvage award?*
A. This is determined by the court and the rules governing it vary from jurisdiction to jurisdiction. Many States have their own salvage laws which have direct bearing on the amount awarded. Just how much you'll get will depend on the circumstances of the case.

Q. *Is there a difference between an abandoned vessel and salvage property?*

A. Yes. A stranded ship may have been on the beach for such a long time as to lose its marine character. In that case, the salvage law does not apply and the finder could claim full possession. But here, too, it must be stressed that only a duly qualified court can make that determination.

Q. *Suppose that you have met all the requirements of salvage. What's the next step?*

A. You may take immediate possession of the property until such time as it can be delivered to a competent court for action, even over the objection of the original owner.

Q. *What other courses of action are open to the salvor?*

A. If the property has been rescued from marine peril, you may take possession and bring it immediately to the nearest port in which an admiralty court sits and place it in custody of the court. You can also allow the vessel to proceed and have it "arrested" at its first port of call. It's at this point that the services of qualified counsel should be obtained. The salvor should watch his step.

Q. *When can't a salvor keep all property he finds?*

A. Where your find is not governed by the "finders keepers" doctrine. The law holds that the original owner of the property lost at sea continues to be its owner, even though it may have been abandoned on the high seas, or thrown overboard and found at the bottom. In salvage cases, the court regards itself as the custodian of the property for the original owner. Salvors, however, are rewarded for their successful efforts.

Maritime law as it pertains to salvage is an engrossing subject. It is also a very complicated one and not easily summarized. We hope the general points outlined above will be helpful should it be your good fortune to find a sunken or abandoned vessel.

APPENDIX B

WHERE TO OBTAIN CHARTS

U.S. Coast and Geodetic Survey Charts

All coastal charts used in this book come from the U.S. Coast and Geodetic Survey. They may be obtained from the Director, U.S. Coast and Geodetic Survey, Department of Commerce, Washington 25, D.C., or from the District Offices listed below:

518 East 32nd St.
Baltimore. Maryland 21218
CHesapeake 3-5654

10th Floor, Customhouse
Boston, Massachusetts 02109
HAncock 6-1481

P.O. Box 2195
Fort Worth, Texas 76101
EDison 5-4211 ext. 782

P.O. Box 3887
Honolulu, Hawaii 96812
HOnolulu 5-8831 ext. 232

Room 4F, Post Office & Court House Bldg...
Chart Distribution Office
811 Grand Avenue
Kansas City, Mo. 64108
BAltimore 1-7000 ext. 2716

535 Subway Terminal Bldg.
417 South Hill St.
Los Angeles, Calif. 90013
688-2838 ext. 318 or 319

315 Customhouse
423 Canal St.
New Orleans, Louisiana 70130
529-2411 ext. 6551

Room 602, Federal Office Bldg.
90 Church St.
New York, N.Y. 10007
REctor 2-9100 ext. 478

102 West Olney Rd.
Norfolk, Va. 23510
MAdison 7-8472 or 7-8285

Room 314, U.S. Court House
620 S. W. Main
Portland, Oregon 97205
CApitol 6-3361

555 Battery St., Room 121
San Francisco, Calif. 94111
YUkon 6-3111 Ext. 2111 or 2317

705 Federal Office Bldg.
Seattle, Washington 98104
MUtual 2-3300 ext. 465 or 466

P.O. Box 190
Tampa, Florida 33601
248-2790

The scales of nautical charts range from 1:2,500 to about 1:5,-000,000. Graphic scales are generally shown on charts at 1:80,000 scale or larger. For convenience or reference, Coast and Geodetic Survey charts are classified according to scale as follows:

Sailing charts, scales 1:600,000 and smaller, are for use in fixing the mariner's position as he approaches the coast from the open ocean, or for sailing between distant coastwise ports. On such charts, the shoreline and topography are generalized and only off-shore soundings, the principal lights, outer buoys, and landmarks visible at considerable distances are shown.

General charts, scale 1:100,000 to 1:600,000, are for coastwise navigation outside of outlying reefs and shoals.

Coast charts, scale 1:50,000 to 1:1000,00, are for inshore navigation leading to bays and harbors of considerable width, and for navigating large inland waterways.

Harbor charts, scales larger than 1:50,000, are for harbors, anchorage areas, and the smaller waterways.

Intracoastal waterway (inside route) charts, scale 1:40,000, are a special series of charts embracing the inside route in New Jersey, the route from Norfolk, Virginia, to Key West, Florida, on the Atlantic Coast, and from Carrabelle, Florida, to Port of Brownsville, Texas, on the Gulf Coast.

The two maps at right are reproductions of portions of U.S. Coast and Geodetic Survey Diagrams showing the geographical coastal areas covered by selected Coast and Geodetic Survey Charts. The upper map details Atlantic and Gulf Coastal water areas covered by the 1,000 series charts shown on Coast and Geodetic Survey Diagram No. 1. The lower map depicts the Pacific Coastal water area covered by the 5,000 and 8,000 series charts shown on Coast and Geodetic Survey Diagram No. 16. These two maps provide a general reference for longitude and latitude. Applicable charts are listed in the tabulation for each chapter.

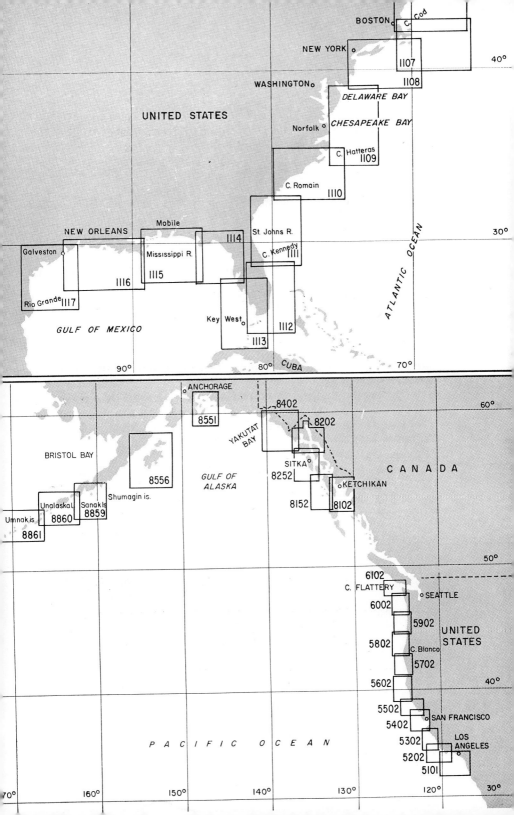

Great Lakes Charts

Great Lakes charts may be obtained from offices of the U.S. Army Corps of Engineers listed below:

U.S. Army Engineers, Lake Survey, 630 Federal Building, Detroit 26, Michigan (mail orders and counter sales)

St. Mary's Falls Canal Office, Corps of Engineers, Sault Ste. Marie, Michigan (counter sales only)

U.S. Army Engineer District, Buffalo, Corps of Engineers, Foot of Bridge St., Buffalo, N.Y. (counter sales only)

U.S. Army Engineers District, Chicago, Corps of Engineers, 536 South Clark St., Chicago, Illinois (counter sales only)

A catalog of charts is revised annually and is available without charge. To avoid error, orders should designate the chart number and title. Payment is requested in advance with order. Charts are not shipped C.O.D. Postage stamps will not be accepted. Remittances sent with mail orders should be in form of money orders or checks made payable to the *Treasurer of the United States.* Remittances from foreign countries must be redeemable through a U.S. bank. All mail orders should be sent to the Lake Survey Office at the Detroit address above. Unless otherwise indicated by the purchaser, charts will be mailed without charge for ordinary postage. Material sent in conformity with order is not returnable for exchange or refund. The purchaser may have the parcel registered by prepayment of $.55 per parcel. Normally packages are limited to 25 charts each. All above references to mailing of publications apply only to the United States and U.S. Possessions. For mailing beyond these areas, regular postage charges as determined by the Post Office Department will apply.

Complete sets of charts are filed and may be inspected, but not purchased, at the following offices of the Corps of Engineers:

U.S. Army Engineer District, St. Paul, 1217 U.S. Post Office and Custom House, 180 E. Kellog Blvd., St. Paul, Minnesota (Minn. — Ontario Border lakes charts only)

U.S. Army Engineer District, St. Paul, Lake Superior Office, Canal Park, Duluth, Minn.

U.S. Army Engineer District, Chicago, Milwaukee Area Office, 428 Federal Bldg., Milwaukee, Wis.

U.S. Army Engineer District, New York, 111 E. 16th St., New York, N.Y.

U.S. Army Engineer District, New York, Albany Area Office, 322 Federal Bldg., Albany, N.Y.

Navigators are cautioned not to use obsolete charts as the information thereon may not represent current conditions. Natural and artificial changes, many of them critical, are occurring constantly, and it is important that navigators obtain up-to-date charts at regular intervals, and correct their copies by hand from changes advertised in the weekly *Notice to Mariners* issued by the U.S. Coast Guard and Canadian Department of Transport, and the monthly Supplement to the *Great Lakes Pilot* issued by the U.S. Lake Survey. Navigators are cautioned that when charts are obtained, the aids to navigation are correct only to the date stamped in the center of the lower chart margin. Charts obtained directly from the U.S. Lake Survey have such corrections posted to date of sale.

Great Rivers Charts

Great Rivers Charts may be obtained as indicated below:

Illinois Waterway (Lake Michigan to Mississippi River) or Upper Mississippi River (Cairo, Illinois to Minneapolis, Minn.)
    U.S. Army Engineer District, Chicago
    536 South Clark St.
    Chicago, Ill. 60605

Lower Mississippi River (Cairo, Ill. to Gulf of Mexico)
    U.S. Army Engineer District, Vicksburg
    P.O. Box 60
    Vicksburg, Mississippi 39181

Kanawha or Cumberland Rivers
    U.S. Army Engineer District, Huntington
    P.O. Box 2127
    Huntington, West Virginia 25721

Tennessee River (ask for sheet covering mile number)
    Tennessee Valley Authority
    Knoxville, Tennessee 37902

Missouri River
    U.S. Army Engineer District, Omaha
    215 North 17th St.
    Omaha, Nebraska 68101

Allegheny or Monongahela Rivers
    U.S. Army Engineer District, Pittsburgh
    Manor Building, 564 Forbes Ave.
    Pittsburgh, Pa. 15219

Ohio River and tributaries
    U.S. Army Engineer Division, Ohio River
    P.O. Box 1159
    Cincinnati, Ohio 45201

NOTES